GETTING THE BOOT

GETTING
THE BOOT

Italy's Unfinished Revolution

MATT FREI

TIMES 𝕋 BOOKS

RANDOM HOUSE

Library of Congress Cataloging-in-Publication Data

Frei, Matt.
Getting the boot : Italy's unfinished revolution / Matt Frei.
p. cm.
ISBN 0-8129-2387-1
1. Political corruption—Italy. 2. Italy—Politics and
government—1976– I. Title.
JN5641.F74   1995
364.1'323'0945—dc20   94-47381

Manufactured in the United States of America on acid-free paper

9   8   7   6   5   4   3   2

First Edition
Book design by Mina Greenstein

TO PENNY

"It is not impossible to rule the Italians.
It is unnecessary."

— BENITO MUSSOLINI

PREFACE AND ACKNOWLEDGMENTS

Most of us have been caressed by Italian culture at one time or another, but few of us have been initiated into the heady pleasures of Italian politics. This book is neither a history of modern Italy nor a purely political chronicle—I leave that task to more qualified observers. This is an idiosyncratic portrait of a very eccentric democracy in one of its greatest periods of upheaval and revelation. Part of the book is a postmortem of the First Republic, in which a culture of almost feudal political patronage degenerated into a system of corruption and graft. Like Japan and Germany, Italy was a country much conditioned by the Cold War and—in her particular case—the need to keep the West's largest communist party from power. When the Berlin Wall crumbled, so did Italy's rigid but moribund edifice of power. The old regime was unceremoniously given the boot; thousands of its exponents, from business leaders to Cabinet ministers, were jailed and interrogated by a crusading judiciary. They were replaced by a bizarre array of political experiments, from Silvio Berlusconi, the world's first media tycoon–prime minister, to the regionalist Lombard League, which was inspired by a twelfth-century revolt against a German emperor. Some thought Italy was witnessing a democratic revolution. Others, like myself, describe the changes as a bloodless vendetta by an electorate that turned against its democratic rulers when corruption ceased to benefit a large number of people.

Italy may not have found a cure for the multiple sclerosis that seems to be afflicting many Western democracies at the end of the millennium, but at least it has not shied away from experimenting. The country is still in transition, and some events have come too late to be captured in print here. I also apologize for dwelling too little on the Italian left, an omission justified by the fact that the most novel developments have been on the right.

I recall the warning words of my history tutor at university, who told me not to lose my readers in the thicket of too much dense detail. All I can say is that covering Italy for the BBC and writing a book about this extraordinary and wonderful country has been a very pleasurable experience. It goes without saying that all errors of fact or judgment within it are entirely my responsibility.

I am indebted to many people who have helped in the creation of this book. My colleagues and friends at the BBC in Rome—Patti Partee, Cecilia Todeschini, Claudio Tondi, Jon Dumont, John Arden, Sean Salsarola, David Willey, and Derek Wilson—encouraged me and provided entertaining company throughout. Thanks also to Charles Richards, Alan Cowell, and Robert Fox for the same. In London my editors—Jenny Baxter, Chris Wyld, and Malcom Downing—were kind enough to let me off the leash. Special thanks to my friend Robert Graham from *The Financial Times,* who found time to comb through the manuscript and pointed out some of the more glaring errors, and to François and Shirley Caracciolo for providing an idyllic setting in which to plug in my Toshiba. Piero Ottone, Franco Pavoncello, Franco Ferrarotti, Franco Venturini, Sergio Romano, Gianfranco Pasquino, Rodolfo Brancoli, Roberto Lasagna, Livio Caputo, Luigi Berlinguer, and many others all provided great wisdom and insight, while tolerating the musings of a foreigner. I am also grateful to the scores of journalists from RAI and numerous regional Italian newspapers for their expertise and help in ushering me through thickets of bureaucracy. Finally I would like to thank my editor, Peter Smith, for his patience, my agent, Bill Hamilton, for his enthusiasm, my friend Tom Weldon for his advice, and my parents, Anita and Peter, for their encouragement. My girlfriend, Penny, who grinned and bore the arduous labor of a book birth, I thank for all the above and much more.

Rome
July 1995

CONTENTS

PROLOGUE

Humble Beginnings

In this country you are a nobody if you haven't
been investigated. To be a suspect in Italy is something like belonging to the House of Lords in your
country.

—GIULIANO FERRARA

The largest corruption scandal in postwar Europe started in Milan in
February 1992 with a cleaning contractor, the head of an old people's
home, his wife, and her alimony. Mario Chiesa ran the Pio Albergo
Trivulzio, Milan's oldest and most venerable retirement home, a
beautiful nineteenth-century palazzo with an ornate garden. He was
also a member of the Socialist Party of former Prime Minister Bettino
Craxi, who had turned Milan into the party's stronghold. For someone
occupying a relatively humble position in the civil service, Chiesa
had a remarkably luxurious lifestyle. He lived in a spacious apartment
on the Via Monte Rosa and was often seen dining out at Savini, Milan's most expensive restaurant. He had several holiday homes and
dressed expensively. Nevertheless, Chiesa could also be stingy, especially toward his ex-wife. Lara Sala was not only aggrieved by the
fact that her estranged husband had jilted her for a woman twenty
years her junior, she was also annoyed that he had not been paying
his alimony, despite all his other expenses. So she complained to the
police. Her *denuncia,* or denunciation, would surely have been buried
in a mountain of yellowed paper at the civil dispute section of the

city's Palazzo di Giustizia had Chiesa not also become the subject of another complaint.

Luca Magni ran an industrial cleaning firm and was negotiating with Chiesa about a contract to clean the Pio Albergo Trivulzio. What annoyed Magni was that Mario Chiesa asked for a 10 percent "commission," payment of which would have halved the cleaning contractor's profits. Magni went to the police, who referred the case to a medium-rank investigating magistrate named Antonio Di Pietro, who had spent several years looking into a local bribery racket. Chiesa, with his wealth, his secure job in welfare, his "commissions," and his connections in the Socialist Party was just the man they were looking for. Di Pietro told Magni to go back to the old people's home and hand over the "commission." Only this time he would be wired with a tiny microphone hidden in his ballpoint pen and a High 8 camera concealed in a black briefcase. Magni met Chiesa in his ornate office decorated with red leather armchairs and old master paintings and handed over the arranged sum of 7 million lire (about $5,000). The stack of notes included ten marked 100,000-lira bills, an old trick that Di Pietro had learned while working as a policeman and a detective. The meeting, which was watched and listened to by the police, went smoothly, and shortly afterward Chiesa was arrested. When he heard from the porter at the front gate that policemen had entered the old people's home, Chiesa suspected that something was wrong. He was caught flushing 100,000-lira notes down the toilet.

Chiesa's arrest helped to unravel a whole regime. A year later the political establishment that had ruled Italy for almost five decades collapsed; whole political parties, with their deputies, prime ministers, and pretensions, were tipped into one of the grubbier dustbins of history.

Further investigations revealed that Chiesa had deposited at least 12 billion lire in bank accounts belonging to his secretary, who was also his girlfriend. He turned for help to the people who had always acted as his benefactors and protectors, the Socialist Party. After all, Chiesa had friends in high places, friends like Paolo Pilliteri, a former mayor of Milan and brother-in-law of Bettino Craxi. He was also on first-name terms with Bobò, Craxi's then twenty-eight-year-old son, who was the head of the party in Milan. But help wasn't forthcoming.

Chiesa was on his own. Taking revenge, he decided to spill the beans, and what he told the investigators went well beyond their most lurid expectations. It emerged that every contract at the old people's home, from the funeral arrangements to the cut flowers for the dining room, had been subject to a fixed commission, or what the Italians, in a wonderful example of verbal obscurantism, call a *tangente,* a tangent, a sideways approach. In other words: a bribe. Thus "Tangentopoli," or "Bribesville," the scandal to beat all Italian scandals, was born. For it wasn't only the old people's home that had been run on bribes. Chiesa gave the magistrates a floppy disc containing the names of seven thousand people who had been involved in the systematic exchange of kickbacks for business in Milan. Chiesa himself had acted as a kind of middleman, a broker of bribes. The disc confirmed that the Socialist Party and the other mainstream parties that had ruled Milan were lining their pockets with *tangenti* from members of the business community vying for public works projects. No overpass, hospital, highway, airport, subway, or sewage plant could be built in Milan without bribes being paid.

Watching the scandal spread was like observing a virus mushrooming under a microscope. At first most of the investigations concentrated on Milan, a galling fact for the rich, hardworking city that had always considered itself to be a bastion of honesty in an otherwise dishonest country. The magistrates who made up the investigation pool involved in the "Mani Pulite" or "Clean Hands" affair—one of several names for the scandal—didn't have to dig for further evidence, they were showered with it. Confession became fashionable as one businessman after another saw which way the wind was blowing and surrendered to tell tales of *tangente.* Those who were reluctant to talk were softened up with a spell in Milan's notorious San Vittore jail. The list of *indagati,* or those under investigation, now includes not only politicians but businessmen, administrators, civil servants, journalists, academics, judges, soccer managers, insurance brokers, spies, doctors, game-show hosts, and opera singers. The five thousand or so suspects in the "Tangentopoli" saga—it is impossible to keep up with the exact number—represent a cross section of Italy's elite. It's as if the entire cast list of *Town and Country* magazine had suddenly ended up on the criminal register. In fact, the Italian *Who's*

Who struck 1,800 names from its 1994 edition, including such grandees as Bettino Craxi, former Foreign Minister Gianni De Michelis, and the Ferruzzi family, celebrated as one of the country's most glamorous business dynasties two years ago but described today by the judiciary as an *associazione a delinquere,* criminal conspiracy. This label is normally reserved for Mafia families. Roberto Mongini, a cynical Milanese lawyer and former Christian Democratic Party hack, who was escorted in police handcuffs from one of the smartest restaurants in Milan—he had been accused of collecting bribes for the Malpensa Airport project—put it like this: "You never meet anyone at La Scala these days. That's because they're all serving time in San Vittore jail." VIP has come to mean not "very important person" but *visto in prigione*—seen in prison. Preventive custody, one of the many sweeping powers bestowed upon Italian investigating magistrates by the Penal Code, became a widely used and controversial means of extracting confessions. Isolation cells that had not been used for years were opened up to make room for the new breed of white-collar criminals. Chiesa, however, was one of the very few to be tried and sentenced. He got six years in prison and had to pay a fine of 6 billion lire, which would have left him with a mere 6 billion to scrape by on when his sentence was over.

But the great majority of those arrested were nothing more than suspects, who were never formally charged or tried, let alone found guilty.

In the summer of 1992 a blue-chip PR firm tried to cash in on the new population of inmates that was overcrowding the Italian prisons. It advised them to take smart casual clothes—"stretchy trousers for many hours spent sitting on uncomfortable chairs"—several long books—"to avoid brooding," and shaving cream and razors—"you might be released at any moment and have to look decent for the cameras waiting outside the prison gates." No tie—"it may tempt you to hang yourself." The joke turned sour when Gabriele Cagliari, the former head of ENI, Ente Nazionale Idrocarbure, the state-owned chemical giant, took his life by suffocating himself with a plastic bag a day before he was due to be let out of preventive detention. Although the main judge in his investigation had decided to release Ca-

gliari, another judge had felt it necessary to continue with the questioning and had canceled the release order indefinitely. The bureaucratic blunder had tragic consequences, and Cagliari's suicide briefly created a wave of public indignation against the judiciary.

But in general the spectacle of seeing Italy's great and good dragged in handcuffs from their elegant restaurants and luxurious holiday villas was mesmerizing. The nightly newscasts' ratings shot up as the roll call of suspects became longer and more illustrious. American soap operas were eclipsed by programs like *Un Giorno in Pretura* (A Day in Court), which had previously only attracted a small audience of trial junkies. Italy now had its own homemade soap opera. The Milan judges, led by Antonio Di Pietro and Francesco Saverio Borrelli, his softspoken, sophisticated boss, became Italy's Jacobins, leading the revolution against the corrupt "palazzo." A rash of graffiti declaring GRAZIE DI PIETRO covered walls, monuments, and lavatory doors all over the country. When Di Pietro walked down the streets of Milan or Rome, surrounded by his posse of bodyguards wielding machine guns, he was celebrated like a pop star or soccer idol.

The scandal quickly crept up the political ladder. Bettino Craxi, who had once been hailed by *Time* magazine as the Italian "maestro" for presiding over the economic boom of the 1980s, was suddenly cast as a villain. The boom had not only been forgotten in the recession of the early 1990s, it now also appeared that much of it had been financed by corruption. Craxi became the subject of seventeen different inquiries into bribery and fraud and was finally forced to resign from the leadership of his party in February 1993. Other former prime ministers followed suit. Ciriaco De Mita, a Christian Democrat, came under investigation for channeling billions of lire earmarked for an earthquake relief fund in his native Irpinia region to the bottomless coffers of his party. The third former prime minister to come under investigation and eventually face trial was Giulio Andreotti. It seemed as if a biblical plague were spreading through the ranks of Italian politics. More than a hundred city councils were disbanded because of corruption. By 1994, a third of Parliament had come under criminal investigation.

The voters reacted accordingly. Parties that had ruled Italy without pause since 1945 were being deserted. The Socialists, who had taken part in every government since 1963, plummeted to barely 1 percent in regional and national elections. The number of voters for the Christian Democrats, for four decades the single largest party, declined by half. Eventually the party was disbanded and its shriveled rump reborn under a different name—the Popular Party—with a new leader.

In May 1993 Carlo Ciampi became prime minister. It was an indication of the acuteness of the crisis and the popular disgust with politics that Ciampi, a former governor of the Bank of Italy, had never even been a member of a political party, let alone an elected deputy. His government of "technicians" was surprisingly successful, and some Italians even began to ask themselves whether the country needed to bother with elections if the unelected politicians were more competent and spent less time feuding with one another.

The once-rigid tectonic plates of Italian politics had been shattered, burying the old rulers and giving birth to a bizarre new generation. The Northern League, until the scandal little more than a medium-sized regional party, rode the wave of political protest to become the largest party in Italy's rich industrial North. Like a poltergeist from the darkest corner of Italy's history, the neo-Fascists now burst from the lunatic fringe of Italian politics to become the biggest political force in the poor South, absorbing millions of voters who had been left homeless by the collapse of the Christian Democrats. Was Italy experiencing a revolution, a counterrevolution, or neither?

Events rolled on. By the end of 1993 everyone was preparing for general elections. In January 1994, out of the blue, a man took the political stage and declared that he would save Italy from communism, even though communism had ceased to exist. Instead of being laughed off stage, he was taken seriously and became brazenly confident of winning. His confidence—some called it arrogance—might have had something to do with the fact that he owned most of the country's commercial television channels, controlled a third of its advertising, and owned its biggest real estate empire, its most popular chain of supermarkets, several magazines and publishing houses, and the national soccer champions, AC Milan. Silvio Berlusconi was a

master of mass psychology and a brilliant salesman. He launched a political movement the way you would launch new deodorant and called it "Forza Italia," or "Go, Italy," a rallying cry borrowed from soccer. It was a catchy title and appealed to millions of voters who were bored and confused by names like Christian Democrat, Liberal, Socialist, and Social Democrat. The man then turned his company into a party, using his managers to orchestrate the election campaign and to run as candidates. He boasted that none of his candidates had ever sat in Parliament. Overtly antipolitical politics had been born, articulating the widespread disgust with old-style politicians and their parties that was spreading all over the West but was particularly virulent in Italy. All over the country people were beginning to mutter the mantra of Forza Italia: "Old is bad; new is good." In April 1994 Silvio Berlusconi became prime minister.

Italy had embarked on yet another political adventure. In two years a curious alliance of voters and judges had staged one of the most remarkable political rebellions of any modern democracy, had rewritten the rules of modern politics, and had given the world its first tycoon prime minister. Was this an eccentric abberation Italian style, or has Italy once again become the laboratory chamber of politics, a role it had also played in the early 1920s, when the collapse of its democracy and the onset of fascism preceded similar developments in Germany and Spain? Has Italy again become the first in a long line of nations that reject traditional politics? The whiff of *fin-de-siècle* decadence is everywhere: in the television/soccer politics of Silvio Berlusconi, in the byzantine plotting of his ruling coalition—lurid even by traditional Italian standards—in cute eccentricities such as porn queens being elected to Parliament, in the media tycoon's plotting to return to power at all costs, in the widespread disgust felt for politics of all kinds. Where better to stage the opening scene of the end of an era than amid the moss-covered ruins of ancient Rome?

Political voyeurs have flocked to Italy to prod the body politic for answers and left even more confused. As for the Italians themselves, many of them had expected their political experiment to yield more. They had seen the changes as the big chance to turn Italians into real citizens and redefine the meaning of "Italy," a country whose very existence is still under debate more than a century after it was founded. But then, ordinary Italians *had* voted for the politicians that ruled them. They too had been on the take, dodging taxes or subverting the state in myriad ways. The nation's failure was, in a sense, their failure—but with a difference. The people had managed to remain separate from the state—so much so that when the state crumbled, the people continued, willy-nilly, to go about their business as usual. Had this separation not existed, Italy's "revolution" might have turned out to be a lot less sweet.

In 1992, as a foreign correspondent who had just arrived in Italy and who had initially spent much time covering the former Yugoslavia, I found it almost impossible to keep up with events. A week's absence from Italy meant missing several instalments of the "Tangentopoli" drama. The Italian newspapers would have discovered new scandals and new names, which they didn't always bother to explain. The media and the country were becoming totally self-absorbed. And who could blame them? Italy, a place where politics had become tediously predictable, was being rattled by one bombshell after another.

No one knew quite what to call the extraordinary upheavals and contortions of Italian politics. I remember sitting together one balmy summer evening with friends trying to come up with the right description. One thought of *"La Dolce Rivoluzione,"* "The Sweet Revolution." But there were victims, too. Giovanni Falcone and Paolo Borsellino, two leading anti-Mafia judges, had been killed in Palermo. Car bombs had exploded in Milan, Rome, and Florence, killing civilians and destroying part of Italy's cherished cultural heritage, including a twelfth-century church in Rome and part of the Uffizi Gallery in Florence, home to some of the most famous Renaissance paintings. As the evening got livelier and the bottles emptier, another person came up with "The Sweet and Sour Revolution." Then we moved into textiles. "The Velvet Revolution"? No, the Czechs had a copyright on that. "The Cashmere Revolution," because of the smooth, expensive nature of the material? But that sounded too much like an upheaval in the rag trade rather than political change. The drunken conclusion of the evening was that the events in Italy defied description, partly because they were so unique and still evolving. Moreover in the warm embrace of a Roman evening in May, with fountains playing to the baroque façades of a piazza full of attractive people, revolution just seemed the wrong kind of word. Life for Italy's Armani-clad *sans-culottes* wasn't so miserable after all. The events seemed more like a vendetta by the electors against the elected than a revolution.

Like many of my friends and colleagues, I have been bowled over by Italian politics. The scandals have seemed farther-fetched than anywhere else in the western half of the Northern Hemisphere, the bribes bigger, their recipients more illustrious, the corruption more systematic, politics more outlandish, and the backdrop more beautiful. In the words of Italian playwright Ennio Flaiano, who died in 1972, "Things are tragic but not serious!"

In his 1964 book, *The Italians,* Luigi Barzini put his finger on one of the eternal questions of Italian history:

> Many begin to admire us today, listen to us, imitate us, and even envy us. Why? We are, of course, still great in the things which always came easy to us. We have improved, to be sure, in many fields, but not perceptibly in those which made us the object of foreigners' scorn in the past. We are not more honest, reliable, and law-abiding than we were, we are badly organized and badly governed. . . . Could it be that foreigners are no longer certain that their virtues are best? Or could it be that our vices have turned out to be desirable advantages in the modern world, qualities essential for survival? Did we or did the rest of the world change?

Getting the Boot is my attempt to seek, in the chronicle of the events of the last few years and in some of the verities of the Italian character, today's answers to some of these questions, which are perhaps more significant now that Italian politics have melted down and been recast.

GETTING THE BOOT

Poggiolini's Hassock

In a sense, many of the questions the corruption scandals raised about Italian society—How could such corruption have come to be? How could it have lasted for so long? Who was responsible? What next?—can be expressed in a single question: Did Pierr di Maria, the wife of the head of the Pharmaceutical Department of Italy's Ministry of Health, get an upholsterer to stuff the treasury bills worth $10 million into her living room hassock, or did she do it herself?

The brown leather hassock, stuffed to the point of explosion, was discovered by the police when they raided her villa on the outskirts of Rome. It was sitting near the coffee table on the Poggiolinis' shag carpet. Mrs. Poggiolini had never dabbled in upholstery. The hassock showed no signs of having been slit open, clumsily stitched back together, or generally tampered with. So how had the neatly bundled bills gotten into it? It must have been a professional job, the police concluded. The search for the upholsterer continues.

This was just one of the questions discussed shortly after Dr. Diulio Poggiolini's arrest in September 1993. Others concerned the origins of the money, why it had been hidden in the first place, and how it related to the other $120 million found in the Poggiolinis' three homes and their fourteen Swiss bank accounts. How, above all, had it been possible for a civil servant to steal so much money without the connivance of others? Although the Poggiolinis' case turned out to be one of the most lurid examples of corruption, it was typical in many other ways: Professor Poggiolini remained convinced of his own innocence. As he told his investigators, "I was merely bending the rules a little."

Poggiolini, like so many other suspects in the corruption scandals, saw himself as little more than the average tax-dodging Italian, forced to live a life of petty illegality by a terrifyingly complex and cold-blooded *stato*. The fact that Poggiolini was himself a representative of the much-loathed state didn't seem to bother him. What the Italians, who congested the phone lines of the Ministry of Health or wrote stinging letters to the newspapers, hated him for wasn't the fact *that* he had taken money—that was almost taken for granted—it was the *amount*. Poggiolini, like hundreds of other politicians and civil servants, had offended the thieves' honor of Italian society. He had been too greedy.

The hassock was not the only piece of evidence the Guardia di Finanza, the state's Financial Police, stumbled across in the Poggiolinis' luxury villa in EUR, a Fascist-built suburb between Rome and the polluted Mediterranean. During their search they also came across a collection of sixty paintings, including several canvases by Amedeo Modigliani and Giorgio De Chirico. One of the works, a small canvas attributed to the German painter Hans Rottenhammer (1564–1625), had, as it later turned out, been stolen from the private collection of a Florentine businessman in 1992. How the painting had ended up in the hands of Professor Poggiolini is still a mystery. There is no suggestion that he had stolen the work himself, merely, according to the investigators, that he had bought it with stolen money. Investing in art or stolen art is the postmodern way of laundering dirty money in Italy.

Three weeks earlier, the police had searched another Poggiolini residence in the center of Rome. This had turned out to be an Aladdin's cave of riches: the family safe contained hundreds of Kruger-rands, old Roman coins, diamonds (cut and uncut) in small pouches, and cash worth $30,000 in a bizarre array of currencies: dollars, deutschmarks, francs, Dutch guilders, and European Currency Units (ECUs). The latter, one newspaper mused, might have been given to Professor Poggiolini in his capacity as a member of the European Union's Pharmaceutical Commission.

Next to the safe the police found a pyramid of shoeboxes: the beginnings of a footwear collection inspired by Imelda Marcos, perhaps? Not so. The boxes contained not shoes but more than a hundred neatly stacked gold ingots. "Forty years of personal savings," Professor Poggiolini told the investigating magistrates. They didn't believe him. Nor did they believe his wife, who dismissed a checking account containing $300,000 dollars' worth of lire as "shopping money." All in all, according to the most conservative estimate, the Poggiolinis had squirreled away the equivalent of $130 million, well beyond the savings capacity of an official in the Italian Ministry of Health, even one as high-ranking as Professor Poggiolini.

As the head of the Ministry of Health's Pharmaceutical Department, the professor had been in charge of approving medicines, setting their prices, and putting them onto the national register. In his ten years in office he had sat in judgment over hundreds of medicines that had to receive his seal of approval in order to be sold in Italian pharmacies. His pricing policy determined how many lire consumers had to pay for their medicines. Professor Poggiolini was arrested in September 1993 on charges of taking bribes, as well as of approving medicines that were faulty or had not been thoroughly tested. Magistrates believed that the $130 million in accumulated assets was the fruits of years of graft—the professor's reward for helping the drug companies.

Newspaper cartoonists had a field day depicting the professor as a Dracula figure, sucking the blood out of his victim, the Italian consumer of medicines. Caricaturists were helped by Poggiolini's stoop, his thin hooked nose that hails from Etruscan cave murals, his subtly crossed eyes, and his crest of gray hair on top of a very high forehead. His wife, who is gaunt in a ghostly way and wears thick glasses, was depicted at various stages as Dracula's bride, Lady Macbeth, or a very large rodent.

What particularly puzzled the investigators was that the couple hardly spent their ill-gotten gains. The millions could easily have elevated the Poggiolinis to the jet-set status enjoyed by so many other grandees of corruption. A villa in Capri or Porto Ercole; a yacht or private plane; expensive hotel suites. Instead, most of their treasures were stashed away where even they couldn't see them. Their paintings were not proudly displayed on their walls but packed away in cardboard boxes. The couple's lifestyle was parsimonious and dull. They lived frugally, did their shopping in the cheapest supermarkets and department stores, and redeemed coupons. They rarely ate out. "Why," the investigators asked Mrs. Poggiolini, "did you *need* so many billions of lire if you weren't spending them?" "Billions?" the professor asked. "I don't even know how many zeros that is!" The investigators pressed on until Mrs. Poggiolini, who came from a wealthy Sicilian family, relented. "We did it for our son!" she said, weeping. Perhaps this was an attempt to soften the heart of her inquisitors by appealing to their sense of filial love. Giovanni, the Poggiolinis' son, is physically handicapped and nursed at home by one of his aunts. The money the couple had "saved" had been meant to provide a secure future for their only offspring. The Italians are perhaps more willing than other nations to flout the law for their children's sake, but the Poggiolinis had turned their parental love into an unacceptable *crime passionnel*.

The couple were kept in separate Neapolitan jails for six months without appearing in court. Italian magistrates have wide-reaching powers and can keep a suspect in "preventive custody" for more than a year without filing charges and do so frequently as a way of extracting confessions. In the Poggiolinis' case, it worked. Every week the location and number of another secret bank account were revealed. Professor Poggiolini even offered to pay back a sizable fraction of his "savings." Unlike his cell mate, a garrulous engineer who had been accused of diddling the state over an earthquake-relief fund, the professor never became acclimatized to the dank austerity of the infamous Poggioreale jail in Naples. He complained of cataracts and high blood pressure and couldn't understand why he wasn't allowed to leave even though he had cooperated with the police so willingly.

He told reporters that all the blame was being loaded onto his shoulders when the real culprit, his boss, former Minister of Health Francesco De Lorenzo, had been allowed to escape arrest. The magistrates followed the professor's advice. In April 1994 Francesco De Lorenzo, another professor, was also arrested on charges of bribery. The investigators were satisfied that Poggiolini had confessed everything he knew, and his health was beginning to deteriorate. After several prominent detainees had killed themselves in custody the year before, the judiciary had taken care not to provoke more suicides. The professor and his wife were released. Soon afterward he was discovered standing in line in a social security office in Rome, wearing sunglasses, cowboy boots, and a blue teddy-boy suit. No disguise, however ridiculous, could hide the distinctive features of this professorial fraudster with the extraordinarily high brow. This man, who still had millions of dollars stashed away in various bank accounts, was lining up for his pension. He was spotted by one of the officials behind the counter and hounded out of the social security office by an angry crowd.

Professor Poggiolini wasn't just a single villain acting on his own. His pricing policy had been fully endorsed by De Lorenzo, a leading member of the now-defunct Liberal Party. De Lorenzo, who in December 1994 was released from Poggioreale jail after almost a year of custody, looking alarmingly haggard, went on trial for corruption and fraud. He was accused of receiving millions of dollars in kickbacks from drug companies whose products he had agreed to put on the market with the help of Poggiolini. It takes at least two to bribe, and, as was widely expected, the pharmaceutical industry also became embroiled in the scandal. Senior executives from at least three leading pharmaceutical companies were arrested for allegedly having paid the bribes that had allowed their products to be sold at inflated prices. Although Italian medicines are heavily subsidized by the state—up to 90 percent for the most essential drugs—the number of products available is relatively small. German pharmacies have 70,000 products on their shelves. In Britain the figure is 35,000; in the United States, well over 50,000. The Italian Ministry of Health is far more restrictive about which medicines it releases onto the official list; in 1987, for example, Italian pharmacies were allowed to have only 5,455 products on their shelves. A bribe was one way of securing a place. As soon as the scandal erupted, the arguments started about who had corrupted whom: Had the pharmaceutical companies tempted the civil servants at the Ministry of Health with a bribe, or had they been the victims of extortion, forced to pay up when faced with the prospect of being banned from the Italian market? This argument has become a leitmotif of the corruption scandal, not just between briber and bribee but as it pertains to all of Italian society.

The case of Diulio Poggiolini, his wife, and the minister of health shocked a nation that had already become hardened to the flagrant abuses of public office disclosed over the previous eighteen months: a former foreign minister accused of stealing money earmarked for third-world aid; a former prime minister charged with taking millions of dollars that should have gone into an earthquake-relief fund; a former interior minister who was—so the investigators believe—in cahoots with deviant extremists in the secret service who were plotting to overthrow the state; a former minister of justice who dealt with the Mafia in order to win seats for his party; a third of Parliament under criminal investigation. In short, a world record of alleged corruption, very little of it proven in court but almost all of it taken seriously enough to file criminal charges, lead to arrests, end political careers, produce suicides, and persuade millions of Italian voters to turn their backs on the parties that they had reelected year after year for four decades.

Considering the sheer number of people under investigation and the extent of the abuse, it is baffling that Italy's "revolution" is considered to have been so "sweet." Bureaucrats were hardly the only, or even the primary, targets of the investigations. Hundreds of politicians were also involved in the "system." But because they were protected from prosecution by parliamentary immunity, they could not be arrested. Like so many other pieces of legislation in Italy, the immunity law had been introduced with the best of intentions in 1945 as a safeguard for democracy: Benito Mussolini had frequently arrested politicians who had refused to toe the Fascist line. Gradually, however, the immunity law became a shield of impunity behind which hundreds of deputies took refuge from the law. Revoking a legislator's parliamentary immunity is a lengthy process involving an application by the judiciary, consideration by Parliament's Commission of Immunity, a report, a recommendation, and finally a vote in the Chamber of Deputies against which the subject in question could appeal. Every count of an indictment required a new application by the judiciary to lift the immunity. It was a laborious procedure, especially in the case of someone like Bettino Craxi, who was investigated under sixteen separate counts.

As the corruption scandal gathered pace, the law on parliamentary immunity increasingly caused outrage. It was doomed when, in May 1993, the Chamber of Deputies voted to maintain Bettino Craxi's immunity. It looked to the Italian public as if the former prime minister, the chief villain in the scandal, was being protected by his chums. The Palazzo Montecitorio, the home of the Chamber of Deputies, and the lavish Hotel Raphael, where Craxi used to reside with his traveling court of sycophants and advisers, were besieged by demonstrators. Carlo Ciampi, the prime minister at the time, immediately began to prepare legislation to scrap parliamentary immunity.

The corruption scandal unfolded during Italy's eleventh Parliament, which turned out to be the shortest in the country's postwar history. By the time the country went to the polls again in March 1994, both chambers of Parliament had received 619 different requests from the judiciary to lift the immunity from prosecution. Parliament's information office has become so used to inquiries about which deputy is being investigated for what crime that it has compiled a list that is regularly updated. On request, the information officer will deliver two heavy tomes that make hair-raising reading. For instance, Severino Citaristi, a Christian Democratic senator who has been accused of acting as the party's principal collector of bribes, occupies fifteen pages in the catalogue of crimes. He is being investigated in no fewer than 175 cases. Most of those concern "an act of corruption that contravenes the duties of office" and "violation of the law on the public financing of political parties," that is, collecting bribes on behalf of the party. Out of 630 deputies in the Chamber, 228 had received an *avviso di garanzia,* the warrant that notifies a suspect that he is under investigation by the judiciary. In the Senate the count was 93 out of

315. In fact, the only political parties still believed to have been immune to the system of corruption were the Radicals of the maverick politician Marco Pannella, the Greens, and the neo-Fascist Italian Social Movement—though that's not to say that the neo-Fascists were squeaky-clean.

There seem to be no political virgins in Italy. Temptation is always nigh. Even the Northern League, a relatively new party that had established itself as the alternative to "politics as usual," was investigated for taking bribes from the Montedison conglomerate, the prime temptress of the "Tangentopoli" scandal. The sums involved were relatively small—a total of $350,000—but the way in which they were handled was amateurish and squalid. The League's treasurer, Alessandro Patelli, first denied that he had received the money from Carlo Sama, the disgraced chief executive of the Ferruzzi empire, then admitted it but said the money had been stolen from party headquarters. The episode became farcical when the League's fiery leader, Umberto Bossi, appeared in court with a check for 1 billion lire and tried to foist it upon one of the judges. Checkbook absolution has been tried by numerous politicians and reveals a perturbing misunderstanding not only of the rule of law but of the notion of personal responsibility.

Many Italians I have met in recent years have combined a loathing for their own corrupt system with a sense of indignation that Italy has been singled out as the most corrupt country in "the democratic world." It goes without saying that Italy doesn't have a monopoly on sleaze. In Germany, where the same coalition of Christian Democrats and Free Democrats has been in power for thirteen years, unaccountability has festered and the fungus of corruption has blossomed. In Spain, the Socialist Workers' Party of Felipe González has also contributed lavishly to the annals of European corruption. The former deputy prime minister, Alfonso Guerra, used air force jets to fly him and his family to their holiday destinations. His brother ran a business empire from an office provided free of charge by the party. And last year a woman who worked as a secretary for the Socialists and whose mother had been a housekeeper in party headquarters rose through the ranks to become the linchpin in a network of bribery. Aida

Álvarez, who is today a fugitive from justice, is accused of having pocketed millions of pesetas in kickbacks for major arms contracts. She also owned six expensive fur coats, which she stored in a special refrigerator at just the right temperature. In 1994 the political elite in France also became implicated in a corruption scandal that had dramatic consequences. Several ministers were forced to resign and one was arrested because of bribes allegedly paid by industry.

In Italy there was a sense of glee and relief when it was discovered that the British establishment and in particular the ruling Conservative Party, so ready to occupy the moral high ground, had not just displayed a penchant for sexual sleaze but had also succumbed to the temptations of lucre. A number of junior ministers were forced to resign because they had received payments of several thousand dollars from companies in return for asking about the firms in question in the House of Commons. This gentle form of subliminal advertising, let alone the sums involved, would scarcely have raised an eyebrow in Italy. To one Italian friend of mine, the outrage in London over a £2,000 payment and some undeclared hospitality courtesy of a generous businessman only confirmed his impression that "the Brits are prudes."

So perhaps the other European democracies ought not to cast the first stone. Corruption *is,* no doubt, universal. Clearly, the longer a party stays in government, the greater the temptation to misbehave. This rule applies as much to the British Conservatives, who came to power in 1979, as to the French Socialists under President François Mitterrand—elected in 1981—or the Spanish Socialist Workers' Party—ruling since 1982—not to mention Japan's Liberal Democrats, which ruled for almost five decades. But Italy is clearly in a class of its own.

Corruption had a longer time to flourish in Italy, where the Christian Democrats came to power in 1947 and stayed there until 1993, precisely forty-nine years. The Socialists, the second party of government, deserted the Communists in 1963 and joined the ruling coalition soon afterward. The Italian political system had never allowed for an alternation of power between government and opposition and thus allowed various forms of corruption to become institutionalized. The Vatican, the United States, and the ruling parties worked together to preserve the status quo in order to keep the Communists out of office during the Cold War. But this collusion, which fostered corruption, was also compounded by other factors. One was an all-pervasive disrespect for the state and the rule of law. The Italian state, which is only just over a hundred years old, twenty-two of which were spent being abused by the Mussolini dictatorship, has never earned the respect from its citizens that the state enjoys in France or the United States. In Italy the state is either feared or flouted. It is not the sum of all its citizens but an alien power imposed from above on a society of individuals, families, clans, and cliques. This is one reason why personal contacts, family ties, and other social bonds are much more important in Italy than is adherence to the laws imposed by the state for the supposed benefit of society.

However, contrary to expectations, the Italians are very legalistic. This is, after all, a country of brilliant lawyers who have invented a web of laws so complex and contradictory that one is almost forced to break them in order not to get hopelessly entangled. As anyone knows who has tried to get a phone bill checked, a parking ticket challenged, a tax assessed, or a residence permit stamped, Italian laws were invented not to benefit society but to provide a devious bureaucratic challenge to the physical and mental stamina of every individual who wishes to exist in the realms of legality. To the ordinary Italian the law seems more like a complex board game invented by Franz Kafka, with consequences as devastating as they are illogical. A friend of mine who set out to be honest and pay his taxes on his real declared income ended up being fined to the hilt for not listing benefits such as a company car and a cell phone that had been provided by his American employers. In Italy being legal is a nerve-racking business—not surprisingly, for many the easy solution is to flout the law and thus expose oneself to the terrors of an unreliable and slow judicial system and other malignant organs of state. The solution has always been to take refuge in the tribe. Even politicians see themselves primarily as members of a political party rather than as representatives of the state. In Italian politics the party became an extended family or tribe for whose survival, well-being, and power breaking the laws of the state is justified. This is part of what the Italians call *partitocrazia*—partyocracy, or the supreme rule of the parties.

As the bittersweet perfume of *fin-de-siècle* decadence wafts through one Western democracy after another, corruption scandals of even greater proportions than Italy's may be in the offing. But for now the Italians have the Gold Medal of Sleaze. The number of people and the sums involved are, so far at least, unique in a Western democracy. So is the political fallout. No country has dealt with its corrupt politicians in as ruthless a manner as Italy has. An entire governing class has been toppled as a result of "Tangentopoli." Political parties went from omnipotence to oblivion in a matter of months. Politicians, senior civil servants, business magnates, and captains of industry were incarcerated and humiliated in a way that would have been unthinkable in Britain or the United States. It was the collapse of a regime. But there is one other way in which Italy has distinguished itself in the field of corruption: the complete lack of personal responsibility exhibited by nearly all the suspects in the scandal. The Japanese politicians caught with their hands in the till gave tearful resignation speeches in parliament and committed political hara-kiri in front of their colleagues. The French, British, and German politicians under investigation all resigned, overcome by shame or bitterness that they had been more sinned against than sinning. The Italians blamed "the system" and claimed they had been the victims of original sin and universal temptation.

Indeed, accusations, charges, and sentences that would have been enough to shame politicians elsewhere into obscurity brought out the fighting spirit of some of the most notorious villains in the scandal. Bettino Craxi preferred to stay in his holiday home in Tunisia rather than face an eight-and-a-half-year sentence for fraudulent bankruptcy or a corruption trial over the funding of the Milan Metro. But from his sumptuous seaside villa at Hammamet the former prime minister has battled the courts and public opinion by firing off faxes and giving interviews in which he has threatened to "reveal all." Giulio Andreotti, another former prime minister, was preparing to go on trial in December 1994 on charges of being associated with the Mafia, but he still found the time and the serenity of mind to edit a religious monthly entitled *30 Giorni* (Thirty Days).

The embodiment of thick-skinned serenity is Italy's former Foreign Minister Gianni De Michelis. With his gargantuan girth, long locks of greasy black hair, and gourmand's taste for food and women, he looks more like a corrupt prince of the Church in the age of the Borgias. Before he was investigated, the former foreign minister was well known for enlivening dreary European Union summits with his sense of humor. He had also written a guide to the best discothèques in Italy. De Michelis left his position as a chemistry professor at the University of Venice to enter politics. Following the traditional pattern, he built up a regional power base in his native Veneto and used this to exert his influence on the Socialist Party, to which he belonged. At the height of his power, De Michelis was revered as the doge in his native Venice. He married and later divorced a member of one of the most prominent Venetian families, the Bernabaus. Today De Michelis still lives in a palace on the Grand Canal next to the apartment occupied by his estranged wife. It happens to be the same palazzo in which Giovanni Casanova once resided.

In July 1995 De Michelis was found guilty of corruption and got a four-year sentence from a court in Venice. He had been charged with receiving a bribe of $500,000 for the construction of a motorway near the Venice airport. Other charges still pending concern the alleged "rechanneling" of millions of dollars of third-world aid money into the Socialist Party's coffers. Every contract that needed the approval of the state and therefore of the political parties required a "commission." This was the rule at home as well as abroad. If a company wanted to take part in a lucrative overseas project financed by Italian State Aid, it had to pay a *tangente* to the party to which the country in question had been "allocated." Businessmen thus found themselves in the unenviable position of having to pay bribes not only to the relevant authorities in the country where the project was being funded but also to the political party at home that had appropriated the funds. This had less to do with an aggressive Italian trade policy and more with the parties' greed to siphon off money from business, even if it meant going to the far-flung corners of the world. The system of rakeoffs was fair, ensuring that all the major players would get their share and no one would be left out. For these purposes the Italian Foreign Ministry had its own imaginary map of neocolonial influence. Sitting in one of the drafty marble-clad rooms of the "Farnesina," the Fascist-built Foreign Ministry, officials carved

up the world for the parties they represented. The Christian Democrats controlled most of Latin America. The Socialists were "allocated" North Africa and most of the oil-producing states in the
Middle East, because the party also controlled the state chemical giant, ENI. The Communists were given Nicaragua, Mozambique, and
Angola. In each of these fiefdoms a political party not only had the
right to appoint the ambassador and other senior diplomatic staff, it
also called the shots over aid policy. An Italian business project in
China or Chile would most likely have meant a bribe for the Christian Democrats. A contract with "Socialist" Tunisia benefited the Socialists. The system had been well established by the time Gianni De
Michelis became foreign minister. He merely perfected it.

The Horn of Africa was one example of Italian aid policy at
work. Since Mussolini invaded Abyssinia in 1935, Italy has had a
special interest in the region. Ethiopia was given to the Christian
Democrats, Somalia to the Socialists. Italian is still widely spoken in
Somalia, and during the U.S.-led operation "Restore Hope" in the
country, the Rome government took the most unusual step of not toe-
ing Washington's line over the treatment of General Mohammed
Aidid, the renegade warlord who repeatedly escaped U.S. arrest and
finally contributed to the United States' swift and clumsy departure
from Somalia. But Italy's claims that it knew what was best for Somalia became ridiculous in the light of Italian aid policy toward the
country in the 1980s. Between 1981 and 1990 Italy backed 114 projects in Somalia costing a total of $1 billion. But few of the projects
ever got off the ground or served any real purpose other than to generate a "commission" for the Socialist Party. A three-hundred-mile
highway built in the middle of the desert was occasionally used by
zigzagging nomads. A hospital in Mogadishu equipped with state-of-
the-art machines soon sank into ill repair. The list of wasted projects
is probably no longer than in many other developing countries receiving the wrong kinds of aid. The difference was that the conspicuous
expenditure was fueled by the parties' desire for funds. During his
four-year stint as foreign minister, De Michelis is accused of having
siphoned off hundreds of millions of dollars. His tactical mistake was
to start "colonizing" countries that "belonged" to other parties. He
appointed his own favorites to prestigious ambassadorial postings,

flouting the time-honored rules of seniority, experience, and party-political affiliation. Much like the party he belonged to, De Michelis was too greedy and therefore upset the delicate balance of the system. In 1993 the "Doge" became another grandee fallen from grace. When he emerged from his first pretrial hearing in Venice last year, he was greeted by a crowd of angry Venetians and excited cameramen, who filmed him getting pelted with tomatoes and insults. The "Doge" was seen dodging the crowd and scuttling from one canal to the next in search of a water taxi.

The first time I interviewed him was in the lobby of his Rome residence, the Plaza Hotel. (Many of Italy's prominent politicians, especially those who were not from Rome, used the capital's luxury hotels like lavish headquarters for their traveling entourage. De Michelis was billeted in the Plaza, Craxi in the Raphael. The Christian Democrats used the Grand and Excelsior.) De Michelis had chosen the perfect backdrop for a guest who embodied the excesses and demise of an old era. The hotel porters greeted a visitor like undertakers at the mouth of Hell. The chief doorman was frighteningly imperious until he too was arrested, charged with receiving the bundles of illicit money destined for the illustrious guest on the third floor. The lobby was draped in heavy tapestries of scarlet velvet. The leather armchairs were designed for people who never wanted to get out of them again, and the sickly Chopin coming from the piano acted as a sedative.

"Are you still dancing?" I asked the former groover of the European Union Foreign Ministers' Conference. "This is not a time for dancing," he replied lugubriously. What did he make of all the charges against him? I asked. "Absolute rubbish," he replied in perfect English. "There was never any corruption, not in my case, at least. . . . Yes, we received contributions from business. But that was necessary to run the campaigns, to pay for all the advertising, the posters, the badges, the television. How else were we to compete in elections?" The former foreign minister was indignant. His large round face was getting redder. Pearls of perspiration glistened on his nose. "The only thing we were guilty of was violating the law on the financing of political parties." The charges had arisen because of the amounts involved, the methods of extraction—which in many cases amounted to downright extortion—and what had happened to the money afterward.

"Did all the money you received from business end up in the party coffers, or did some of it make its way into a Swiss bank account or into your own pocket?" There was a moment's silence while I waited for De Michelis to combust. But the answer was a simple "No," an avuncular smile, and an explanation: "You see, Mr. Frei, there has been a conspiracy against us. There is a plot against the Socialists all over Europe, not just in Italy." He listed a number of his Socialist friends from other countries who had been toppled by allegations of corruption. Then he leaned back in the deep armchair, let the Chopin wash over him, and, looking me straight in the eye, said, "Mr. Frei, there is an unfortunate appetite for justice in Europe these days!"

Giulio Andreotti, a devout Catholic with a knack for the apothegm, once remarked that "In Italy there are neither angels nor devils, only average sinners." Forgetting for a moment the remark's exquisite cynicism, coming as it does from the man accused of being the godfather of the Mafia in Rome, Andreotti's observation is deeply perceptive. It is easy to imagine why the Poggiolinis, De Lorenzos, and De Michelises, as well as thousands of others who thrived on the system, might remain blissfully unaware of any sense of culpability. If six thousand people are guilty, no one is. Italy's corruption suspects enjoy the safety of numbers and the tolerance of a Catholic society nurtured on the concepts of original sin and universal temptation.

For the individuals involved, if not for Italy herself, the rituals of confession, penance, and absolution provide the time-honored solutions; they are, after all, just average sinners.

Average Sins

I t is hard to understand the profound effects the corruption has had on Italy's politics, its people, and its landscape, without a better sense of its scope. The sleaze that flourished in Italy was as varied as the people who benefited from it. The most common category involved the payment of bribes by businesses that wanted to secure public works projects. When you land at Milan's unfinished Malpensa Airport, you have to think of the billions of illicit lire mixed into the fresh cement. The taste of a cappuccino in Verona is soured by the *tangente* that was necessary to build the milk-processing plant. Venice has a water purification plant thanks to murky money. A motorway tunnel in Genoa, which took five years to build and was essential for relieving the city's congested traffic, was finally completed in March 1993 at a cost of $14 million. Unfortunately, the tunnel was too low for the lorries that rely on the motorway. Other examples are too numerous to mention here. It seems that no public works project was started anywhere in Italy without someone paying a bribe. The system was straightforward: if a municipal or regional government decided that a new motorway, sewage plant, or rail link had to be built, the bidding for the contract was based not on who could present the most competitive deal but on who could come up with the biggest bribe.

For companies selling to the state, the bribe was as normal as a corporate tax. The difference is that it was one of the few Italian taxes that couldn't be dodged. The system of virtual extortion was described in detail by one of Italy's most famous businessmen, Carlo De Benedetti, the chief executive and main shareholder of the computer and office-equipment giant Olivetti. De Benedetti tried— unsuccessfully, as it turned out—to avoid arrest by going directly to the judges with an eleven-page dossier in which he personally accepted all responsibility for the payment of bribes. It was a rare admission of personal culpability, albeit one designed to get him off the hook. In his dossier he described how party henchmen from the Socialists and the Christian Democrats had browbeat, cajoled, and blackmailed his company into paying *tangente*. The money would be handed over in cash by a representative of Olivetti, not De Benedetti himself, and received by a party henchman. The message from both parties was: Pay up or no business! De Benedetti pointed out that the Christian Democrats had behaved like gentlemen thieves. The Socialists, who were less burdened by moral pretensions, had been gruff extortionists.

Much of the Italian economy is owned by the state and therefore controlled by the parties. Before it embarked on a program of privatization, Italy had the biggest public-sector economy in the European Union. The threat to uncooperative businesses therefore wasn't idle. For those who could afford the bribe, corruption had its rewards. In his confession De Benedetti described how the turnover of one of his office equipment companies with the Ministry of Post and Telecommunications had increased from 1 billion to 100 billion lire a year in 1984 after paying a bribe of 10 billion lire. Olivetti had thus acquired an exclusive contract to supply the ministry with typewriters, photocopiers, computers, and other office equipment. Magistrates who questioned De Benedetti when he finally did go to jail for half a day in November 1993 accused him of having inflated the prices and sold faulty products. At the time of the deal, this hadn't mattered: the money had been paid, and the political parties and

Olivetti were all happy. Quality didn't really come into the equation. As Sergio Romano, a historian, newspaper columnist, and former high-ranking diplomat, pointed out in his book *Spaccato da Mano,* on the roots of corruption in Italy, "The exchange of bribes for contracts fits neatly into the long-established pattern of relations between Italian industry and politics. These relations were based on compromise: industry helped the rulers of the day to stay in power, the rulers helped private industry to make money."

The genius of Italian corruption was its pluralism. The bribes were shared out among a large number of parties. Whenever possible, no one was made to feel left out. This was corruption based on consent, very democratic and strictly in accordance with the country's electoral system of proportional representation. The size of the bribe often corresponded uncannily to the electoral strength of the party that received it. Roberto Mongini, the "collector" for the Christian Democrats in the Malpensa Airport project in Milan, told me how his party had received 20 percent of the money, the Socialists (who ruled Milan) 30 percent, the Republicans (who were a small but loyal coalition ally) 10 percent, and so on.

Nationally, the largesse was spread widely, as well. The "super-bribe" of $100 million paid in 1991 to close the ill-fated merger of the petrochemical concern ENIMONT even took into account the feuding factions of the Christian Democratic Party. The company paid 4.75 billion lire ($3 million) to Arnaldo Forlani, the secretary of the party, and 5 billion lire to Paolo Pomicino, a former minister of industry and leading figure of the Neapolitan faction of the party. (Neither Forlani nor Pomicino was ever charged with a crime.) Giulio Andreotti's faction, whose power base was in Lazio and Sicily, got 2.48 billion lire ($1.5 million). The smaller parties weren't ignored either: the Liberals got 205 million ($125,000), the Republicans and the Social Democrats 300 million lire ($180,000) each. The newcomers, Umberto Bossi's anticorruption Northern League, also joined the ranks of "average sinners" when they were given the small but compromising sum of 200 million lire (about $120,000).

All the bribes were paid by Raul Gardini, head of the Ferruzzi agro-industrial empire, which owned ENIMONT. Their purpose was to ensure that he would be able to end the merger of his chemical company, Montedison, with the state's chemical giant ENI, once it became obvious that the project was not working. Gardini became Italy's paymaster of bribes. By paying off as many parties and factions as possible, he tried to broaden the base of complicity. Once the racket was unmasked, Gardini, a passionate sailor and playboy with a perpetual tan, preferred to take his own life rather than face the judges and the humiliation of arrest.

The pluralist system of kickbacks mirrored the consensus in Parliament. Despite their sense of moral rectitude, the Communist opposition accepted the occasional sum. Although their corruption was quantitatively smaller than that of the ruling parties, they were also shareholders in "Tangentopoli." Business cooperatives set up by the Communist Party shared in lucrative state contracts, so the party's connivance, or at least tolerance, of malpractice could be bought. But because it was not in power and therefore not in a position to commission as many public works projects as the Christian Democrats or Socialists, it had by default to be less corrupt. The fact that its reputation was "cleaner" than that of the other parties had more to do with a lack of opportunity than with moral rectitude.

The system of corruption was based on a mutually beneficial contract between the political parties and business. The parties needed to pay for election campaigns, party workers, and, most important, the increasingly lavish lifestyle of the party bosses. In the heyday of "Tangentopoli," the party secretaries and their armies of flunkies lived like princes. In her kiss-and-tell account of life with the Italian Socialists, actress Sandra Milo describes the dreary routine of orgiastic parties in exclusive Roman hotels, the luxury apartments allocated to hangers-on, and the state's executive jets used for private purposes. Businesses didn't mind financing this lifestyle as long as they could increase their own profits.

The cost to the taxpayer and to the country's economic health was enormous. It was calculated that between 1980 and 1992, $20 billion had been paid out in bribes. Because businesses treated *tangente* like any other legitimate expense, the $20 billion was added on to the state's bills for public works projects. Naturally, because the *tangente* had not gone into the state's coffers, the increased outlays were not matched by increased revenue that could cover the inflated prices.

About 15 percent of Italy's colossal budget deficit is made up of such shortfalls. The state in turn made up the difference by increasing the prices paid by the consumer—a motorway that should have cost 10 billion lire, for instance, ended up costing 11.5 billion lire. This, of course, had a trickle-down effect on the growing mountain of debt and on ordinary Italians, who had to pay a higher motorway toll or an extra 2,000 lire to see the Uffizi Gallery in Florence or an exorbitant electricity bill. The man or woman in the street had gained nothing from the bribes circulating at the top of the pyramid. They had little in common with "average sinners" like Bettino Craxi or Carlo De Benedetti. But the recession, which began in 1990, meant that they too had become less tolerant about the sins of their rulers.

The system finally collapsed not because of moral outrage but because of lower profit margins. At its annual conference in 1992, Confindustria, the Italian Employers' Federation, a naturally conservative body that had always shown a self-interested loyalty to the government, finally turned its back on the parties it had supported for five decades. There were two reasons. First, in a recession companies could no longer afford to pay the 10 to 15 percent bribe on major contracts or ask for an equivalent markup in their own prices.* Second, the Italian budget deficit—at 115 percent of GDP—was no longer just embarrassing. It had become unviable and posed a serious threat to Italy's place in the first division of the European Union. The Maastricht Treaty, which had just been signed, had committed its twelve signatories to a reduction of each member country's budget deficit of 6 percent per annum by 1997, in preparation for monetary union. For Italy this meant halving the debt in five years, an impossible task. The grandees of Confindustria saw their own businesses losing out.

Two other economic factors helped precipitate the collapse of the system. First, the international community had lost faith in Italy's ability to get its affairs into order. The U.S. credit-rating institute Moody's downgraded Italy from the top AAA category, reserved for the members of the Group of Seven (G-7) club of industrialized pow-

*This was the main reason hundreds of businessmen lined up outside the judges' offices in Milan to confess. Without their admissions the "Tangentopoli" scandal never would have been uncovered to its vast extent.

ers, to the second group, which included countries like Spain and Portugal. The reaction from a country that had always prided itself on being the world's fifth or fourth richest nation, depending on whom you believe, was one of indignation. "Who is this Moody, anyway?" snapped the newspaper *La Repubblica*. For a whole week columnists and politicians heatedly debated the merits of Moody as if he were some cocky *agent provocateur.*

The fact was that Italy *was* becoming less creditworthy. In September 1992 the lira was taken out of the European Exchange Rate Mechanism and devalued by approximately 20 percent. The government of Prime Minister Giuliano Amato was staring bankruptcy in the face. Stefano Micossi, the head of Confindustria's planning and research staff, told me at the time that the government had been gripped by sheer panic. "Something had to be done. They had to save money, otherwise we would have faced financial collapse and a massive crisis. You can imagine the social consequences." In fact, Amato's government had already begun to cut public spending. Ironically, the devaluation of the lira that was one of the consequences of the international dismay with Italy's inability to whittle down its public expenses led to an export boom. Italian products had become much cheaper. But the damage that had been done by the system of corruption was lasting. The crisis of the lira left no one in any doubt that the party was over.

The domino effect was dramatic. With the country unable to borrow any more money, the ruling parties could no longer afford to finance the system of political patronage they had set up. They could no longer build highways, office blocks, tunnels, hospitals, or car parks whose sole purpose had been to generate bribes and power. In short, they could no longer buy votes.

The other great source of money, especially for the depressed South, had been the European Community. The flow of money was reduced by 20 percent between 1991 and 1993 because of German unification. The German government spent billions on restructuring the economy of the former East Germany and thus reduced the amount of money it was sending to Brussels. As a consequence, the outflow from the European Community's regional development fund, from which the poor and most Mafia-ridden areas of Italy had benefited in the past, suddenly dwindled to a trickle. Money was running out everywhere.

The system of corruption hadn't just consisted of a few hefty bribes; it had lubricated the whole machinery of politics, from the upper echelons of the parties to the lower ranks, where loyal party workers were paid off with jobs, flats, or cash. The illicit money had even trickled down to voters in regions like Sicily or Campania, where reluctant voters had simply been bought by the parties. During the 1992 national elections, for instance, the price of a vote for the Christian Democratic Party in Naples was 50,000 lire (about $30). In subsequent elections, as the party became more desperate, the price of a vote increased, but the ability to pay had declined. The party's share of the vote in the Naples municipal elections of November 1993 crashed to 5 percent. The *tangente* had been the lifeblood of the *partitocrazia;* without them, its metabolism simply packed up. Corruption was largely killed off by its own excesses.

The "system" had several unhealthy consequences. The first was that Italian democracy was undermined. The second was that the growth of a freer market and fairer competition was prevented. Some would say that it took Italy's instinctive distrust of the free market to create a system based on deals and kickbacks. Indeed, it has become common for Italian industry to lament the absence of a genuine free market. Carlo De Benedetti, for instance, had frequently made such a complaint. In an interview in 1992, well before he himself was sucked into "Tangentopoli," he told me, "We Italians dislike genuine competition among ourselves . . . in politics as well as in economics." This was ironic since De Benedetti was one of those who had benefited from the system.

In this sense the *tangente* was more than a bribe. It was a peace offering to a potential enemy, the modern equivalent of a feudal tithe. Those who couldn't afford to pay it were excluded from the market. In April 1992 I went to Milan to see one such outcast. Giovanni Gadola was the owner of Italy's oldest construction company, founded in 1857. The offices of this diminutive but immensely proud entrepreneur were located in a nondescript housing block. The rubber plants seemed self-consciously rubbery. The yellowed walls were decorated with photographs of the company's projects: a small sandal factory, an office block, a footbridge. The company clearly wasn't doing very well. Anywhere else in Europe this fact would have been put down to the firm's own failings, but Gadola came up with a different explanation. "Our business isn't thriving," he lamented, "because we haven't got the funds to pay the *tangenti* that get you the big projects. All the lucrative public works projects in Milan demand a *tangente*." Gadola, who was perched on a huge swivel chair, had become angry. "My family refuses to take out loans to pay bribes!" The construction industry was one of the most difficult sectors for an honest entrepreneur to thrive in, since the most lucrative contracts came from the state and therefore from the greedy parties. This company had probably been denied its share of the market because it wasn't corrupt.

The lack of a free market may have been a misfortune for small businesses, but it didn't hinder the Italian economy from blooming. Compared to the United Kingdom's or Germany's, Italy's recession was short-lived. By mid-1994 growth rates had risen above 2.5 percent and thanks to the low value of the lira Italian exports were booming. To some this proved that Italy was still a success story despite its widespread corruption. But this ignores the upheaval created by the collapse of the old regime. Corruption created genuine political instability and shook the brittle foundations of Italian democracy.

It also left visible scars on Italy's spectacular landscape and cultural heritage. This is a sad and lengthy catalogue of mutilation. The story of ancient Rome was told in marble, granite, and travertine, that of modern Italy in reinforced concrete, cement, and asphalt. A whole coffee-table book could be filled with the unfinished highways, the unused canals, the abandoned building sites that litter the Italian landscape.

The further south you head, the less harmless the abuses. Broadly speaking, what distinguishes southern Italy from the North is that the bribe was not only used as a lubricant for business, it was often its sole purpose. En route from Rome's Fiumicino Airport to the center of town an uncompleted cloverleaf sprouts out of a cabbage field next to the existing highway like some luxuriant cement Triffid. This excrescence of modern civic engineering has been there for ten years.

It is a building site without builders. The roads look like amputated stumps. Metal girders stick out at odd angles like bristles. Meanwhile, the never-ending construction site creates a nerve-racking traffic jam on the existing highway. Beyond the stranded cloverleaf is a collection of what look like futuristic grain silos off the set of the film *Blade Runner.* These, in fact, are housing blocks. The protest banners and flags hanging from the windows next to lines of washing denounce the local housing authorities and plead for better accommodations. Most Italian cities are ringed by such housing developments that have never even experienced a bat's squeak of *dolce vita.*

The stunning coastlines of Calabria, Puglia, and Sicily are scarred with unfinished multistory car parks and tower blocks. One of the most shocking examples of the surreal genius of overconstruction is the Bay of Palermo. At the end of a sweeping valley that hangs like a hammock between two mountain ranges, this bay was once one of the most beautiful in Italy. Even allowing for the urban expansion of Palermo, a city of one and a half million inhabitants, there is no excuse for the abandoned housing developments that stick to the mountainside like solidified lava. The houses, built on a perilous slope, were never meant to be lived in. Their *raison d'être* was generating business for the local construction company that was in the hands of the Mafia and a bribe for a politician who was also in the hands of organized crime. The superstrada from Palermo to San Guiseppe Iato that rings the bay is built on sixteen-foot pylons, even though it crosses no rivers or valleys. The motorway could just as well have been built on the ground. The pylons were an ingenious way of using more cement and therefore generating more money and bigger bribes. In Sicily, cement rules. Just two hundred yards from where the anti-Mafia judge Giovanni Falcone, his wife, and their five bodyguards were killed by a car bomb in May 1992 is a sign put up by the Sicilian cement company, bidding visitors welcome to the island. The bomb, which had been planted in a drainage shaft under the highway, left a crater six feet deep and a hundred wide. Within days the crater was filled and the motorway patched up. The Mafia, they say, is in construction. The bomb not only removed the country's leading anti-Mafia judge, it also created a demand for more cement.

If much of Italy is littered with what the Italians call *cattedrali nel deserto,* cathedrals in the desert, the Saint Peter's amongst them is the European container port at Gioia Tauro in Calabria. This is a monument to the corruption, mismanagement, delusions of grandeur, and misplaced hopes of the local population. What was once one of Calabria's most fertile agricultural plains, filled with orange orchards and with some of the peninsula's oldest olive trees, is now a vast expanse of concrete, empty and desolate. The trees were mowed down in 1969 to make room for twenty square miles of industrial park. The centerpiece was going to be one of Italy's largest steel mills. Gioia Tauro was selected over eleven other potential sites against all technical advice. The area had no port, it was predominantly and profitably agricultural, and it had no industrial tradition. There was no substantial demand for steel within a 125-mile radius, and it was situated in a high-risk earthquake zone. None of these arguments mattered. They were outweighed by the needs of the local Christian Democratic and Socialist Party bosses for public money to renew their sources of patronage and thus their power.

After the 1973 oil crisis the demand for steel in Europe dropped sharply. But work continued on the infrastructure of the project, which has become one of the most expensive industrial skeletons in the country. The nearby industrial zone lies vacant. Arms manufacturer Oto Breda built a plant in the 1980s to produce a new missile for NATO, but by the time the plant was finished, the missile had been superseded. Later projects to build a power station were thwarted first by the local environmental lobby and then by the involvement of the local Mafia, the 'Ndrangheta, which was angry that it wasn't getting its cut of the business. Gioia Tauro has one of the highest rates of infiltration by organized crime, with around sixty 'Ndrangheta families operating in the area. In 1990 magistrates froze all construction contracts on suspicion that the business had gone to front companies of the 'Ndrangheta. In January 1993 thirty-nine people were arrested on corruption charges in connection with the power station, including the chairman of ENEL, the Italian state electricity company. (That same day, I almost had my electricity cut off for being a week late with the payment of a bill. The man from the electricity board agreed with me about the injustice in the face of greater crimes and let me off the hook.)

Today an artificial port is linked to Gioia Tauro by a country road that turns into a dirt track, a cruel irony when you consider that so many deserted parts of the region that never had even the dimmest hope of industrialization are endowed with three-lane highways. First you come across an abandoned village of workers' huts made of corrugated iron. Then you see a trawler beached on a sandy dune, rusting into oblivion. From the dune you get a spectacular view of three miles of virgin quayside. In the distance three large blue cranes stand idle. To their right is a vast container parking lot. It's completely empty except for one broken-down gasoline truck stranded right in the middle. The salty wind whistles across the industrial plain. The only human activity is two urchins driving a flock of sheep across the building site of the steel mill, now covered by a threadbare carpet of grass. A lone fisherman, sitting on a yellow mooring post, lazily flicks his rod into the still, serene waters of what was supposed to have been Europe's biggest container port. So far the only things produced by the billions of dollars sunk into the project have been a handful of arrest warrants and a lot of disillusionment among the local population.

The empty building site stands in lurid contrast to the ramshackle town of Gioia Tauro, a name that means "Jewel of Taurus," inappropriate in 1994 but I suspect not in 500 B.C. Although the town started its urban life as an ancient Greek settlement, it bears an alarming resemblance to a South African township. Most of the labor in the nearby orange plantations is provided by black African immigrants from Ghana or Senegal. You will not find any immigrants in the few local bars or restaurants or in the Benetton clothes shop on the main road. At dusk, when they have returned from the plantation, the workers huddle around small campfires on the side of the road. They live in abandoned cottages or makeshift huts and get paid 30,000 lire a day, about $20, much less than an Italian worker could ask for.

The male population of Gioia Tauro still pins its fading hopes on the container port. "Five thousand jobs, one quarter of the local population, that's what they promised us when they came to chop down the orange trees in 1969." Giancarlo Calucci, a local journalist, told me that the project was only temporarily on hold. "Once they have sorted out all this political mess," he continued, "they'll carry on working. They've got to." What Giancarlo didn't want to admit to himself was that the only reason for building a container port in Gioia Tauro, hundreds of miles from any industry or commercial center, was political. Once the political system that had produced the building site imploded, the project too was doomed.

C H A P T E R   3

Couch Confessions
of an *Ancien Régime*

U ntil he was sacked on April 22, 1992, Dr. Piero Rocchini re-
joiced in the title of "Health Consultant for Clinical Psychology to the Italian Chamber of Deputies." Dr. Rocchini, who is in
his forties and has a dense beard and glasses with thick lenses,
worked for ten years on the medical staff that ensured that Italy's parliamentarians were in the best shape to represent the needs and
wishes of the people who had elected them. The medical and psychological care was free of charge, a service provided by the taxpayer.
Having listened to the fears, dreams, and desires of more than two
hundred deputies who had regularly sought the solace of his couch in
his practice behind the Coliseum, Piero Rocchini became deeply anx-
ious. What he found was a Parliament on the edge of a nervous
breakdown: tired deputies unable to carry out their duties because
they kept waking up at night in a cold sweat, an increasing number
of persecution complexes, identity crises, cyclic depression, nervous
rashes, and chain-smoking. Tranquilizers had become the most popular item sold over the counter at the Parliament's in-house drugstore.

Dr. Rocchini has never revealed the names of his honorable clients. But in April 1992 he wrote of their collection of symptoms in
an article. He wanted to warn the Italians about the mental state of

their elected assembly. Unfortunately, this was seen as an act of gross indiscretion; it incurred the wrath of his patients and led to his dismissal. The position was never filled again. With more time on his hands, the doctor then turned his mind to a book, *Le Nevrosi del Potere* (The Neuroses of Power). It was published, and the launch party was held in a hotel next to Parliament. Many of the guests had been Rocchini's patients. In fact, most of the deputies have remained on the doctor's register, unable to sever the strong emotional bond established over the years. Out of power and in disgrace, many seek his advice these days about how to deal with the stresses of unemployment.

In 1992, just as the old party-political regime was collapsing, the doctor was dealing with different stresses. His office always got overcrowded during election campaigns. In the weeks before the spring elections of 1992, which have gone down in Italian history as the calamitous "5 Aprile," the parliamentary shrink was in greater demand than ever. The deputies' anxieties were justified: the Christian Democrats and the Socialists, the parties that had exercised an almost divine right to rule for decades, suffered their worst-ever hemorrhage of votes. Only a handful of Rocchini's patients were reelected. According to his diagnosis, this reflected the breakdown of communications between the politicians and the people they represented.

While the umbilical cord between the electors and the elected was being severed, another emotional tie was getting stronger and stronger. The patients' energies were concentrated to an unhealthy degree on their relationship with their party. This gave rise to what Dr. Rocchini called *partito mamma sindrome,* or mother party syndrome. The party had become the ersatz mother or, in the doctor's words, "a perverse place of refuge, a kind of political womb, which allows the deputy to play out his private fantasies." Devotion to the party is so great that it stifles any other affiliations or affections. The deputy is unable to have normal relationships with his family, his friends, and, most important, his voters. This politically induced Oedipus complex is seen by the opponents of Italy's *partitocrazia* as one reason why the all-powerful parties had become so corrupt and lost touch with those voters who voted for them but didn't owe them their jobs, bribes, or other material benefits.

But the party wasn't just *mamma*. She was also an increasingly fickle mistress, thanks to an electoral law that was passed in 1991. This produced the so-called "single-preference syndrome," perhaps the only time in the history of psychology that an electoral law has created its own neurosis. The law abolished the existing system whereby voters were allowed to vote for four preferred candidates from one party. Now they could vote for only one. The struggle to be *numero uno* led to furious bouts of jealousy, infighting, intrigue, and backstabbing among those deputies who were nurtured, as it were, by the same *mamma*. In a survey conducted by the Center for Sociopsychological Studies of 250 politicians from five Italian cities, it emerged that the interviewees feared members of their own parties more than they did the opposition.

By far the most serious psychological disorder afflicting the Italian Parliament was the so-called "Di Pietro syndrome." Dr. Rocchini named it after Antonio Di Pietro, the Milan magistrate who has led the judicial crusade against corruption. When the extent of corruption was first uncovered and Antonio Di Pietro started issuing the famous *avvisi di garanzia,* warrants that notify a subject that he or she is under criminal investigation and may soon be taken into preventive police custody, Dr. Rocchini's workload also increased exponentially. His couch became crowded with parliamentarians fearing disgrace.

In spring 1992 the Socialist Sergio Moroni resorted to suicide as the only way out of his humiliation. Under Parliament's immunity law, he was in no danger of going to jail. But he had been issued with a warrant. His was the first in a long line of suicides provoked by the stresses of the corruption scandal. After Moroni's death a collective nightmare began to keep Parliament awake. "My patients started having recurring dreams," Dr. Rocchini said. "They're locked in a house at night. There's a loud knock on the door. The door is suddenly flung open, and a policeman is waiting outside with a pair of handcuffs. In another common nightmare my patients dream that they are being led in handcuffs from an expensive restaurant filled with their family and friends." The dreams were remarkably lifelike and, it seemed, prophetic. Perhaps they were inspired by a guilt complex, whose origins may be explained by the findings of another survey conducted by the Center for Sociopsychological Studies. Asked why they had wanted to go into politics in the first place, 38 percent of the politicians said they had done so in pursuit of power and public office, 34 percent admitted they were in it just for the money, and only 16 percent said they had become politicians because they believed in the ideological principles represented by their parties—a remarkable display of honesty for a group one third of whose members were under indictment.

Where did these politicians come from? It is implausible that Italian politicians are constitutionally incapable of integrity or inherently flawed psychologically. A system as corrupt as the one that has been in power since the end of World War II is not composed of hundreds of individual bad apples. Instead it is the result of deeper currents, a type of original sin that no one can escape.

By 1992, the year in which Dr. Rocchini's couch was fully booked, Italy's regime had degenerated into smoldering decadence. The psychiatrist's couch had become the symbolic deathbed of the *partitocrazia*. It was easy to forget the fact that Italy had prospered under that system. Whether because of or in spite of the *partitocrazia*—to this day people can't really make up their minds—Italy emerged from fascism and civil war to become a stable democracy and one of the seven wealthiest nations in the world. The system under which it achieved this was one of the most bizarre acts of political acrobatics in modern history. Like the Tower of Pisa, which leans more and more every year but never falls, Italy's "democratic regime" has defied almost every rule in the handbook of democracy. Between 1945 and 1992 the country had fifty-one governments, creating the impression of permanent chaos among those who don't understand the genius of the system. In fact, the chaos masked a rigid continuity that verged on rigor mortis. This was one of many paradoxes. Another was that Italy's election results seldom changed despite a consistently high turnout and a lively political debate. For millions of Italians voting became a regular ritual, as ceremonial and meaningless as going to Midnight Mass on Christmas Eve. A 2 percent swing in results for or against the Socialists or Christian Democrats was considered a political earthquake. But however violent the tremors, Italy's coalition governments barely changed. Italian voters saw their votes less as a means of political change that could enable them to throw out a government they might not like and more as a statement of creed. Many Italians adopted a political party for life, just as the party often adopted them for life too. The livelihoods of millions of voters depended on the patronage of one party or another. The town of Crotone in Calabria was a case in point. The town's only large-scale employer was the local sulfur factory. This factory was run by a Christian Democrat who had been placed there by the party. Through the hierarchy of patronage he "persuaded" most of the factory's employees and their families to vote for the Christian Democrats. The party was seen as the local benefactor.

The system was quasi feudal. The ruling parties carved up the country's bloated public sector, from the steel industry to the railways, as if they were private domains. This culture of patronage created its own vocabulary of political abuse, as peculiarly Italian as it is untranslatable. One of the key concepts was *sottogoverno,* literally "undergovernment." This was the alternative power structure that had been nurtured by the parties to provide them with patronage and votes. Although it had been set up by the governing parties, it undermined the influence of government itself by making the executive branch less important than the parties. The purpose of government was not so much to legislate as to preserve the fiefdoms set up by the parties and to ensure that the spoils were shared out fairly.

Sottogoverno was created by *lottizzazione,* or parceling out. This was the widespread practice of giving jobs to the boys, even if the boys weren't particularly qualified. Perhaps the most bizarre word in the warped vocabulary of Italian power is *consociativismo* (literally, "associationism"). This untranslatable term was coined after Italian unification in the 1860s and describes the traditional acquiescence of the opposition to the party of government. It stems from the instinctive fear of conflict and the preference for compromise that have become a ground rule of Italian politics. This was another Italian paradox. Despite the fact that the ideological fault line of the Cold War ran right through Italian society, with Catholic conservatives in government and the biggest communist party in the West in perpetual opposition, the two reached a modus vivendi soon after 1948, when the Christian Democrats swept the elections and established themselves as the ruling party. In the late 1970s the Communists stopped being a genuine party of opposition and became a minority shareholder in the system of patronage. Italy was thus deprived of an alternation between government and opposition. When the electorate changed its mind in 1992, it threw out the whole regime.

The extraordinary continuity of Italian postwar politics is best exemplified by a man who was a founding member of the Christian Democratic Party in 1942 and took up his first cabinet post at the same time as Winston Churchill became prime minister for the second time. He served his last term as president of the Council of Ministers in 1992, the last Christian Democrat to do so before the party was disbanded and reborn as the Popular Party. Giulio Andreotti had helped to write Italy's 1946 Constitution, had sat in twenty-seven of fifty-one postwar cabinets, and had been prime minister seven times. He is also a devout Catholic who goes to Mass every morning at seven and once wrote a book entitled *Popes I Have Known.* There were four! This close association with God and his highest representatives on earth has not protected Andreotti from what the Italians call *odore di mafia,* the smell of the Mafia. At the time of completing this book, Andreotti was preparing to go on trial for alleged collusion with the Mafia, a fact that brought him the dubious honor of being perhaps the only statesman in the world commonly referred to as "Beelzebub" in the press. Before losing his parliamentary immunity from prosecution in 1993, he had already fought off twenty-six separate parliamentary inquiries into a variety of peccadilloes concerning the abuse of power and corruption. He has always been suspected of forming a pact with the Devil, and once upon a time was even mildly flattered by these whispers. "I have been blamed for every possible disaster in Italian history," he once lamented, "with the possible exception of the Punic Wars [264 B.C.–241 B.C.]. And that's because I was too young at the time."

Andreotti has survived every other European statesman of his generation.* His longevity used to impress Italians, who saw in him the incarnation of a quality that they have always highly valued:

*He first joined the Italian Cabinet when the British prime minister John Major was three years old, and he was still sitting opposite his British counterpart in 1992.

furbo, or cunning. He proved to be a masterful negotiator during all-night sessions of the European Community and more than a match for someone like Margaret Thatcher. He was also a rounded personality with diverse interests. Gifted with an elegant but simple Italian, he wrote a weekly newspaper column and several biographies. But none of them could compete in intricacy and suspense with the story of Andreotti's life.

The "Old Fox" was also a quintessential Roman. One could imagine him as a wise and cunning senator in ancient Rome or as a cardinal at the Vatican, the *éminence grise* behind a weak pope. The more power Andreotti possessed, the more discreetly he wielded it. His other nickname was "Zio," or uncle. Until recently Andreotti used to conduct an avuncular morning ritual that seemed like a scene from *The Godfather.* At the crack of dawn he would gather a group of his closest advisers and friends in his bathroom to discuss world affairs or party politics or just to gossip. While the others sat on stools or the edge of the tub, Andreotti would lean back in a reclining chair and be shaved by his favorite Roman barber. Once the conclave was over, he would go to Mass in his local church in Rome's Via Giulia. Andreotti was a peculiarly Roman mixture of Machiavelli and incense. While half his schoolmates became bishops or cardinals, he became the high priest of the *partitocrazia.*

Now shriveled by illness and abandoned by party and friends, he still stalks the Senate as one of seven life senators. A gaunt, ghostly figure with an increasingly hunched back, he has become the death mask of the old regime. Some of the charges against him seem literally unbelievable. Andreotti is currently under investigation for allegedly ordering the murder in 1979 of Mino Pecorelli, an investigative journalist and blackmailer who threatened to expose the fact that Andreotti allowed his friend and colleague Aldo Moro to be killed by the Red Brigades. According to one theory—and there are many!—Moro had opened the way for the Italian Communist Party, the biggest in the West, to participate in government, a fact that enraged the United States. It's about as outlandish as if President Bill Clinton were being investigated for colluding with the New York Mafia to murder the head of the Democratic Leadership Council. Wild stuff, but not too wild for the Italians!

If Mafia turncoat Baldassare Di Maggio is to be believed, Andreotti not only let himself be manipulated by organized crime, he also allowed himself to be kissed by its bosses. Di Maggio told judges how he had personally witnessed a meeting between Andreotti and the boss of all the bosses, Salvatore "Totò" Riina—who is currently in jail—in Palermo in 1988. At that meeting Riina is alleged to have kissed Andreotti on the right cheek, an avuncular but highly symbolic Mafia gesture that establishes the superiority of the kisser over the kissed. The former prime minister has rejected these charges as ludicrous and part of a plot to ruin him.*

But even if these charges are groundless, Andreotti himself is partly responsible for them. Massimo Franco, his biographer and a personal friend, told me, "Andreotti consciously nurtured the mystique around him by promoting a sense of ambiguity about everything he did. He has become the victim of his own ambiguity." Part of this mystique is an archive, kept in a cellar somewhere in Rome where all the dark secrets and shady names of the First Republic have been stored by the former Vatican archivist. Rome is full of journalists, newspaper readers, and politicians who are in awe of Andreotti's personal archive, crammed full of dark secrets and potential incriminations, although I have never seen the archive and have never met anyone who has seen it. In fact, it may not even exist. Perhaps that was the intention. The implied threat, which Andreotti has never spelled out himself but which others have made on his behalf, is that some of these secrets will become public should the former prime minister be put on trial. The archive has become like the secret Italian state library of dirt and a Delphic oracle: a universal key to understanding the mysterious bombs, kidnappings, and murders of illustrious citizens that scar recent Italian history and that have never been fully explained. It is thus part of the rich undercurrent of mysteries and conspiracies that flows through Italian politics and that expresses a common obsession with hidden truths. The Italians even have a word for this: *dietrologia,* literally "behindology."

---

*When I interviewed him in his office, which was filled with thousands of pages of evidence that he hopes will prove his innocence, the "Uncle"—who was wearing slippers and a cardigan—dismissed Di Maggio as a "poor old fellow" who had been forced to lie in order to stay in Italy's witness protection program.

The secret of his power was not that he tried to impose his will on everyone around him, but that he left them to their own resources. In that too he embodied the old regime. One of the biggest crimes of the old political elite was that they didn't govern but allowed malignancies to spread in the interest of preserving power within their own party. "Power tires only those who do not possess it," the sibylline Andreotti once said when asked how he had managed to stay at the helm for so many decades. The reason is that his type of power demanded the minimum of exertion. It was power without responsibility. But to understand fully how he came to be the master practitioner in such a warped system, one has to return to the making of Italy after the collapse of fascism.

Don Giulio was brought into politics by his mentor and Italy's greatest postwar leader, Alcide De Gasperi. In the 1930s and early '40s De Gasperi was the chief archivist of the Vatican Library in Rome. One of his assistants was Andreotti, a devout young Catholic who was as studious as he was reclusive. It was said that the two used to go to Mass together: De Gasperi would speak to God and Andreotti to the priest. A Roman by birth, Andreotti had a humble upbringing. His father, an elementary school teacher, died when Giulio was only two. He was brought up in religious schools and had his first personal encounter with a pope at the age of eight, when he crashed an audience that Pius XI was giving for a Belgian delegation. As a student Andreotti became a member of the Catholic Graduates' Association together with Aldo Moro. Both were recruited by De Gaspari into the Christian Democratic Party soon after it had been founded in Milan in September 1942.

The party itself was not new but recycled. Its ancestor was the Popular Party, a mass Catholic party founded in 1911 and modeled on the German Center Party. The Popular Party had been killed off in 1926 by internal divisions, by Fascist repression—Mussolini banned all opposition parties that year—and by the fact that the Vatican, the party's main source of influence and inspiration, was coming to terms with Il Duce. Three years later this resulted in the Lateran Treaties, which gave the Catholic Church massive financial compensation for the properties it had lost during Italian unification in the previous century and established Vatican City as an independent state.

Alcide De Gasperi, who had been the last general secretary of the Popular Party, was motivated first by anti-fascism—he had been imprisoned by the Fascists in 1927—and then by anti-communism. Once fascism collapsed in most of Italy in 1943, De Gasperi considered the battle between communism and Christianity the principal struggle of his lifetime. He saw it as a war between two visions: the broad social solidarity of the Catholic Church on one side and the domination of one class by another, as interpreted by Marxism, on the other. De Gasperi wanted to turn the Christian Democrats into a Catholic party of the masses that would appeal to capitalists and landowners as much as to workers and peasants. He managed to achieve this thanks to help from two quarters: the Vatican and the Allies, who occupied Italy at the end of the war.

Pope Pius XII, who was elected in 1939, ideally wanted to see Italy become a Franco-style dictatorship, undemocratic and very Catholic. When he realized that this was impossible, he started casting around for political support elsewhere. Gradually and somewhat begrudgingly, he adopted the Christian Democrats as the Church's party, helping it in several crucial ways. In 1944, after the liberation of Rome by the Allies, the Vatican instructed priests to speak out in favor of the Christian Democrats and encouraged Catholic groups like Catholic Action and the Coldiretti, a peasants' association, to give their allegiance to the fledgling Christian Democratic Party. Within weeks the party was handed the support of millions of Italian Catholics and their grassroots organizations on a platter. Much of this support came from rural and urban working-class associations. The fact that they backed the Catholic right as opposed to the left undermined the Communist Party's hold on large swathes of the working population, especially in the staunchly Catholic Veneto region, Lazio, the Campania, and much of the South. This too was part of the instinct for *consociativismo,* the ability to create a consensus amongst people or groups that in other countries would have battled one another. The Christian Democrats not only championed socially progressive issues such as land reform and the rights of factory workers, they also appealed to the traditional instincts of Italy's family culture with a "mission to restore the family to health and morality" after the devastation and uprooting of the war. This campaign was aimed above all at women, and it reaped its dividends in the 1946 elections, the first in Italian history in which women were allowed to vote. Significantly, the Communist Party also tried—far less convincingly—to become the champions of a wholesome family life. But doing so did more to expose them to ridicule. Father Riccardo Lombardi, known as "God's microphone," made his broadcasting career by pointing up the differences between the Communists' family policy and the Marxist belief that the family should be abolished.

If the Vatican gave the Christian Democrats moral help, the Allies, in particular the Americans, provided invaluable material assistance. As the British historian Paul Ginsborg has described in his excellent book, *A History of Contemporary Italy,* Washington played a crucial role in ensuring that the foundations of modern Italy were built on Christian Democracy. As early as June 1945, Joseph Drew, the acting secretary of state, had written, "Our objective is to strengthen Italy economically and politically so that the truly democratic elements of the country can withstand the forces that threaten to sweep them into a new totalitarianism" (for "totalitarianism," read "communism"). Acting through the United Nations Rehabilitation and Relief Administration (UNRRA) in 1946, Washington was already providing the majority of imports into Italy. Furthermore, the committee that ran the UNRRA in Italy was headed by the U.S. chief of mission and by a close associate of De Gasperi's, who was also the brother of the future Pope Paul VI.

The brunt of American intervention in Italy's internal affairs, however, came to be felt after 1947. There were two reasons. First, the Christian Democrats and De Gasperi were rapidly losing support among the electorate. The rate of inflation had risen to an alarming 50 percent in the first six months of 1947. Second, in February a peace treaty was finally signed. It was a massive blow to De Gasperi's prestige: Italy lost all her colonies, including those acquired before World War I; the country had to pay $360 million dollars' worth of reparations to the Soviet Union, Greece, Albania, and Ethiopia, among others; the Istrian Peninsula went to Yugoslavia; and the city of Trieste became a so-called free territory under international supervision. Regional elections in Sicily showed that the damage to the Christian Democrats was severe, and national elections were due in

1948. Meanwhile, the Americans had formulated the Truman Doctrine, the Cold War had begun, and everything needed to be mobilized to ensure a victory of the right. And it was.

In the first three months of 1948 the United States gave Italy $176 million in interim aid, while the U.S. embassy and the Christian Democratic authorities made sure this injection of money received the most intense publicity. The arrival of every one hundredth ship bearing food, clothes, and medicines was celebrated in a variety of ports from Genoa to Reggio di Calabria. The goods were then loaded onto special "friendship trains," often accompanied by the U.S. ambassador. If clarification were still needed, George Marshall declared on March 20, 1948, that if the Communists won the Italian elections the plan that bore his name would stop immediately. Meanwhile, the Western Allies managed to remove the most-hated clause of the infamous peace treaty by promising the Italians months before the elections that Trieste would after all remain Italian.

Hollywood was also enlisted in the election campaign. Film stars recorded messages denouncing the Communists. More than a million letters were sent by Italian immigrants to family members in the "old country," urging them to vote anti-Communist, that is, Christian Democrat. And in a cosmetic but effective gesture, the U.S. fleet in the Mediterranean reinforced its presence around Italy. U.S. warships anchored off the coast of Naples, just in case the "wrong" party won.

The Vatican weighed in behind the Americans. On March 29, 1948, Pius XII told the Romans that "the solemn hour of their Christian conscience has sounded." The episcopate warned that "It is a mortal sin to vote for lists and candidates who do not give sufficient assurances of respecting the rights of God, the Church, and mankind"—in other words, the Communists. Local parish priests echoed the message from the pulpit, virtually threatening deviants with excommunication. The Christian Democrats waged a crude campaign, exaggerating the threat of communism and fueling the fears it produced. One poster showed a giant Joseph Stalin trampling on the "wedding cake," the white marble monstrosity in the center of Rome that had been built as a monument to Victor Emmanuel II and Italian unification. The party also enlisted the help of the stomach. "Don't think," one poster proclaimed, "that you'll be able to flavor your pasta with the speeches of Togliatti [the Communist Party leader]. All intelligent people will vote for De Gasperi because he has obtained free from America the flour for your spaghetti and the sauce you put on it." The culinary propaganda paid off. The Christian Democrats received 48.5 percent of the vote and 305 out of 574 seats in the Chamber of Deputies, an absolute majority.

Although the Christian Democrats were never again to repeat such stunning results, the elections of 1948 and the help provided by the Vatican and the United States established them as the party of government for the next four decades. Equally important to the future shape of Italy was the behavior of the Communists, which essentially was acquiescence toward their electoral enemies, the Christian Democrats. The Communists never managed to capitalize on the fact that they had dominated the anti-Fascist resistance movement and the several hundred thousand Italians who had taken part in it. Under the leadership of Palmiro Togliatti, they abandoned working-class militancy and started the transformation from a revolutionary movement to a mass party. The decision was made—much to the dismay of the more eager and dogmatic comrades—at a meeting in Salerno in 1944. It became known as *svolta di Salerno,* the turning point of Salerno, and set the party on a course of cooperation rather than confrontation. Like the future leaders of the Communist Party, Togliatti was hamstrung by the Western Allies, whose troops were still based in northern Italy as late as 1947, and by the hold of the Catholic Church over the Italians. The Communist "Church" simply couldn't compete, a fact Togliatti admitted when he arrived in Rome in 1944. "We the Communist Party have declared—and I repeat this declaration here in Rome, the capital of the Catholic world—that we respect the traditional faith of the majority of Italian people." Meanwhile, Togliatti was convinced that the Christian Democrats, who had managed to capture the support of a significant part of the working class, were committed to social reform. This turned out not to be true, but the fact that the Communist leadership was fooled had as much to do with their own delusions as with De Gasperi's ability to exploit them. As Paul Ginsborg has pointed out, "It was part of De Gasperi's political genius that he continued to inspire the respect and even the faith of the left, while consistently denying them their objectives."

Even after Stalin had called the Italian Communists to heel in 1947, Togliatti, who had been minister of justice under De Gasperi, refused to adopt the path of militancy and chose to fight the Christian Democrats on their own terms, namely at the ballot box. As we have seen, however, the playing field was far from level.

From then on the Italian Communist Party was torn apart by the need to preserve its left-wing identity and the desire to become accepted as a mainstream party of government. It became a masterpiece of ambiguity—some called it institutionalized schizophrenia. As the party moved from ideology to pragmatism, the only way to preserve its unity was through some masterful intellectual juggling. In this the party leadership was helped by Italy's chief philosopher, Antonio Gramsci. One of the founders of the party and its secretary from 1924 to 1926, Gramsci had been imprisoned by the Fascists until his death in 1937. While in prison he jotted down his thoughts on literature, philosophy, history, and the party. The writings, published as *Prison Notebooks,* were often so muddled and disjointed that they produced a veritable cottage industry of interpretation. Some chose to see the *Notebooks* as a celebration of Stalinism, others as an affirmation of a watered-down socialism.

In any case, Gramsci was dissected and borrowed to underpin whichever line the party's leadership chose to paper over the cracks. For its friends the party's stance was constructive ambiguity, for its enemies a policy of *doppiezza,* or duplicity. The party, it was claimed, was engaged in a duplicitous double game of seducing the voters with the respectable mask of a constitutional party, only to reveal the hidden face of Soviet-style communism once in power. Historians are still divided about whether this accusation was fair or not. The fact is, however, that the Communist Party was always mistrusted—in the words of its own official historian, Paolo Spriano, "like a Trojan horse in the bourgeois citadel." This mistrust was so deep that it re-emerged during the elections of 1994 and deprived the successors to Italy's Communist Party of an election victory they had assumed would be theirs after four decades in the wings.

The most important political contribution to postwar Italy made by the Communists was the modus operandi that they had established with the ruling Christian Democrats and their allies, which reached its most sophisticated form in the 1970s. Using the "grand coalition" that had been set up in West Germany between the Social Democrats and Christian Democrats as a model, Communist Party leader Enrico Berlinguer announced a policy of "historic compromise." Although not part of the governing coalition, the Communist Party would vote with the government on key issues of foreign and domestic policy. For the first time since 1947, the Christian Democrats began to reintegrate the Communists into the governing system. The reconciliation was engineered in 1976 by, among others, Giulio Andreotti, who was now prime minister for the third time. In return for their indirect support in Parliament, the Communists were given some sizable crumbs of power, including the presidency of the Chamber of Deputies and the chairmanship of seven parliamentary committees.

Behind the scenes, party leaders hammered out common policy programs that were then presented to the parties as a *fait accompli*. In the abstruse language of Italian politics, the parties had established a "constitutional arch" of cooperation among all the parties in Parliament that had taken part in the drafting of the Italian Constitution in 1946. This comfortable arrangement would have continued to flourish had it not been for the unjustified fears of the U.S. White House that the Christian Democrats were opening the doors of government to the Communists. The kidnap and murder of Aldo Moro by the Red Brigades finally pulled the rug out from under the Communists' feet and the government's strategy. Pressured by discontent among the rank and file, who complained that the price of compromise had been the rights of workers, the Communist Party abandoned its support of the government in 1979 and forced new elections.

But even this was only a temporary phenomenon: the Communist Party never, in fact, fully turned its back on the policy of acquiescence it had set out three decades earlier. Instead of taking power at a national level, it proved to be a very effective force of local and regional government.

Unlike the Fascists, the Communists really did make the trains and buses run on time. Bologna, a stunningly beautiful city and home to Europe's oldest university, is the capital of Italy's traditional "Red belt." The city is a shining example of municipal efficiency. The streets are spotless, the transport system works—there is even a housing policy for gay couples, in a country that barely recognizes the existence of homosexuality. Bologna, called *"la Grassa,"* or "the Fat One," by Italians because of its obsession with food, is not so much a Socialist Workers' Paradise as a monument to bourgeois good living and civic values. In many parts of central Italy like Umbria, Tuscany, and Emilia-Romagna where the Communists have always run local administration, the party is seen not so much as the ideological heir of Karl Marx as an opponent of clerical misrule. Before the unification of Italy these regions were part of the Papal States and as such were notorious for their bad administration, poverty, neglect, and high taxation.

The back-scratching between those in power and those in opposition was further consolidated by an electoral system of pure proportional representation that allowed no party to gain an absolute majority in Parliament and that kept the four-party coalition in power until 1993. Italy became a country deprived of the balancing act of government and opposition taking turns. This is what finally inspired the electoral reform referendum of 1993, when 38 million Italians, more than 85 percent of the electorate, opted for a British-style majority "winner-takes-all" voting system. The irony was that this system had been tried at the beginning of the century and had been scrapped because it was blamed for giving too much power to local party bosses, who ran their constituencies like Mafia fiefdoms.*

Since its unification, Italy's history has been signposted with different incarnations of the same *consociativismo.* Under Camillo Cavour, the first prime minister of a unified Italy, it was the *connubio,* or marriage, between government and opposition. Then it became the "transformation of parties" under Agostino Depretis, the "national government" under fascism, the "conciliation" between the Church and Mussolini in the late 1920s, the center-left coalition between the Socialists and the Christian Democrats in the 1960s, the "historic compromise" between the ruling coalition and the Communists in

---

*Even after the 1993 referendum, legislators took care not to scrap the old system entirely. Twenty-five percent of parliamentary seats were still elected by proportional representation, and brittle government by coalition was doomed to continue. The instinct for compromise and consensus prevailed.

1973, Aldo Moro's famously twisted "converging parallels" and "national solidarity" in 1976, and the *partito trasversale,* or crossover party, of the 1980s. The leitmotif was compromise and cohabitation.

I came across one rather amusing example of this phenomenon last year, during the political party conference season. It was a Sunday morning, and I had set off to the outskirts of Rome to report on the congress of the neo-Fascist Italian Social Movement. The party that for years had hovered uneasily in the twighlight zone of Italian politics was in the process of changing its name to the less menacing "National Alliance." The congress was taking place in a huge hotel turned conference center. As I walked into the lobby of the Hotel Ergife, I was perturbed to find a riot of red flags, badges of Karl Marx and Vladimir Lenin, a banner with the face of Che Guevara. I knew the neo-Fascists were trying to change their spots, but wasn't this going a bit far? When I asked an official what was going on, he told me that I had landed—unbeknown to me—at the national conference of the orthodox Communist Party, Communist Refoundation. "I'm looking for the neo-Fascists!" I said, somewhat irritated and convinced that I had written down the wrong location. "Oh, you mean the blackshirts," said the official. "They're over there, come with me." We descended into the bowels of the hotel and walked through cellars and darkened corridors, emerging ten minutes later in a room decked with pictures of Mussolini and crowded with young men wearing bomber jackets, black armbands, and extremely short haircuts. We had crossed from one end of the political spectrum to the other without leaving the building. I can't think of any other country in which parties representing the two political extremes would stage congresses at the same hotel.

The lack of alternation between the perpetual parties of government and the toothless opposition had several consequences. The first and most obvious one was an extraordinary degree of continuity. Italy may have had more than fifty postwar governments, but until recently every one of them was dominated by the Christian Democrats and their allies. The cabinets were like a game of musical chairs in which no one ever removed the chairs. Giulio Andreotti and his seven prime ministerships were not an exception. Amintore Fanfani, who served three times as president of the Senate and twice as secretary of the

Christian Democratic Party, formed his first government in 1954 and his last in 1982. Emilio Colombo entered the Cabinet for the first time in 1955 and left it for the last time in 1992. Amintore Fanfani, Aldo Moro, and Mariano Rumor each served as prime minister five times. One study showed that between 1946 and 1976, 1,331 ministerial and sub-Cabinet positions were held by no more than 152 politicians. The only other governments that have illustrated such a high degree of continuity have been those of President Hastings Banda of Malawi, who was ousted in 1994 at the age of ninety-two, and of Erich Honecker in East Germany. The only modern statesman who has outgoverned Giulio Andreotti is Fidel Castro, and that's probably because the Cuban leader was a late starter by comparison.

This exclusive club of ministers was reappointed over and over again not because of their exceptional qualities but because they represented certain political factions. Factionalism became the dominant characteristic of the Christian Democratic Party, the amoebalike alliance of shifting interest groups. In a classic example of Italian *sistemazione,* or systemization—a favorite word, especially in Italy's distinctly unsystematic South—the appointment of a Cabinet, as well as of junior ministers and under secretaries of state, was worked out through a mathematical calculus known as the "Cencelli manual." Massimo Cencelli was a Cabinet official who administered and established the criteria by which certain factions would receive certain posts according to their strength. For instance, the Christian Democrats' Dorotei faction, named after the Santa Dorotea monastery in Rome, where the founding members of the group had first met, were almost always given the Interior and Public Works portfolios. Another rule was that a minister who leaves a Cabinet post during the lifetime of a government had to be replaced by another minister from the same faction, whether that person was qualified or not. For instance, between 1986 and 1989 the man in charge of Italy's notoriously bedlamesque health service was Carlo Catin, a former trade unionist who had no qualifications for the job of minister of health other than that he belonged to the right faction. In 1984 he decided not to attend the first global AIDS summit in Florence because he was "too busy with other things."

If the moderate-conservative character of the Christian Democrats was determined by its wartime leader, De Gasperi, the structure of the party as an alliance of factions sometimes at war, sometimes at peace with one another was the legacy of his successor, Amintore Fanfani. In his attempt to loosen the ties between the party and the Vatican and to turn the Christian Democrats into an independent party controlled neither by the Church nor by big business, Fanfani did what Mussolini had done before him: he "colonized" the state's industries and banks and turned them into reservoirs of political patronage. In 1956 Fanfani set up the Orwellian-sounding Ministry of State Participation to consolidate the party's control over the public-sector economy, which was expanding rapidly during Italy's economic miracle of the 1950s. By the end of the 1980s the state controlled 80 percent of the country's banking, more than a quarter of its industrial employment, and half its fixed investment.

These vast public corporations, described by Swiss journalist Theodor Wiener in *Italy: A Difficult Democracy* as "a byzantine archipelago of some 45,000 companies," became the main sources of patronage. Theoretically, they were independent. Some were even commercial and had private stockholders. But in reality the public corporations were controlled by the different factions of the political parties as though they were fiefdoms. They included not only the state's banks and large industrial firms, such as the Ilva steel factories, but also television and radio, theaters, museums, and universities. Through the public corporations the political parties, first the Christian Democrats and then also their coalition partners and the Communist opposition, reached every corner of society. This was the "party-state" apparatus. The difference between Italy and, for instance, East Germany was that it was in the hands of several parties, not just one.

A brief look at the Institute for Industrial Reconstruction (IRI) illustrates the system. IRI was set up in 1933 by the Fascists. Before its gradual privatization in 1992, it was one of the largest state holding companies in the world. It was a vast, impenetrable forest of six hundred holding companies that controlled the country's iron and steel production, most of its shipbuilding, its telecommunications and electronics industries, much of its engineering, road and motorway construction, city planning, the national airline Alitalia, national broadcasting, and most of the shares in Italy's three largest banks. In many sectors sound economics were replaced by pure Machiavelli. The fact that the party literally "colonized" large areas of the state economy encouraged the formation of factions competing, or in many cases warring, to secure their chunk of patronage. For example, four large chemical groups were set up in the 1960s and '70s, each allied to a specific faction. Italy's map of motorways still reflects the country's political map of factions. A stretch of highway near Avellino in the Campania is called the "De Mita," because this was the home region and power base of Ciriaco De Mita, the former Christian Democratic prime minister. The Arezzo stretch of the A1 between Florence and Rome is known as "the Fanfani," the superstrada from Rome to Latina as "the Andreotti."

Only a few parts of IRI, such as the Banca Commerciale Italiana, escaped the stranglehold of the parties. The rest became dominions of *lottizzazione.* Many public corporations became giant electoral factories, serving their party-political patrons. The bond of patronage trickled right down to the lowest level. For instance, until four years ago the administrators, doctors, nurses, and even patients at Palermo's Civic Hospital could be "expected" to vote en masse for Salvatore "Salvò" Lima, Andreotti's man in Sicily. The hospital alone was good for something like 8,000 votes. This was possible because the head of the hospital—appointed, naturally, by the Christian Democrat authorities in Palermo—was Lima's brother.

With millions of people employed in the state sector and millions more dependent on those people's salaries, it's not difficult to envision the number of votes that were determined not by ideology, persuasion, or habit but by money and patronage.

Although many companies managed to do well despite being under the thumbs of the parties, in other cases the quality of products or services suffered. It only takes a stint in an Italian state hospital to discover this. Since the basic services in so many hospitals are deplorable, most Italian families become nurses in residence when one of their members is taken ill. Go, for instance, to any ward in Rome's San Giacomo Hospital, a crumbling terra-cotta palazzo that takes all the romance out of crumbling terra-cotta palazzi, and you will find family members fussing over the patients. They bring in food, drink, and clean sheets. They often administer the medicines. They do most of the nursing, partly because they are suspicious of anyone who is not "family," partly because the available care simply isn't good enough.

The distrust of the Italian health system doesn't just apply to ordinary citizens. When Pope John Paul II was shot in Saint Peter's Square in 1982, the ambulance preferred to fight its way through Rome's rush-hour traffic to the private Gemelli Clinic at the other end of the city rather than to take the Pontiff to the Santo Spirito Hospital behind the Vatican. The pope's advisers obviously thought he stood a better chance of surviving in an ambulance stuck in traffic than in a state hospital. If more proof were needed of the damage of *lottizzazione* and *sottogoverno* to public services, I would advise a trip on Alitalia. The inefficiency, surliness, and high cost of the airline have landed it somewhere at the bottom of the ladder, not far above Aeroflot, according to a 1993 survey in *The Economist* magazine.

The public corporations weren't just carved up to renew the patronage of the governing parties, they were also bequeathed to the opposition as a price for their acquiescence. Thus the Communists were given control of the railways and much of the public arts. Again, the results were not always favorable. Perhaps the best example of how the parties have devoured the state sector is Radiotelevisione Italiana (RAI), the national television and radio network. Until 1993 RAI 1 was still in the hands of the Christian Democrats, RAI 2 belonged to the Socialists, and RAI 3 belonged to the Communists (who had renamed themselves the Democratic Party of the Left). One consequence was a discernible political bias in the news reporting on each channel, especially in the hours devoted to the patron party and its leaders' declarations, which were reported punctiliously. Until recently the three parties tried to exclude a number of other political movements, seen as a threat to the cozy but corrupt status quo, from their coverage. Lilli Gruber, a feisty, attractive newscaster on RAI 1 who leans into the camera like a flirtatious barmaid and who led the newsroom rebellion against the old editorial nomenklatura, told me how she had been ordered not to include news about the Northern League, despite or perhaps because of the fact that the League was fast becoming the most popular protest movement in Italy. Understandably, in the absence of fair reporting by the state channels, Umberto Bossi, the cantankerous leader of the Northern League, demanded his own television station. Even today RAI television news broadcasts often sound more like political gossip sheets than a national information service. Newscasters still tend to refer to political figures by their surnames without bothering to remind viewers of their positions or titles. The bulletins buzz with jargon picked up in the lobby bars. Miss two days of news gossip in the ever-unfolding saga of Italian politics, and it's like leaving the country during a long-running television soap opera: You return feeling completely lost and bewildered, though closer inspection reveals that very little has really changed.

The other consequence of appointing news editors because they represent the right faction rather than have the right qualifications is that the quality of much of the broadcasting on RAI is sloppy and substandard. News footage tends to look as shaky and out of focus as a holiday video. The reports are thin on facts but dense on comment, and despite its generous state subsidies and license fees RAI has produced little television drama or documentary material of any lasting value. This may now change, as the leadership of all three RAI channels has been taken out of the hands of the parties that once controlled them. Indeed, in the case of RAI 1 and 2, the parties no longer exist. Nevertheless, it will be more difficult to remove the deadwood of middle management that has accumulated over years of *lottizzazione*. This is a problem faced by many public corporations that are now being privatized or becoming independent.

Rome's hapless opera house became the victim of one of the more absurd examples of *lottizzazione*. In 1991 a new director, Giancarlo Cresci, was appointed. Cresci had been a television producer, but his main qualification for the job as opera director was that he belonged to the Christian Democrats and was a close friend of Rome's mayor. In less than two years Cresci managed to turn a $300,000 annual profit into a $50 million debt. It was mismanagement on a truly operatic scale. Cresci tried to improve the reputation of Rome's lackluster opera house by throwing money at it. He dressed the ushers in eighteenth-century brocade uniforms and made them learn English in private lessons that cost $30 a head per hour. He decked the lobbies in Persian rugs and commissioned one of Italy's most famous architects to build a canopy over the main entrance. By the frugal standards of the Rome Opera, he paid exorbitant fees to singers, including $15,000 to the Spanish tenor José Carreras for a single performance. The director hired private planes to fly in violinists. For an ill-fated production of Verdi's *Aïda* he recruited the services of several monkeys and camels at $3,000 apiece per night. The camels became incontinent at the brassy sound of fanfares.

Cresci had thought his funds were unlimited. He swore he had never kept a single lira for himself. But this didn't help him when the new city administration was elected in November 1993. Cresci was sacked, and the opera house, one of the oldest in Europe, was almost closed down. Bailiffs confiscated several rows of chairs in the front stalls because the rental fee for the seats had not been paid in months. To recuperate some of the losses, the number of productions was slashed and the budget halved. On my only visit to the Rome opera house, I was amused to find that the ushers in livery had been replaced by traffic wardens in white uniforms, parading up and down the aisles as if they were looking for parking offenders.

If Giulio Andreotti the elder statesman embodied the subtle nature of power in the old regime, another prime minister personified both its successes and its self-inflicted failure. Bettino Craxi has fallen further than perhaps any other politician in Italy. After rising through the Socialist ranks, Craxi became the party's leader in 1976 at the age of forty-three. For sixteen years he ruled the Italian Socialist Party (PSI) like a personal bailiwick until he was ousted at a raucous party congress last year, disgraced by corruption charges and abandoned by those who had for years treated him like a prince. Craxi transformed the nature of the PSI. He stopped its flirtation with the Communists and established the principle that the ignominy of government was preferable to the nobility of opposition. From then on the Socialists attracted voters who were looking for an alternative to the Communists and the Christian Democrats. A master tactician, Craxi played off one party against the other and finally became the indispensable kingmaker of governments, able to topple an administration at a whim. His price was an increasing number of *poltrone,* or "armchairs," of power for his party. Although the PSI received no more than an average 14 percent of the vote at the height of its popularity, it ended up holding almost 40 percent of key government and administrative positions.

While Andreotti wove a subtle web of power, Craxi imposed his will on the party like a feudal overlord. He strengthened his own position in the party, which up to then had been a mercurial alliance of factions, selecting and ejecting leaders with alarming regularity. In 1981 Craxi changed the party's constitution. The party secretary would no longer be elected by the central committee but by the congress, made up of 200 local party representatives, 100 parliamentary deputies and 100 Socialist celebrities, intellectuals, veterans, actors, singers, and other luminaries selected by Craxi himself.

The last remaining scraps of socialist ideology were buried in the unabashed pursuit of power. Occasionally the party still paid lip service to the socialist belief in the equitable distribution of wealth, but in reality it started to redistribute an ever-larger quantity of money to itself. The party's new pragmatism had become a self-fulfilling prophecy. Dwarfed by the Communist Party, the Italian Socialists had always found it difficult to convince others of their ideological integrity. Communist philosopher Antonio Gramsci called the PSI a "Barnum's circus . . . which never takes anything seriously." In 1920 Lenin wrote a damning letter to the Italian Socialists: "You seem to yourselves so terribly revolutionary . . . but in reality you are frightened." It was Filippo Turati, the man who founded the PSI as Italy's first mass party in Genoa in 1892, who said: "What a beautiful thing socialism would be if there were no socialists."

His remark turned out to be prophetic. Since most of the genuine Italian socialists could be found in the Communist Party, the PSI has always suffered from an identity crisis. The party has swung like a pendulum from extremism to moderation, losing credibility every time. In the 1980s the Socialists and Craxi were to Italy what the Conservatives and Thatcher were to Britain: upwardly mobile and motivated by the pursuit of wealth and happiness, a hedonistic escape from the doldrums of the seventies.

Craxi became prime minister in 1983. His rule, hailed as one of the most effective in postwar Italy, lasted four years, longer than any other government before or since. As he pointed out to me during an interview, "The history of modern Italy, which is Europe's youngest country but one of its oldest civilizations, has always been fraught with instability since unification in the 1860s. There have been only two periods of stable rule in more than a hundred years. One was the authoritarian episode of fascism, and the other was my prime ministership." Most other politicians would have shied away from such a comparison. But not Bettino Craxi.

On the surface the economic successes of his four-year rule were remarkable. The Milan stock exchange, the only one in Italy, increased its capitalization fourfold. Inflation came down, and the national economic growth rate increased from 0.85 percent in 1982 to 2.5 percent in 1984. In January 1987 Italy experienced the so-called *sorpasso,* when, according OECD figures, its gross national product ($599.8 billion) overtook that of Britain ($547.4 billion). Italy moved from sixth to fifth place on the G-7 ladder of world economic powers—after the United States, Japan, Germany, and France—and Italian newspapers started referring to their country as *il quinto potere economico mondiale,* the fifth global economic power. Italy had finally become richer than the country whose soldiers had helped liberate and occupy it forty years before. Not surprisingly, the *sorpasso* produced an unprecedented degree of self-congratulation and national pride. "Made in Italy" became a coveted hallmark of style and quality. By the end of the 1980s Italy's export boom had transformed the lifestyle of northern Europe. From Sunderland to Stuttgart people were paying a small fortune to buy extra-virgin olive oil, tomatoes dried in the Calabrian sun, and Armani clothes. But as in Britain, Italy's economic growth ultimately depended on the United States and the reflation of the U.S. economy à la Reaganomics. Economists now believe that Craxi rode the wave of economic growth created by someone else and used the euphoria of the day to overexpand and ultimately lay the foundations of his own demise. According to most of the testimony that has emerged so far in the "Tangentopoli" scandal, the mid-1980s saw the exchange of bribes for contracts flourish unfettered. As the power of the parties, especially the Socialists, swelled, so did their demand for money to oil the wheels of patronage. The collection of *tangente* for public works contracts turned into systematic extortion. One consequence was a renewed building boom. The other was a mushrooming debt. By 1989 Italy had accumulated the highest mountain of debt in the European Community. As a percentage of the gross national product, its debt was beaten only by Belgium's and Ireland's. While the government was preaching the virtues of closer European integration and the Maastricht Treaty, it was laying the foundations for its own exclusion from Europe's first division. By the time the treaty was signed in Maastricht in December 1991, Italy failed to meet all of the seven economic requirements set out in the document. This was the legacy of Bettino Craxi's prime ministership.

The grandees of the Christian Democratic Party wore their power like the gold-embroidered humility of the princes in the Vatican. They were remote and aloof. In deference to their creed they maintained a degree of restraint. The Socialists of Bettino Craxi, on the other hand, soaked themselves with abandon in the luxurious bubble bath of power. The party leadership became notorious for jetting from one Socialist International congress to the next in a fleet of chartered planes with scores of family members, hangers-on and *portaborse,* or bag carriers, in tow. Meanwhile, the collection of *tangente* became increasingly crude. Silvano Larini, a close aid of Craxi's, told the judges that he had regularly stacked bundles of billions of lire in cash in Craxi's own office at party headquarters.

As Craxi's power grew in the party so did the influence of his family. His portly son Bobò became the head of the Socialist Party in Milan at the age of twenty-eight, before resigning because of an investigation into illegal party funding. Craxi's brother-in-law, Paolo Pilliteri, was mayor of Milan twice before being charged with corruption.

At the height of his power Craxi enjoyed a personality cult that was unusual for Western Europe. At the Milan party conference in 1989, delegates were greeted at the door by a sign inviting "Comrades" to "Wait here if you want to pose for a photograph with Party Leader Craxi." While Craxi's family preened itself on stage, delegates to the conference sang "Long Live the Red Carnation." Meanwhile, the head of the family was meeting his close friend, media tycoon Silvio Berlusconi, in his camper van. The conference program reassured delegates that the beautiful hostesses hired by the party for the occasion had been chosen for their good looks and their height, which "varies from 5 feet, 6 inches to 5 feet, 8 inches." The Socialist magazine, *Mondo Operaio,* celebrated the purveyor of tall women as "a politician with eclectic human and cultural interests, avid in his research as well as his imagination, lucid in thought and tenacious in deed." He was referred to in the party press as "the impresario." Even *Time* magazine hailed him as "the Maestro" on its front cover. As the tall, bulky Craxi became increasingly puffed up with power, admiration gradually turned to ridicule. Giorgio Forattini, the well-known cartoonist of the newspaper *La Repubblica,* always depicted him as the "Duce" figure in jackboots and uniform, accentuating Craxi's jowls and assertively fleshy lips. His first name, Bettino, was changed to "Benito," as in Mussolini.

The pretensions of the former prime minister were proportional to the wrath he later incurred. No politician was more loathed at the height of the corruption scandal. Craxi and his cronies no longer dared to show their faces in public. Waiters refused to serve them at Maiella, their favorite restaurant behind the Piazza Navona in Rome. The night the Chamber of Deputies voted not to lift his immunity from prosecution, Craxi walked out of his Rome residence, the Hotel Raphael, into a hailstorm of coins and verbal abuse. (When convicted thieves were paraded through the streets of medieval Rome, throwing coins was one way the public expressed its disgust.) Shortly afterward, Craxi was ousted as the leader of the party he had dominated like a feudal retinue for sixteen years.

Before his downfall Craxi rarely gave interviews, especially to foreign journalists. I was thus pleasantly surprised to hear from his office that the honorable Craxi would be prepared to see me and my colleague David Willey at his Rome residence, the Hotel Raphael, in September 1993. He clearly had time on his hands. The Raphael is a medium-sized hotel tucked behind the Piazza Navona on a dark street. It is completely covered in ivy, which gives it a rather forbidding, mysterious air. For fear of bombs there were no cars parked in front of it, apart from one police van filled with bored carabinieri, and the two armored cars that Craxi and his bodyguards still used until he fled the country in the summer of 1994. The lobby is decorated with carved wooden statues and precious antiques. Sitting alone among the artifacts, slouched into a sofa in front of a coffee table groaning with empty glasses, coffee cups, and overflowing ashtrays, was the former prime minister. He looked at home in the lobby and seemed to treat it like his own living room. His bodyguards and a cluster of hangers-on, including a very large man in a shiny gray suit, pigtail, and sunglasses, occupied another part of the foyer.

Craxi looked disheveled. He wasn't wearing a jacket. His tie was undone and hung lazily around his neck, like a noose. His shirt was creeping out of his trousers, which threatened to slide down. The former prime minister had lost weight. Were these the withdrawal symptoms of power or just the self-neglect of a man who was no longer in the public eye? Craxi was extremely friendly, beckoned us to take a seat, and offered us a coffee. He wasn't so much sitting as lying on the sofa, smoking one cigarette after another. I watched with fascination as the tip of ash grew longer and longer and finally dropped onto his shirt, onto his trousers, onto my trousers, into the orange juice, onto the floor, onto my bag. Craxi didn't seem to mind. The front of his shirt was covered with ash stains. When the ashtray became too full, you could hear the cigarette butts sizzle as he stubbed them out in the dark sludge left at the bottom of a coffee cup. "The Maestro" was defensive. "I have been in politics for twenty-two years. I was elected seven times to the Chamber of Deputies, three times to the European Parliament. I was prime minister for four years. And I have never had a brush with the law. No one has ever proven, or will ever prove, that I have deviated for one second from the path of legality." Craxi inhaled to the bottom of his lungs. "I have never, I repeat, *never* been bought by anyone."

There was a brief silence. Then Bettino Craxi took us on a guided tour of his conspiracy theories. "There are so many liars, so many hypocrites today. Just think of the big industrialists, who have always financed our political system and now pretend to be victims and saints. They are such terrible liars, I call them extraterrestrial." Craxi shook with laughter, spilling ash everywhere. The voice of the former prime minister rose and fell in a mesmerizing melody. "Of course power corrupts," he admitted. "In Italy there has never been a genuine alternation of power; a certain degree of degeneration is bound to have occurred." "The Communists are the worst," he suddenly said. "They behave like Goody Two-shoes, but they were *the* extraterrestrials." I was trying to imagine the leader of the former Communist Party in a space suit. What did Craxi mean? "They were paid by Moscow," he thrashed on, "controlled by the KGB. Stooges. Spies. The lot." Ash landed somewhere near my right shoe. Did he have any evidence to prove this, I asked. "Evidence? Evidence! Mountains of it! All will be revealed in good time." "Why not now?" "The time is not ripe. Not just yet."

Like Andreotti, Craxi has been around for a long time. He knows or pretends to know everything about everyone. He will probably never go on trial, let alone to jail. The man who a year before was still able to make or break governments had already received his worst punishment. He had been stripped of his power. His court had vanished. For Craxi, personal enrichment was much less important than the influence inherent in extracting a *tangente* from the business community.

A week before the interview, moving men had taken the last pieces of furniture out of the Socialist Party headquarters in the Via del Corso. The party that is alleged to have stolen tens of billions of lire was now bankrupt with debts of more than $180 million. The Socialists could no longer afford to pay the rent, and the landlord had had them evicted. So who, I asked, was paying Signor Craxi's bills at the Raphael? "I still have many friends, many more than you think." "Who?" "Friends in the Middle East. They pay the hotel. They have also given me a plane for my travels. I spend a lot of time in the Middle East." Lurid thoughts crossed my mind. No names were mentioned. It was churlish to ask.

"What do you do all day?" "I give advice, a lot of advice. Many people still come to see me, you know. And I write. I'm currently writing reports to the judges to clarify my situation . . . and the situation of others. I have started on my memoirs, I'm writing a book called *Tunisian Thoughts*. These are things that occurred to me while I was in Hammamet. I am also writing a novel." "Is that all?" I asked. "No," said Craxi. "I'm also thinking of *re*writing a number of little-known Italian authors from the last century. Wonderful books. Everyone should read them, but they are written in an Italian that few understand." Here was a picture of unruffled confidence, serenity in the face of adversity, and, some would say, Olympian arrogance. But then he fumbled for another cigarette. Half of it turned into glowing ash immediately, as he inhaled with a vengeance. The interview was over. Craxi accompanied us outside. "Do you dare show your face in public?" my colleague asked. "Of course. But yesterday I was walking from my car to the hotel when two boys came up to me and called me a thief." "What did you do?" "I punched them," said the former prime minister.

Like Bettino Craxi, most of the patients who used to frequent the couch of Dr. Rocchini, Italy's parliamentary shrink, are now unemployed, voted out of power by an electorate bent on vengeance. Some, like Craxi, are brooding in exile and trying to avoid the courts. Others have discovered new vocations. Gerardo Bianco, the former floor leader of the ruling Christian Democratic Party and a respected Latin scholar, is writing a book about the animals in Virgil. Gianni Prandini, a former minister of public works, is learning Spanish and helping his wife, who is an insurance broker. Claudio Martelli, a former minister of justice, has enrolled as a mature student in an economics course in London. He attends class whenever he doesn't need to attend his own or other people's trials in Italy. Others are learning how to paint or play the piano. One former Liberal has taken up deep-sea diving. Some are hatching new plots or have been recycled as "new" politicians for one of the new parties like Silvio Berlusconi's Forza Italia. The people who ran Italy two years ago, and who represented five decades of rigid political continuity, are suddenly nowhere to be seen. They have been toppled by their own excesses. They destroyed the source of their own power: the party. In Dr. Rocchini's words, "They killed *mamma.*"

After five decades it was perhaps to be expected that a political system in which the parties in power never swapped places with those in opposition would become stale and corrupt. But when the Italians got rid of the old ruling class and its *partitocrazia,* many of them had forgotten that the system had virtually been imposed on them by the Vatican and the Americans, whose paramount desire was to keep Italian communism at bay. Considering the potential for conflict in a society that had just come out of one civil war and now found itself on the fault line between East and West, it was a stroke of genius to let the Italian Communists share power without ever formally handing them the reins of government. Not only did the Italians avoid internal conflict, Italy also became a stable democracy and one of the seven richest nations of the world.

In 1992 it was fashionable in Italy to blame the lack of political accountability and of healthy political alternation between government and opposition on the electoral system of pure proportional representation. Mario Segni, a reform politician and renegade Christian Democrat, led a successful movement to change Italy's electoral system. The movement culminated in a referendum in April 1993 that was meant to give Italy a British-style voting system in which all the deputies are elected in single-member constituencies or electoral colleges. The candidate with the largest number of votes would win. The party or parties with the largest number of seats in Parliament would form the ruling majority. It was a nice idea. But then the Italian spirit intervened. It took months to hammer out the new law in Parliament. The final result was a typically Italian fudge. Seventy-five percent of the seats in the Chamber of Deputies were now to be elected in single-member constituencies and 25 percent according to the old proportional system. The minimum threshold to get into Parliament would be 4 percent of the vote. Thanks to this small window of opportunity, many parties still thought they had a chance of getting into Parliament on their own without having to merge with others. In the 1994 elections sixteen parties fielded candidates, producing a dizzying array of emblems and candidates, and ten parties entered Parliament. The result was more unstable government under Prime Minister Berlusconi and a ruling coalition that was more brittle and fractious than most of its predecessors had been. Another bout of reform became inevitable. Those who saw electoral reform as the panacea for Italy's problems had clearly forgotten the fact that the British-style voting system had been tried at the beginning of the century. It had been scrapped in 1919.

The reason why Italy has never been able to adopt the Anglo-Saxon system is that Italy is neither Britain nor the United States. The Italians are ill at ease when too much power is concentrated in the hands of too few. The tribes that make up Italian society, be they political parties or powerful families, distrust one another too much and have too little faith in the institutions of the state. Power therefore has to be shared. This is the real reason for the *consociativismo* between opposition and government, or what Aldo Moro elliptically and absurdly called the "converging parallels" between the Christian Democrats and the Communists. This is also why the Italians began to chip away at the power of Prime Minister Berlusconi. During the election campaign, his wealth and influence had impressed them. But they were angered by his apparent attempts to silence the troublesome judiciary and to control the state media when he already enjoyed a monopoly on commercial television. Berlusconi threatened to become too powerful. On the other hand, he had also promised to be the "Man of Destiny" the Italians have yearned for since Niccolò Machiavelli wrote *The Prince:* a charismatic figure who could unite Italy and restore the glories of the old Roman Empire. History had encouraged the Italians to dream of such a man. Bitter experience, especially in the form of Mussolini, had taught them to distrust him. As Silvio Berlusconi has shown, this remains the conundrum of modern Italy.

One of the reasons why this riddle cannot be solved is that 130 years after its creation Italy is still a country in the making. Corruption in Italian politics is as old as united Italy. The difference is that the postwar republic developed and perfected a particular system of corruption. The *tangenti* were not just generated by greed, they also became the currency of an unwritten pact in which as many interest groups as possible were paid off for the sake of maintaining peace, stability, and their own power. The justification for this system was that the divisions of the Cold War were mirrored in such a grave way in a country that harbored the biggest Communist Party in the West that a degree of corruption was permissible if it meant keeping the social peace. The First Republic, as the Italians now like to call the period between 1945 and 1992, provided stability at the increasing price of corruption. Its collapse left an institutional vacuum and an alarming degree of confusion. It's as if Italy has been sent back to the drawing board once again, just as it was in 1918 after World War I, under Mussolini and after Mussolini's histrionic experiment to "make

Italy" had suffered its miserable failure. As an elegant woman who spoke excellent English once put it to me at a diplomatic dinner in the breathing space between the veal cutlets and the lemon sorbet, "All this upheaval is nothing but a renewed attempt to turn us Italians into proper citizens. The trouble is, you can't create Italy without the citizens, and you can't create the citizens without Italy. Until we've solved that one, we remain nothing more than the world's best-dressed and best-fed tribesmen and -women."

Jacobin Judges

T he region of Molise, stuck between the wild mountains of Abruzzi and the fertile plains of Puglia, is one of Italy's poorest and smallest. The village of Montenero di Bisaccia is typical of the area. It clings defensively to the side of a mountain. It has only a few asphalt roads. A fierce wind blows dust and rubbish through the maze of squat farmers' houses. In the summer the earth is bone dry and cracked like an old man's face. In the winter rain turns the dust and earth into rivers of mud and sludge. The majority of Montenero's inhabitants are over the age of fifty. The younger ones have either left the village to work in the Fiat factory near Campobasso, the regional capital, or moved to another part of Italy. But for the cars, mopeds, the Dalek sounds coming from the fruit machines in the Bar Centrale, and the unavoidable rash of cement construction, Montenero di Bisaccia has changed little since 1933. It was in that year that Giovannino Palma, one of the village's farmers, took his flock of sheep, his son, and his favorite horse, Regina, to the neighboring town of Cannita for the monthly fair. At the fair everyone admired Giovannino's horse and made offers to buy it, but Giovannino only wanted to sell his sheep and refused. That night, while the farmer and his son were sleeping in a barn, thieves came and stole the horse.

Giovannino was distraught, because the horse had been his most precious possession. He and his son gathered their sheep and headed home to Montenero. The following night, the farmer dreamed that the horse had been taken to the village of Sannicandro. At dawn he set off, and in a fenced paddock outside the village he discovered twenty horses. One of them was his own horse, Regina. Giovannino went to the local carabinieri, told them that he had discovered his stolen horse, and asked them for permission to take it back. The carabinieri refused, saying that Giovannino didn't have enough evidence to claim the horse. The farmer sought the advice of lawyers, who told him to secure the return of his horse through the courts.

Giovannino Palma waited in vain for two years for his case to go to court. Fed up with lawyers, the sluggish court, and the creaking machinery of justice, he decided to take matters into his own hands. He returned to Sannicandro and discovered his horse in the same paddock. He was about to open the gate and grab Regina when three men appeared, armed with shovels and pickaxes. They called him a horse thief and threatened him with the weapons. Giovannino refused to back off and explained why he had come, but the men stood firm. Finally Giovannino took out a picture of the Madonna of Montenero, which he had kept concealed in his shirt, and showed it to the three men. At the sight of the Madonna, they dropped their weapons and ran away. Giovannino opened the gate, took his horse, and rode back to his village.

On hearing the news, almost the entire village gathered in the main square and a photographer was summoned from the neighboring town to commemorate the occasion. Once a picture had been taken, the villagers, Giovannino, his wife, whose nickname was "Pazienza" because of her long-suffering nature, and the children all went to church for a thanksgiving mass, taking the horse with them. The photograph was pinned up next to the picture of the Madonna. Later in the year Regina had two foals.

The most extraordinary aspect of this story is the man who tells it. Antonio Di Pietro is the hero of Italy's "sweet revolution" and the grandson of Giovannino Palma. He and the horse are part of the living legend that has been woven around this investigating magistrate whose crusade against corruption has toppled the country's political elite. According to one biography, the story of the horse explains "his resilience, his thirst for justice and truth, his disdain for the sluggishness of Italian law." These points and others are listed from one to ten.

Antonio Di Pietro is proud of his peasant origins. He still looks like one of the villagers in the yellowed black-and-white photograph taken at his parents' wedding fifty years ago. He is stocky with a kind, round face with two small but intelligent eyes set far apart, his hands are large, and he speaks with the slightly stilted and clipped accent of his home region.* Before he resigned from the pool of anti-corruption magistrates in Milan on December 6, 1994, Di Pietro led the crusade against political corruption and the toppling of an entire ruling elite. Di Pietro and his colleagues caused a revolution by doing little more than applying the law.

Like millions of other Italians who have migrated to the wealthy North, Di Pietro frequently returns to Montenero. Most of his extended family still live there. When he and his bodyguards arrive in their armored motorcade, they are greeted by graffiti. GRAZIE DI PIETRO is scrawled on a wall near his family house, as it is on thousands of houses, buses, laboratory doors, monuments, and park benches all over Italy. Antonio Di Pietro is worshipped more than any film, rock, or soccer star. His face adorns T-shirts, plates, and coffee mugs. He has inspired films, novels, and even a musical. A ten-foot effigy of him has been paraded through the streets of Italian cities during Carnival. When Di Pietro came to Rome for the first time after the eruption of the corruption scandal, women rushed into the street to kiss and hug him. He was showered with carnations. The number of students enlisting in university law courses has shot up, not only because a degree in jurisprudence is a useful qualification for the civil service—the traditional reason—but because the adulation of Di Pietro has launched a thousand trainee magistrates, yearning to follow in their hero's footsteps. Had Di Pietro stood for Parliament as thirty magistrates did in 1994, he would have been elected with a resounding majority. Many Italians wanted him to become prime minister.

---

*His language, even in court, was refreshingly blunt compared to the usual grandiloquence of Italy's legal profession.

Media tycoon Silvio Berlusconi tried to cash in on his popularity by asking him to become minister of justice or interior minister, but Di Pietro turned him down, saying he had more work to do in cleaning up politics. A country that is notorious for flouting the law at every level worshipped an enforcer of the law. However, Di Pietro's fans are applauding not his punctilious application of the law but his political role. In this, Italy has once again started a trend. In France and Spain anticorruption judges have been holding the political class to account. In all three countries the legal system is based on the Napoleonic Code and its tradition of magistrates as politicized but unelected civil servants. The judiciary in Italy has evolved from an instrument of law and order into the battering ram of political change to an extent unparalleled in other democracies.

Di Pietro, the son of a humble peasant, has become a Jacobin hero, a Robespierre who has taken on the arrogant "palazzo," the Italian establishment, and brought it crashing down. He and his team of *mani pulite,* or "clean hands," judges spearheaded the investigations into "Tangentopoli." Their weapons were pieces of paper, the so-called *avvisi di garanzia.* Although they do not automatically lead to criminal charges, trials, or sentences, they have become a potent force for change. At the height of the corruption scandal, one of these *avvisi* was issued to a powerful politician or industrialist almost every day. Every time the delivery became a spectacle, often broadcast live on television. Paolo Cirino Pomicino, a Christian Democrat and former minister of public works, received his *avviso di garanzia* in Naples. It was delivered in an armored police van. Many others were first leaked to the press before reaching their recipient. Scores of ministers resigned on receiving one. Italy's elite were presumed guilty, as they always had been. Even in 1983, 84 percent of Italians had considered their politicians to be dishonest and inept, even if they were not interested in doing anything about it. But ten years later the conditions for their judicial beheading were ripe. The end of the Cold War had finally removed the excuse for the perpetual reelection of the Christian Democrats and their allies as the protectors against the Red Peril, the budget deficit had become big enough to threaten Italy's standing in Europe, and the parties had run out of money with which to buy votes. While Antonio Di Pietro and his colleagues issued warrants, the Italian electorate voted their former leaders and their parties out of power. Judges and voters egged each other on without a single guilty verdict having been issued. The Christian Democrats and Socialists began to implode at the ballot box before the first "Tangentopoli" trial had even started. Whether the defendants are guilty or not, justice in Italy has always been a political tool.

Antonio Di Pietro's team and their suave boss, Francesco Saverio Borrelli, work in Milan's Palazzo di Giustizia, the Palace of Justice, a granite monstrosity built under Mussolini. The word "Giustizia" is sculpted in large, uncompromisingly square letters on the front façade. Like most other "palaces of justice" in Italy—every large town or city has one—the size of the building doesn't necessarily reflect the amount of justice that emanates from it. Nevertheless, the austere Milan "palace," guarded by scores of carabinieri and shown every night on Italian television from every possible angle, has become a concrete symbol of the judicial crusade against abuses of power. The giant halls with square marble columns and cold neon lighting echo to the din of litigation produced by hundreds of judges, lawyers, clerks, secretaries, policemen, bodyguards, and desperate citizens milling around, feeding the factory of justice.

Antonio Di Pietro and his pool work on the fourth floor, guarded by carabinieri with machine guns and clusters of bodyguards in civilian clothing, lounging casually near their charges and the scores of cameramen and journalists waiting for scraps of news.

One day my camera team and I joined the fray to try to get a "doorstep" interview with Di Pietro. Unlike many magistrates who are much less famous, Di Pietro doesn't grant formal interviews. This, however, never stopped anyone from trying to get one. Every time the judicial hero came out of his office, seven bodyguards carrying pistols and wearing flak jackets surrounded him as though he were a queen bee and escorted him to the office of one of his colleagues. The human tangle immediately attracted a platoon of cameras and furry microphones on rods, dangling above their heads like Chinese lanterns. They all shuffled frantically along until the magistrate disappeared behind another door. The bodyguards stood in a semicircular formation, barring access. We settled down for another wait. Twenty minutes later the door opened and the circus moved again.

Di Pietro looks more like a private detective from a Raymond Chandler thriller than an Italian magistrate. This is not entirely surprising since before becoming a magistrate he was an ordinary policeman. Before that he was a guest worker in a West German factory. Di Pietro squeezes information and confessions out of his victims with the streetwise psychology of a cop on the beat, the legalistic logic of a magistrate, along with a measure of menacing patience. Roberto Mongini, a Christian Democratic financier and collector of bribes for the Milan Malpensa Airport project, has described how Di Pietro made him sweat during their "talks." With theatrical timing he would take off his watch and slowly dismantle and reassemble it like a watchmaker. The effect was unnerving and the style of interrogation helped Mongini and hundreds of others to confess. If they didn't, a spell in prison could easily be arranged under the magistrate's sweeping powers of arrest and wide latitude for facilitating confessions.

Before becoming a subject of public worship, Antonio Di Pietro spent almost ten years collating the evidence that would allow him to pounce in February 1992. Using a computer, then a revolutionary tool in Italy's archaic legal system, Di Pietro was able to piece together the landscape of "Tangentopoli" like a puzzle. By sifting through company and party accounts, he discovered the systematic exchange of bribes for contracts. He and his colleagues were eventually helped by the political climate, as the parties began losing some of their power in 1990 and disloyalty in the ranks produced a growing number of "confessors." Meanwhile, the recession had made it more and more difficult for businessmen to pay illegal tithes, and they too began flocking in droves to Di Pietro to confess.*

Several judges have told me that they believe Di Pietro the computer whiz kid had collated the incriminating evidence well before the scandal erupted but had been stymied by the parties, who then still controlled a large part of the judiciary. Others feel the bulk of the information about "Tangentopoli" was leaked by the Italian secret services. According to this theory, Milanese Socialists had become too

---

*Since this explanation was too simple for some, the conspiracy mill added its own theories.

greedy; the Christian Democrats wanted to teach them a lesson, and they told the secret services to provide Di Pietro with the incriminating software. If this was indeed the motive, it soon backfired as the corruption scandal spread from the Socialists to the Christian Democrats and from Milan to Rome.

Whatever triggered the investigations, Di Pietro's computer has become part of the living legend. The cover of *Time* magazine showed him sitting next to his electronic tool, holding a floppy disc that was presumably loaded with evidence. The loyal Dr. Watson to Di Pietro's Sherlock Holmes, the computer often sat next to the prosecutor in court, like some daunting oracle that contained all the secrets of "Tangentopoli."

The trial of Sergio Cusani, who was sentenced to eight years in jail and ordered to pay $91 million in damages last year, illustrated the high drama of Italian justice. The "processo Cusani" was the first major trial in the corruption scandal: the roll call of witnesses read like a Who's Who of Italian government. The defendant was found guilty of falsifying company balance sheets, misappropriating funds, and violating the laws that regulate the financing of political parties. The forty-five-year-old Neapolitan nobleman and financier was held responsible for siphoning off $91 million from Enimont and passing $14 million of that to politicians like Bettino Craxi. In 1991 the Ferruzzi business empire was allowed to sell its stake in Enimont, a chemical joint venture with ENI formed two years before, back to the state at vastly inflated prices. It was allowed to do this despite the fact that Enimont had been a catastrophic failure. The price paid by Ferruzzi was a *supertangente* of almost $100 million, which was used to buy the acquiescence of the political leadership to what was essentially a bad deal. The case was a textbook illustration of the fraudulence and waste of "Tangentopoli." It gave the Italian public a firsthand insight into the maze of corruption that had flourished at the highest level of business and politics, and it did so almost every night on prime-time television. Apart from showing long extracts of the trial on the nightly television news, RAI 3 used to screen "the best of Cusani" twice a week. The program regularly attracted audiences of more than 12 million viewers, eclipsing even the most popular soap operas. It made for compulsive, riveting viewing. It is churlish to say that Italians love spectacle. But the Cusani trial made Court TV in the United States look about as exciting as a shipping forecast.

The script of this modern morality play could have been written by Bertolt Brecht and the trial's casting was perfect. Antonio Di Pietro, son of wily Molise peasants who had worked his way up from street cop to magistrate, stretched Cusani, the haughty nobleman from Naples, on the rack of justice. As the trial dragged on, Cusani looked increasingly haggard and noble. Wearing elegant dark suits, he sat bolt upright in the defendant's chair with his legs crossed, a tragic figure of dignity. His long thin neck was tailor-made for the guillotine. Cusani's lawyer, Giuliano Spazzali, looked the perfect Devil's advocate. He had a gray goatee, startlingly alert eyes, and demonic eyebrows that curled up at the ends. His voice was shrill, his comments sharp. Chief Judge Guiseppe Tarantola had the languid, slightly blasé air of a man who had spent a lifetime witnessing the sleazy side of human nature. One of the key witnesses in the trial was the former chief executive of the Ferruzzi empire, Carlo Sama, who had married into the Ferruzzi family. Smooth and handsome, he was the Master Seducer of "Tangentopoli." There was no one, it seemed, whom his company hadn't bribed or incriminated. Every week Sama's revelations, masked by a boyish smile, would be the kiss of death for another politician. Sama told the court that the Communist Party, which had always claimed it was squeaky-clean, had received $600,000 in bribes. Even the Northern League, which had once been alone in occupying the moral high ground of Italian politics and had thrived on its reputation as an honest party of protest, was dragged into the quagmire. Sama told the court that the party's treasurer had been given $200,000. According to Sama, even financial journalists had been paid off to conceal the truth. It was a sorry picture of almost universal corruption and corruptibility.

Di Pietro played his epic part with consummate skill. His unshaven, disheveled look gave him the appearance of a working-class hero in a revolutionary people's court—with dress code to match. Wearing the long black gown of a state prosecutor, he flapped his arms as if they were the wings of a bird of prey. Under the open-front gown he often wore little more than a white undershirt, which gradually rolled up over his paunch as he became more and more agitated. In contemplative moments Di Pietro would rub his stubbly chin on the court microphone as if it were an electric razor. It was a refreshingly raw, uncouth performance. Di Pietro mocked, cajoled, teased, and insulted his victims. He accused Cusani of being a liar, a thief, and a "triple traitor." But he often also joked with him. The performances were always unpredictable. The courtroom frequently erupted in laughter, leaving some to wonder just how serious the trial was and whether, if found guilty, the defendant would actually have to face the consequence of his actions. On occasions Bertolt Brecht was replaced by Luigi Pirandello, the Italian dramatist and master of illusion.

Di Pietro's finest performance was his interrogation of Arnaldo Forlani, the former leader of the Christian Democratic Party. Forlani embodied the Christian Democratic Party's mixture of raw power, paternalism, and Catholic devotion. Over the years his solemn expression under a halo of gray hair had become a rigid mask of aloofness, but in court the mask was shattered. Forlani was only a witness for the prosecution, but he was treated like a defendant and behaved like one. He was literally mesmerized by Di Pietro, unable to utter anything but barely audible denials. He said that the sum total of his knowledge of "Tangentopoli" had come from the newspapers and blamed any deviation from the law on Severino Citaristi, a Christian Democratic parliamentarian who had orchestrated the collection of bribes for his party. As Forlani stumbled through the hearing, white foam, the secretion of fear, appeared in the corners of his mouth. The scene was shown again and again on television. This was the ritual humiliation of the old elite.

Sergio Cusani's punishment was harsh. The prosecution had only asked for a seven-year sentence. The judges gave him eight and ordered him to repay almost $100 million. In his emotional final testimony Cusani accepted personal responsibility but said that he didn't want to become the sole scapegoat for an entire system of corruption. Cusani had already spent five months in custody before being charged. Ironically, he may never go to jail again, now that he has been found guilty. The case will inevitably go through two appeals stages lasting several years. A different judge in a more lenient political climate may well annul the sentence.

Just as Antonio Di Pietro's grandfather tired of waiting for a decision from the courts about his stolen horse, many Italians today regard the law not as a guarantee for justice in society but as an intrusion by a hostile state into the private lives of citizens, and as the Italian judicial system has done little to reassure citizens that this is not the case, the law is either flouted or feared. The country's creaking machinery of justice is notoriously slow and, like so much else in Italy, a victim of good intentions ruined by inadequate application. A disagreement over fishing rights off the island of Sardinia went to trial in 1858 and was settled in 1981. A dispute over the will of Don Carmelo Parisis, the duke of Leucadia and Casalecchio, began in Messina in 1914 and was concluded in 1980, and then only because the property in dispute had become a ruin and the banknotes had lost most of their value. The family finally decided there was no point in pursuing the case. There have also been more serious examples. In 1969 a bomb in Milan's Piazza Fontana killed sixteen people and injured ninety. The trial, in which three extreme-right-wing terrorists were charged with murder, began in Rome in 1972. It was later transferred, first to Milan and then to Catanzaro in Calabria. There it didn't resume until 1974, only to be postponed until 1977. A verdict of guilty was reached in 1979, but the case was appealed. A second verdict was reached in 1982, only to be quashed by a higher court. In 1985 the trial was closed without a verdict and in 1993 a Milan judge tried to get it opened again. The case continues. The 1979 bombing of an Italian airliner over the island of Ustica, off Sicily, in which eighty-one people were killed, hasn't even reached the trial stage yet, because the investigations have consistently been blocked at a higher level. Witnesses have died in mysterious circumstances, and vital evidence has been lost or shredded.

The Italian judicial system frequently does its best to fuel Italy's cottage industry of conspiracy theories and suspected plots. But more often injustice is the result of a mundane but debilitating lack of resources. The Italian Constitution guarantees three trial stages as a means of achieving maximum fairness, though various shortages chronically debilitate the system's efficiency so that the average length of a trial from its first appearance in court to the final verdict is ten years. Italy spends less on its judicial system than most other European countries do. The court administration tends to be crude and understaffed. The filing systems are inadequate. There is a lack of computers, court stenographers, and office space. The judges are often badly allocated, with too few in the lower courts and too many at the appeal level. The geographic distribution of judges dates back to 1941 and today is woefully out of sync with the country's population shifts. There is a glut of judges in provincial capitals, especially in the South, but a shortage in big northern cities such as Milan and Turin. Because the machinery of justice creaks so slowly, only about 5 percent of cases get from the preliminary investigation to the trial stage. Despite this, the total backlog of cases in the three branches of the judiciary—administrative, civil, and penal—is more than 3 million!

Although the judiciary may be slow to bring trials to court, it is quick when it comes to arrests. Thanks to powers that stem from the authoritarian days of fascism and were renewed at the time of the terrorist scare in the 1970s, it is very easy for Italian judges to issue arrest warrants, as no equivalent to habeas corpus exists, and very difficult for those arrested to get bail. More than half of Italy's bloated prison population of over 50,000 inmates is still awaiting trial. They are being held in "preventive" or "precautionary" custody to prevent them from fleeing the country, destroying evidence, or committing another crime; theoretically, a person can be held for up to three years and three months without being charged. Although the recommended time is considerably shorter, even a six-month spell in jail is a terrible punishment for someone who turns out to be innocent. On a visit to Regina Coeli—Queen of the Heavens—Rome's notorious and inappropriately named jail, I found "Tangentopoli" suspects and convicted drug dealers sharing the same overcrowded cells. The prison was built for five hundred inmates but is now home to three times as many. Meanwhile, many genuine criminals are allowed to go free because their cases never make it to court.

Perhaps the most notorious case of pretrial imprisonment took place after a wave of extreme-left-wing terrorist attacks. In 1979 the police arrested twenty well-known Marxist intellectuals suspected of links to the Red Brigades and involvement in the murder of former Prime Minister Aldo Moro. Toni Negri, a professor from the University of Padua, spent four years in jail without being tried. He was released not because the authorities had decided they had no case against him but because the Radical Party, outraged by his treatment, made him a parliamentary candidate. Negri was elected and thus automatically received parliamentary immunity from prosecution and arrest. Parliament subsequently voted to lift his immunity, but Professor Negri didn't wait for the outcome of the vote and fled the country. A few years later he was sentenced in absentia to thirty years in jail.

In another case a well-known television presenter named Enzo Tortora was arrested on the testimony of a Mafia killer who had accused him of being a drug dealer. Tortora spent several years in prison before being released. He was never charged.

"Tangentopoli" has rekindled the debate about preventive custody. More than two thousand suspects have been held without being charged or tried. Many have been kept in custody in order to extract confessions. The government of Prime Minister Berlusconi was particularly strong in describing this as an unacceptable practice. The judges responded, rightly, that without preventive custody no one would have confessed, the extent of corruption would not have been discovered, and reform would not have come about.

"Tangentopoli" has obscured the fact that Italy's judicial system is in a dreadful mess. Although preventive custody is one of the oldest and most fiercely debated ills of the Italian judicial system, it was scarcely touched by the much-vaunted 1989 legal reform known as the "New Code of Penal Practices." This reform was above all designed to limit the sweeping powers of the *pubblico ministero,* the public prosecutor. For instance, the reform has scrapped the old provision of *segreto istruttorio,* or secret proceedings. Previously, a suspect didn't even know what the charges against him were until his first day in court, making it very difficult for the defense to prepare its case. The ambiguous verdict of "case annulled because of insufficient evidence," which helped hundreds of mafiosi to get off the hook, has been abolished. A verdict now has to be either guilty or not guilty. Today public prosecutors also need the permission of a judge to issue an arrest warrant. Nevertheless, the practice of keeping suspects in preventive custody even when they have clearly been cooperating with the judiciary is still very widespread. Consequently, prison overcrowding is so bad that many of the industrialists and politicians arrested in the "Tangentopoli" scandal have been put into the only available space, the solitary confinement cells. The culture shock of going from a boardroom to an isolation cell must be considerable.

On a visit to Milan's San Vittore jail, the premier prison of "Tangentopoli," I wasn't allowed to interview illustrious prisoners. But I was introduced to William Mamone, a long-term resident who was serving ten years for armed robbery. Mamone was born in Calabria but had been named William in honor of an American pilot who had rescued his father during World War II. William had emigrated to the United States, where he had become a rock music producer and then a cocaine dealer. He was also accused of armed robbery in the United States and later that year was due to be extradited—he had allegedly been caught in a shop in Los Angeles with a submachine gun. "I didn't mean no harm to no one, honest!" he told me.

William Mamone was one of those prisoners who can almost make jail seem like a homey kind of place. Having been to two other prisons, he was a connoisseur of coolers. He was kind, witty, articulate, and well dressed. He grew basil and marjoram on his windowsill. The leaves crept up the bars as up a pergola. He knew fifty different pasta sauces and cooked them in the tiny lavatory of his cell, which he had converted with the help of a Bunsen burner into a makeshift kitchen. He also edited the *San Vittore Journal,* the glossy in-house monthly that featured gossip, legal advice, political commentary, features on "life outside," and a special set of horoscopes tailor made for its readers. Example: "Sagittarius: Your sign is in the ascendant. Sentence may be coming up for review!" But above all William Mamone was one of the few prisoners who talked to the people he called "the white-collar criminals," the illustrious arrestees of "Tangentopoli." "I saw many of them cry," he told me. "Imagine the humiliation of suddenly being carted out of a restaurant or your nice home and being taken here. Most of them carry on wearing their suits for a day or two. They can't quite believe they're here. They think they'll be let out the next day. When it dawns on them that they may have as much as six months or more inside, they start wearing more casual clothes. I saw one guy sitting on his own. He was a very well known businessman, I can't tell you his name. Anyway, he was sobbing. I asked him what was wrong. He said his son had been attacked and teased at school because of his father. The arrest was all over the newspapers."

William believed that it was unfair that most of those arrested were businessmen and not politicians, who did not lose their parliamentary immunity from prosecution and arrest until the spring of 1994. "Businessmen make money. They create jobs. Most of them should be let out. I would much rather see someone like Bettino Craxi or Giulio Andreotti here. I could teach them how to cook."

The strain of spending months in jail without being charged, let alone tried or found guilty, was too much for some. Gabriele Cagliari, the former head of Italy's state chemical company, ENI, committed suicide. The former director of one of the world's biggest chemical companies had been in prison for four months without being charged. Although Antonio Di Pietro had signed his release papers, another Milan judge wanted to hold him for further questioning and had the papers annulled. On hearing that his release had been postponed yet again, Cagliari killed himself. Di Pietro was furious. The public's sympathy was in danger of turning against the judges.

"Tangentopoli" has shown once again that in Italy there is no such thing as a single unified judiciary but more than eight thousand individual magistrates, prosecutors, and judges. Some of them are left-wing, some right-wing, some independent. The politicization of the Italian judiciary is partly historical. Most of the senior judges in the immediate postwar era were inherited from Fascism. Consequently, the younger generation became radicalized in the 1960s and '70s as a reaction to their deeply conservative superiors. For some, like the jurist Federico Mancini, the courts become a weapon in the class struggle. "All laws," Mancini wrote, "should be interpreted with this yardstick: partisanship is a virtue and neutrality a misconception or a fraud; so is independence; a judiciary cloaking itself in these sham values is a servant of power . . . judges must defend the oppressed and the downtrodden and cooperate with the labor movement."

If some judges were *pretori d'assalto,* intent on battling the establishment, others were only too happy to serve it. Corado Carnevale, a senior appeals court judge, was known as "the quasher" because he released legions of mafiosi on the grounds that there was insufficient evidence against them. Two years ago Carnevale was forced into early retirement. Since then more than twenty judges have been investigated or in some cases even arrested for allegedly collaborating with the Sicilian Mafia or the Neapolitan Camorra.

Although Italian judges are far more politicized than their counterparts in England or Germany, they are not elected as American judges and district attorneys are. They cannot be held accountable for their political leanings, despite the fact that these leanings often interfere with the process of justice. According to the Napoleonic Code, judges and examining magistrates have to pass a tough public examination just as senior civil servants do. If they're successful, they are appointed for life and enjoy sweeping powers. Some suffer from delusions of grandeur. One magistrate closed down Silvio Berlusconi's three national television networks for a week on a technicality. Another ordered a raid on his headquarters days before the elections that brought Berlusconi to power. This magistrate, from the Calabrian town of Palmi, was looking into the links between politics, Freemasons, and mafiosi and wanted a list of all the candidates put forward by the media tycoon's Forza Italia. She could just as easily have called the Interior Ministry's information department. In both cases Berlusconi suspected a left-wing plot to undermine him. But Italian magistrates don't always need plots in order to exercise their powers. Another magistrate issued an arrest warrant for Yasser Arafat.

Theoretically, the judges are servants of the state whose political independence is enshrined in the Constitution and guaranteed by the judiciary's governing bodies, the Superior Judicial Council and the Constitutional Court. But as usual politics have intervened. The Constitutional Court, which was set up in 1956 and has the power to overturn legislation deemed unconstitutional, consists of fifteen members who serve nine-year terms. The five appointments made by Parliament were traditionally the most partisan, conditioned, like so much else, by *consociativismo*. According to an unwritten agreement, two of the nominees went to the Christian Democrats and one each to the Communists, the Socialists, and lay parties such as the Republicans. The president was allowed five slots, which were also open to partisan influence. In the case of the five appointments made by the judiciary itself, the political leanings were perhaps less difficult to trace but no less real. Now that the Christian Democrats and the Socialists have lost their power, it will be interesting to see how the country's highest judicial posts will be carved up in the future and whether the appointments will be left entirely to the judiciary. So far, at least, the Italian judicial system has always mirrored the country's rigid political pluralism. Within this amorphous body there was a balance between Right and Left, but this didn't help the individual left-wing suspect who was being investigated by a right-wing magistrate or vice versa.

Perhaps the most bizarre aspect of the Italian judicial system is the large number of laws that have been inherited from Fascism and that fill the statute books in total contradiction to the spirit of Italy's very liberal Constitution. A third of the laws are still thought to be of Fascist vintage. The 1931 Rocco Code, which was named after Mussolini's minister of justice, Alfredo Rocco, and formed the basis of the repressive legal code under Fascism, has never been scrapped in full. Only individual laws, like the death penalty and certain aspects of censorship, have been repealed. But others remain. The most notorious law is the old-fashioned-sounding one forbidding *vilipendio*, or vilification. Theoretically, a person showing contempt or disrespect toward state institutions, the national flag, the armed forces, the Italian nation, religion, the president, or the pope can be sent to prison for several years. In 1980 the editor of the satirical weekly *Male* was sentenced to two and a half years in jail for making fun of Pope John Paul II. By a remarkable coincidence His Holiness was speaking to the Rome press corps at the same time about the need to guarantee freedom of speech in modern societies. The most recent and most absurd example of *vilipendio* took place in 1992, when Rome's favorite madman was charged with vilifying the president of the Republic, Francesco Cossiga. A forty-five-year-old doctor of jurisprudence who lives with his mother, the "*ballerino* of Piazza Barberini" has invented what he calls the "universal theory of five dimensions," a key to unlock the mysteries of the universe. He wears a bizarre headdress that consists of a baseball cap fitted with thin metal spokes. His identity and kidney donor cards dangle from the spokes. The *ballerino* prances and pirouettes around the Bernini fountain in the middle of the square every day, preaching his "theory" to pedestrians, tourists, pigeons, and passing cars. He spits and spices his delivery with insults against the president, the prime minister of the day, and a certain Professor Feinstein, about whom he is particularly vitriolic. The man is quite clearly as mad as a hatter. When his insanity was proved beyond any reasonable doubt—in about five minutes—the charges were dropped.

Despite the occasional charge of *vilipendio,* for now one can rest assured that the great majority of these vestigial Fascist laws will not be used. But a future government might choose to dust off some of the old furniture. If they do, they could theoretically find a law for every repressive measure in the complex, contradictory quilt of Italian justice. However remote, the temptation hangs over the country's relatively young democracy like a dark cloud. Genuine reform in Italy must surely involve a complete redrafting of the legal code by Parliament, a redefinition of the rights of the judiciary, and insurance against any political interference.

In fact, all these provisions already exist on paper. The rub is—as ever—in their application. The only way to shrug off the contradictions of the legal system is to start again from scratch. This may be impossible. In Italy the preferred method of change involves the grafting of new layers of legislation onto the old rather than a fresh beginning. Italy is, after all, a palimpsest of all the cultures and civilizations that have flourished on the peninsula. Where else can you see so many medieval churches built into Roman temples, redesigned by the Renaissance, spoiled by the Baroque, repainted at the time of the Risorgimento, surrounded by Fascist lampposts, and restored with late-twentieth-century technology? The seam of continuity runs through this chaotic but profoundly conservative country.

For me the most striking monument to the good intentions and inadequate application of the law in Italy is the Palace of Justice in Naples. If Milan's Palazzo di Giustizia was inspired by film director

Fritz Lang, the Naples "palace" hails from Dante's *Inferno* and Samuel Beckett. The building is a sixteenth-century palazzo with the sturdy, angled walls of a dank, sinister fortress. Situated next to Spaccamapoli, one of the city's most crime-infested streets, it is guarded round the clock by soldiers. Some of them stand in gray armored sentry boxes, others sit in armored vehicles. None of them looks happy to be there. The manic tangle of traffic and pedestrians that is Naples buzzes around them like a stubborn swarm of bluebottle flies. The large entrance to the inner courtyard is as inviting as the Mouth of Hell. In the courtyard, scores of bodyguards, soldiers, carabinieri, and armed men of all descriptions, wearing every conceivable uniform, linger amid scruffy-looking armored cars like private retainers, waiting for their judge to appear. One almost expects to hear a director shouting through the megaphone: "Cut! Next take!" But no film set could be as vivid and colorful as this reality.

I had gone to see Rafaele Marino and Paolo Mancuso, two leading anti-Mafia magistrates who had been largely responsible for disclosing the links between the Neapolitan Camorra and the city's Christian Democratic grandees. The judges were fighting three battles, they told me: one against the corrupt political leadership of the city, the second against corrupt judges, and the third against overcrowding in the jails. Six magistrates and two secretaries shared one small office with three desks. The closets and cabinets were groaning with files. Court records dating back to the 1970s were piled up to the ceiling, leaning precariously. In the sweltering heat the air current from a noisy ventilator was directed strategically so as not to flutter the yellowed papers scattered over every desk. Because of government cuts, there was only one computer among the six. The court stenographers had gone on strike because they hadn't been paid for two months, and many of the judges were being forced to write their dispositions by hand. Others were crouching in the corridors in their flowing court robes, working on laptop computers.

"We're lucky," said Judge Mancuso. "Most of our colleagues work either from home or in portable cabins that have been put up in the courtyard behind the kitchen." There is in fact a brand-new, spacious, fully equipped courthouse only half a mile away in the Centro

Direzionale, an ugly cluster of skyscrapers in the derelict "Manhattan" of Naples. The court building has been ready for three years. Unfortunately, in 1992 the Camorra burnt part of it down. Everything was repaired last year, but the judiciary can't move in until a legal dispute with a neighboring skyscraper about the laying of electricity lines has been cleared up. Faced with this nightmare of surreal pettiness, the death threats from the Camorra, and the stresses of a *vita blindata,* or armored life, of bodyguards and bulletproof cars, I was amazed to find Judges Mancuso and Marino in such good humor. They offered me a coffee. Somewhere behind a rubber plant a machine hissed and spluttered. "We could charge every one of the politicians that we are investigating today, right now," they told me. "But if it came to a trial, we wouldn't have the resources to bring them to court. In Naples the administration of justice is on the verge of collapse. What's more, we have to deal with all these." Judge Marino picked up a pile of papers and dropped them onto his desk with a thud. "Hundreds of cases involving petty crimes, such as cigarette smuggling. We're deluged." It was very sad to think that Italy's "sweet revolution" would flounder because of a mundane but crippling lack of resources.

Many Italian magistrates and judges clearly deserve their status as heroes or, in some cases, martyrs. Giovanni Falcone, his wife, who was also a magistrate, and three of their bodyguards were killed by a massive bomb near Palermo airport in May 1992. Two months later, Paolo Borsellino and his bodyguards were killed by a car bomb in the center of Palermo outside the house of his mother, whom he had just been to visit. These murders, more brazen than any before, galvanized the anti-Mafia struggle in Sicily. They helped to break the infamous *omertá,* the blanket of silence under which the Mafia managed to kill, rob, and extort with impunity for more than a century. They also fueled support for grassroots movements like Leoluca Orlando's Network party, which attacked the Mafia not just as a band of organized criminals but as an affront against civilized society and a cancer thriving on complacency. Today the tree outside Falcone's house in Palermo has become an anti-Mafia shrine. Its trunk is studded with hundreds of messages of gratitude and homage. A lone soldier wearing the feathered hat of the Italian Alpine Regiment guards the tree, probably regretting that he got caught up in the fight against the Mafia, hundreds of miles from home, in another Italy.

In Milan, Antonio Di Pietro and his team have launched an unprecedented crusade against corruption. They forced an arrogant and bloated political elite to recognize what is written in every Italian courtroom: *La legge e uguale per tutti* (Everyone is equal before the law). They proved to the Italians just how wasteful, corrupt, and damaging the old system had been. But they would also be fooling themselves if they thought they could have acted to the same extent without the help of the electorate. Their fight against politics was in itself political. The electorate had become a jury of forty million people. By voting against the old parties, the Italian people had issued a collective verdict of guilty before any trial had even taken place. This had given Di Pietro and his colleagues the courage to bring politicians like Craxi and Forlani to trial. As Di Pietro declared at the beginning of the Cusani trial: "*We* are the people. Not the parties." There are shades of Robespierre in this statement that would probably make any British barrister or American attorney cringe with embarrassment or, for that matter, blush with envy. At a conference on "Tangentopoli" at the European University at Fiesole in the hills above Florence in February 1994, a roundtable of academics was warning about the dangers of a "Republic of the Magistrates." At a time when the old Parliament had still not been dissolved and the honesty of the president had been called into question by a scandal in the deviant secret service, they pointed out that the only institution of state that was still functioning properly was the judges. Unfortunately, everyone agreed, the judges were too divided to form one homogeneous body. Politics should not be left to them.

An episode from the Cusani trial illustrated the fact that the law is still feared as a means of repression and not respected as a guarantee of liberty for every citizen. However liberal Italy's Constitution may be, the country has not been able to shake off some of its authoritarian instincts, fifty years after the end of Fascism.

On January 4, 1994, a businessman named Domenico D'Addario

sat in the witness chair in one of the cold granite-and-marble court-rooms in Milan's Palazzo di Giustizia. Dressed in his black robe, Antonio Di Pietro began the questioning. "Who are you?" "I'm Domenico D'Addario," said the witness. "What are you doing here?" asked Di Pietro. "I thought you would know. I'm here to give evidence, I presume." "No, no," said the prosecutor. "We wanted Amadeo D'Addario, not Domenico. You've got nothing to do with this trial." (Laughter from the spectators.) "Does that mean I can go?" (More laughter.) "Yes, go!" The court had accidentally called in the wrong D'Addario, a distant relative of the man it actually wanted to question. What was astonishing was that Domenico D'Addario had actually turned up in court without even bothering to inquire what he could possibly have witnessed. He had just assumed that he was guilty of something.

The Catholic ritual of regular confession has conditioned Italians—even, it seems, the great majority who no longer go to confession—to think of themselves as perpetual sinners. And the notion of universal temptation and original sin has let the individual off the hook.

The State Versus the Citizen

T he Italians have a reputation for flouting the law, breaking the rules, and conducting their daily lives in a matter that is infuriatingly haphazard but charmingly individualistic. Their easy-going Mediterranean lifestyle is the envy of pent-up Protestants in more sober climates. When I first moved to Italy in 1991, I discovered to my horror that the Italians had been misunderstood and I had been misled. Italy turned out to be hair-splittingly legalistic, a country slavishly obsessed with petty rules and officialdom. Tourists do not stay long enough to get entangled in the legal web of opening a bank account, getting a telephone, a parking permit, a residence permit, or a mushroom-picking permit. They have probably never had the degrading experience of sending a package through the Italian postal system or paying a gas bill, both of which involve hours of queuing and mounds of paperwork. Overawed by the colorful, noisy theater of street life, they are blissfully unaware of the fact that it is they, not the Italians, who are breaking the rules. Take even the enjoyable and deceptively simple act of drinking a frothy cappuccino. This ritual is a minefield of regulations.

Rule Number 1: Never have a cappuccino after 11 o'clock in the morning. It is intended only as a morning beverage, accompanied by a croissant (*cornetto*) or a brioche. If you do order a cappuccino after the deadline, make sure you give the person behind the bar a reason. For instance, you could say that you woke up late because you were working until the early hours of the morning. *Do not* say you are hungover. Getting inebriated, whether in public or in private, is very un-Italian and frowned upon.

Rule Number 2: Never order a cappuccino after lunch or dinner. How can you pour all that hot milk into a stomach filled with pasta, meat, and cheese? A postprandial cappuccino will immediately brand you as a foreigner and possibly lead to an increment on the bill. It would simply not occur to an Italian to have a cappuccino after a meal. If you walk into a caffè and the waiter asks you in broken English if you would like a cappuccino—whether before or after 11 o'clock—leave immediately! The caffè probably caters only to tourists and is therefore neither good nor cheap.

Rule Number 3: Never have your cappuccino sitting down unless you want to pay a large sum of money.

Rule Number 4: When you have found the right caffè at the right time, you can't just order your cappuccino without knowing what *kind* of cappuccino you want. Italians are very particular about whether they drink it *bollente* (literally, boiling hot); *senza schiuma* (without foam); *con cioccolata* (with a sprinkle of chocolate on the top), or *in vetro* (in a glass, as opposed to in a cup). This last is one of the more puzzling concepts, because the barman often actually prepares the cappuccino in a cup only then to pour it into a glass.

Rule Number 5: You can drink espresso all day long. The question again is what kind of espresso: *lungo* (long, or with a dash of water); *macchiato* (with a dash of milk); *lungo/macchiato* (with a dash of each); or *corretto* (with grappa); this is allowed before 11:30 A.M.

Rule Number 6: Never leave the bar without your receipt, even if it's for the trifling sum of 800 lire. You are obliged by law to take the receipt. Not taking it makes you an accessory to tax evasion. The receipt is proof that a purchase has been made and that the purchase will be registered in the cash register, and therefore eventually on the bar's tax returns. In 1992 a ten-year-old boy was fined for leaving a grocer's shop with an apple but without a receipt. The fact that the shop was owned by the boy's father did not impress the Guardia di Finanza, Italy's much-loathed Financial Police, recognizable by their gray uniforms and the emblem of a small yellow flame flickering on their peaked caps.

The Italians are creatures bound by custom, and contrary to their image they can be slavishly conformist. Another example: the *passeggiata,* the ceremonial Sunday evening stroll when a whole town parades up and down the main street in its best clothes of almost identical fashion before dinner. The *passeggiata* takes place according to a strict but unwritten timetable that is different from town to town. In Perugia, for instance, the main street fills up at 7 o'clock on the dot and is jam-packed for one and a half hours until the *passeggiata* suddenly fizzles out at 8:30 as if someone had blown a whistle. In Reggio di Calabria, which is hotter, the same ritual takes place half an hour later. Another example: my local birreria (a restaurant that serves beer and food but no wine or coffee) is popular for lunch every day. At 12:30 P.M. the blue-collar workers eat; at 1 P.M. the white-collar workers from the nearby banks arrive (the managers eat sitting down; the clerks standing up, which is cheaper). At 2 P.M. the civil servants from the nearby ministries and government offices arrive for lunch (their official working day as servants of the state ends at 2 P.M.). Italians take their espresso at "their bar," buy meat at "their butcher," go to "their laundry." If you get caught in another shop, bar, or laundry, this will be perceived by the owner as an act of disloyalty or treason. Get caught twice, and you have declared war.

The Italians distinguish between rules created by society, which are there to be observed, and laws imposed by the state, which are there to be broken. Patronizing the same shop or bar not only stems from the instinct for routine, it also comes from the realization that a personal rapport is essential for survival. In Italy, everything from getting a job to buying a pair of trousers is done on recommendation. When I asked my friend Michele where I could buy a decent pair of jeans, he sent me to the other end of Rome, to a shop owned by a man who was a friend of his uncle's. "You'll get a discount!" he promised. The jeans were very nice, and I did get a 15 percent discount. But the money I had saved went for the gasoline I used to drive there and didn't compensate me for the irritation of crossing

Rome by car. Furthermore, I would have been able to purchase the same pair of trousers around the corner from my apartment; and probably with the same discount, which is taken off automatically to seduce the casual shopper into becoming a regular and which the shop owner has accounted for anyway. The Italians know all this, of course, but to blurt out the truth would spoil the ritual.

Another example: Italians are sticklers for titles. All those who look as if they might have a university degree are called "dottore." Eyeglasses are usually considered to be an accurate indicator. If the "dottore" has gray hair, he is automatically upgraded to "professore," unless we know his real academic title, in which case he might become "avvocato," like Gianni Agnelli, "ingegnere," like Carlo De Benedetti, or "onorevole" (honorable), like Bettino Craxi. (Since the corruption scandal, the title "onorevole" has been used more as an insult.) You can call a woman "signora" if she is a housewife. But try not to call a man "signore." Call him by his professional title. The Mafia use "signore" as a devastating insult. It implies that the addressee has no title, therefore no power and thus no role in society. He is a nonperson. Should you meet a senior mafioso, make sure to call him "Don" plus his first name. Flouting the ritual of respect can lead to trouble. For instance, the Mafia had it be known they wanted to kill the carabiniere who had arrested Totò Riina, the diminutive boss of all the bosses, in Palermo in January 1993. In their minds he deserved to die not because he had arrested the *capo di tutti capi*— that was, after all, his job—but because when the officer had arrested him, he had made him lie down on the street facedown. That was an unpardonable act of disrespect.

Italy has a genius for complication, which is exemplified by the byzantine ritual of drinking coffee as much as by the country's four competing police forces. The Guardia di Finanza deals only with fiscal abuse and contraband, leaving theft, rape or murder to the Polizia. Crimes against the state, such as Mafia killings, flag burning, and attempted coups d'état are on the whole dealt with by the Carabinieri, who answer to the Ministry of Defense, as opposed to the Ministry of the Interior. The cavalry branch of the Carabinieri has been entrusted with the stylish protection of historic monuments such as the

Senate or the Forum in Rome. With their long capes, swords, and knee-high boots, they are the world's most overdressed police force and are uninterested in any crimes that do not directly concern their narrow brief. They are also too decorative to stoop to the undignified act of making an arrest or running after a suspect.

Traffic offenses in cities are the exclusive domain of the Vigili Urbani, whose lowly status in the law enforcement hierarchy is compensated for by their splendid white pith helmets. All the police forces take pride in their dress code, and in 1988 the Carabinieri commissioned Giorgio Armani to design their lightweight summer uniform. The art of surviving in Italy depends in large part on knowing what crimes to commit in the presence of which uniform. An officer of the Carabinieri or the Guardia di Finanza is unlikely to intervene in a traffic offense. For fear of stepping on a colleague's toes, a traffic cop is unlikely to touch a serious crime without deferring to the Carabinieri or the Polizia. Italy's multifaceted police apparatus exists to enforce a myriad of laws, inscribed in one of the world's longest and most complex legal codes.

Why, then, have they done such a terrible job? Why has Italy experienced the most rampant and systematic corruption of any postwar democracy? Why has an entire political elite been toppled from decades of uninterrupted power because of widespread abuse of public office? Why have thousands of business leaders, politicians, and bureaucrats been arrested? Why is tax dodging a national sport in Italy? Greed and power are only two reasons. Another is that Italy's laws are too complicated to be followed and too contradictory to be respected. The country, which invented Roman law and therefore helped to lay the foundations of modern society, has been forced to seek refuge in illegality.

The complex rituals, from the morning coffee to the titles with which one addresses people, prepare the Italians for the most important, durable, and trying battle of their lives: the citizen versus the state. The rituals are a foretaste of the labyrinthine rules imposed by the state on the individual and explain why so many Italians follow the rules or at least are at pains to give the impression they do. They are too terrified not to. Historically, the state has always been distrusted or feared by the Italians. Under the Spanish Bourbon monarchy the state was a foreign power. According to the popular myth, the state under the popes in central Italy was nothing but an excuse to collect high taxes, administer as little as possible, and use God for moral blackmail. Mussolini and the Fascists worshipped the state as a universal remedy. Under them it invaded the lives of citizens more than ever before and suppressed those who didn't worship it. In the postwar republic, the state was abused by the parties who carved it up for political patronage. Its reputation was further tarnished by the fact that the state's highest representatives, from senior civil servants to former prime ministers, stole from its own coffers. Prime Minister Berlusconi became widely mistrusted for looking like a tycoon who wanted to incorporate the state into his business empire. Meanwhile, with public services from the transit system to health care in a deplorable state, only a small majority of Italians feel they are actually getting something in return for their contributions. Who can blame them for trying to dodge their taxes? The relationship between citizen and state in Italy is clearly in urgent need of repair.

Nowhere is this more obvious than in the intricate relationship between the Italian and his tax. Which tax? one might well ask. The income tax? The car tax? The tax on your driving license? The tax on your car purchase? Was that a used car or a new car? The tax on your refrigerator, your television, your first home, your second home, your boat, your helicopter, your pet, your fur coat, your marriage license? Separate taxes exist for all these and many more. Luigi Enaudi, Italy's most eminent postwar economist, calculated that if every tax in the Italian lawbook were collected, the state would earn 115 percent of the nation's total income and wealth. As it happens, the state collects only a fraction of the taxes it is owed. Italy's tax policy owes more to Samuel Beckett than to Franz Kafka. It verges on the surreal. Take the story of the ISI tax imposed in the summer of 1992.

August is the hottest month. In Rome the cobbled streets flicker under an intense heat. They are deserted but for groups of sweaty tourists shuffling like forced laborers in search of the handful of bars and restaurants that remain open. Debilitated and delirious, they are easy prey for the few street vendors and souvenir sharks who sell tempting bottles of mineral water and flat Coca-Cola at exorbitant prices. You hardly ever see the few Romans who have not escaped to the sea or the mountains; they spend all day indoors behind closed shutters that keep the sun out and the flies in. Many of them venture out only before dawn. In August 1992 they did so not because this was the coolest time of day but because they wanted to be at the head of the line that formed every day at sunrise outside the *catasto,* the municipal land-registry office. This was the ISI queue. The ISI, or Imposta Straordinaria sugli Immobili, was Italy's new property tax, levied by Parliament at the beginning of August and due for collection by September 30. It was one of the desperate measures drawn up by the government of Prime Minister Giuliano Amato, who, in the wake of new European Community targets, had the unenviable task of whittling Italy's monstrous budget deficit down to an acceptable European level.

The new property tax was straightforward enough: property owners had to pay 0.2 percent a year on the value of their home above the figure of 50 million lire. The collection of the tax was, however, not so straightforward. You had to fill out a form that you could get only at one of the few designated land-registry offices. You had to pick up the form in person. That is, *if* forms were available. But to join the line for the form, you needed a special ticket, without which you had no right to be in line. A police van was posted outside several offices after there had been angry scuffles. Forms had run out soon after the office had opened—three hours late. Thousands of diligent, law-abiding citizens had forgone their God-given right to be at the beach in order to head back to the steaming capital on the sweltering autostrada, all to pay a new tax. Understandably, they were seething. In Milan a minor riot erupted when the computer system at the municipal land registry office broke down and three world-weary officials had to process the forms of more than two thousand applicants by hand—at a snail's pace, of course.

But the forms that caused all this unhappiness were only the preliminary ones. They merely enabled you to fill out another form—that is, *if* you had located the right documents to back up the information about your property required in the first form. Finding the deed of your property is difficult enough at the best of times. It is impossible if your lawyer is lying oiled and tanned on a beach somewhere on the Mediterranean—unless, of course, he too wanted to pay his ISI tax and you caught him at home. If you were cunning, patient, and above all lucky enough to have filled out all the right pieces of paper and get them approved, you could then pay your tax. But failure to do so would have resulted in prosecution. As the commentator in *La Repubblica* put it, "I don't think there is another country north of the Antarctic where people get up before sunrise just to hand their money over to the state, and what's more at a time when they should be on vacation." A SUMMER OF SHAME, thundered *Corriere della Sera*. A cartoon showed a confused citizen scratching his head in front of a tangle of corridors, revolving doors, and staircases that seemed to lead up and down at the same time: Italy's bureaucratic quagmire, one of the sternest tests of character invented by humankind. The final twist to this woeful tale of taxes—Kafka's own cherry on the cake—was that after having seen your holiday ruined, stood for days in the ISI queue, sweated in the Roman heat, developed an ISI ulcer, and emerged haggard and drawn but nonetheless victorious just before the deadline, the Italian government did what it so often does in these circumstances: only days before the deadline, it decided to scrap the tax. The ISI tax, the government realized, was, after all, unenforceable ... just like the dog/pet tax of the previous summer, which had involved stamping the hind leg of the dog upon receipt of the tax, or the fur coat tax, which had seen thousands of Italian women turning up at the tax office to register their dead mink, rabbit, or sable. In 1993 the authorities, desperate to collect taxes more efficiently, drew up a new income tax form. It was called Form 740, the same as the previous form. And it was so complicated to fill out that special programs were broadcast on television to show people how to do it. Accountants who specialized in tax forms were in great demand. Form 740 became a universal topic of conversation, more feverishly debated than soccer or "Tangentopoli."

The Italian state can play nasty tricks on its citizens. It is therefore not surprising that the citizen has learned how to play dirty with the state. The reason why both are so vicious toward each other is that they know each other's motives and tactics. They are, after all, both products of the same Italian mind. What does the civil servant who devised the ISI tax and Form 740 do every morning? He has to decide among four different types of coffee.

Tax dodging is perhaps the most famous Italian national sport. It is a complex subject that says as much about the way the individual regards the state as it does about how Italians regard one another. The Ministry of Finance has calculated that two thirds of the budget deficit—around $1.4 trillion—could be paid off in one go if the government could collect all the taxes due to it. The main culprits here are the *autonomi,* or self-employed workers, who include everyone from farmers to architects and accountants—everyone whose income doesn't get taxed at its source. SECIT, the special unit of tax inspectors in the Finance Ministry, estimated in 1990 that the average annual income of all self-employed workers—around 8 million Italians—was 8.6 million lire, just under $6,500 each, judging from their own tax assessment. The figure was clearly absurd. This is about one third of the average income of a person whose tax is deducted at source, the *dipendenti.* According to these calculations, a dentist is likely to earn half as much as a worker who stuffs turkeys or welds car parts at a factory. Unlikely! According to the financial newspaper *Il Sole 24 Ore,* the worst tax dodgers are economists and statisticians, followed closely by furriers, accountants, and stockbrokers. Those who dodged least in this category were doctors, who failed to declare, on average, only 20.5 percent of their annual income.

Because the self-employed are so modest about the amount of money they earn, the state has decided to tap their wealth in other ways. When the government announced a tax on second homes, yachts, helicopters, and luxury cars, it didn't just send a ripple of anxiety through the ranks of the super rich, it worried millions of Italians. But it delighted millions more. Italy is not a class-ridden society in the British sense. Social values, airs, and graces do not percolate down the pyramid from an outdated landed aristocracy. Nor does Italy see class as purely a matter of wealth. What counts in Italy is which part of the country you come from and whether you pay taxes, dodge taxes, or abuse the state in other ways. The social hierarchy thus consists of three principal layers: the tax-dodging *autonomi* at the top; the taxpaying but freeloading *statali,* or state employees, in the middle; and on the bottom rung the largest group, the *dipendenti,* who are taxed at source but enjoy none of the benefits of the groups above. What dilutes these divisions is the fact that a single family often contains members of all three.

The tax dodging of the self-employed is sneered at by those who get taxed at source. But even here there are important distinctions. The income of the *statale* may be taxed automatically, but he or she has other means of abusing the state. Take the civil service. In Italy this institution exists to *be* served rather than to serve. With over two million civil servants, Italy has one of the world's most bloated bureaucracies. The category "civil service" is very broad: it includes everyone from the under secretary of state at the Interior Ministry to the man who cleans his lavatory and the porter who doffs his cap to him in the morning. To become a civil servant at even the lowest level, you have to pass a *concorso,* a series of public examinations. If the Ministry of Cultural Goods wants three new lavatory cleaners, it can't just stick an advertisement in the newspaper, it has to set up a national *concorso* and wait for literally thousands to apply. The *concorso* is meant to ensure that the job isn't given to a friend or the friend of a friend. In theory it is very fair; in practice it is not. The complex, highly subtle machinery of bribes, friendships, and favors means that the person best qualified to clean the lavatories in the Ministry of Cultural Goods will not necessarily get the job. But the reason why so many people apply in the first place is that the job is like gold dust, a meal ticket for life, a firm foothold on the greasy pole, a position with status and power.

First of all, the *statale* receives an extraordinary number of privileges denied to all non-*statali.* He or she works only from 8 A.M. to 2 P.M., gets discounts on public transit, and can retire after fifteen years of service on a full pension. If you had started your career as a lavatory cleaner in the Ministry of Cultural Goods at the tender age of eighteen you could retire on 90 percent of your salary at the ripe old age of thirty-three—and millions of "baby pensioners" did before the law was changed in 1993. Of course, their salaries were not very big, perhaps 2 million lire a month (about $1,200) and taxed at source. But that is not the point. The majority of *statali* have at least two or three jobs. After lunch they work in their father's trattoria or in their mother's shoe shop or run their own olive oil export business.

Before 2 P.M. many use the phones at the ministry to set up the "afternoon economy." The *statali* are resented by everyone who is not *statale*. The self-employed think they are lazy, forgetting the fact that most *statali* become *autonomi* after two in the afternoon. Jealousy has no doubt fueled the myth machine. There's the story of the clerk in the Ministry of Finance who ran his sister's Parma ham export business from the office. Not to mention the bodyguard at the Interior Ministry who rented the ministry's limousines and motorcycle escorts to Roman businessmen who wanted to impress their clients at the airport. However apocryphal, these stories are plausible. Many of them are true, including the one of the policewoman in Turin who was discovered working in a brothel during a police raid by her colleagues. She was wearing her uniform as an added "disciplinary" attraction.

Absenteeism and fake sick leave have become endemic in the civil service. In Rome a judge ordered all hospitals to examine thousands of claims for sick leave among staff. Miraculously, they always fell ill en masse just before or after a holiday period. The *dolce vita* of the *statale* has definitely been soured by draconian reforms in the public service. Baby pensions have been outlawed, other state pensions have been frozen or cut, the number of "invalid" pensions, which had produced an army of two million perfectly healthy invalids—all that was needed to become an "invalid" was a certificate from a friendly doctor—have been cut. Today the applications for such pensions are scrutinized more rigorously.

The government has invented a whole array of surveillance measures to make sure that the *statale* actually works for the state when he or she is in the office. Staff at the Ministry of Cultural Goods, Italy's awkwardly named cultural ministry, have been given new electronic identity cards with which they have to clock in for work every morning. A computer gives an automatic readout of the number of absent or sick days. The former minister of public affairs, Giuliano Urbani, a lugubrious professor who has made it his life's task to pull the Italian civil service out of the Dark Ages, introduced the so-called "cappuccino law." This draconian piece of legislation, applicable only to *statali,* has banned the ritual midmorning cappuccino break. The reason was that the ten-minute constitutional often merged seamlessly with lunch. The day before the ban was imposed, I went to see some of its victims across the road from the Ministry of Public Affairs.

The atmosphere in Bar Italia was very heavy with foreboding. The *statali* lounged in disconsolate gloom at the bar. The cappuccinos had been replaced by stiffer drinks to soften the blow. "It's unfair," one of the *statali*, an archivist at the ministry, told me. "We are being made scapegoats for the whole system. I never stay longer than ten minutes, and by eleven I need a cappuccino. Especially if I had to be in the office by eight A.M." Such self-pity has merely fueled the loathing most Italians feel for the *statali*. No group hates them more than the *dipendenti*, who make up the majority of Italy's workforce, counting some fifteen million in their ranks. They get none of the state's privileges and have to work a full day. Many of them seek the protection of trade unions. But this is little compensation at a time when the Italian unions are getting less and less powerful, membership has fallen, and jobs are being threatened by rising unemployment. The *dipendenti* are the foot soldiers of Italian labor, loyal participants in the massive demonstrations and general strikes that paralyzed much of Italy in the hot autumn of 1992. But compared to their French or German counterparts, they are a docile bunch. I have covered countless general strikes in Italy. After the first one, I realized that these strikes are not nearly as daunting as they sound. They tend to last no longer than four hours, and they are called either before lunch or after lunch, rarely during lunch.

The difference between the three categories—*autonomi, statali,* and *dipendenti*—are further underlined by their political affiliations. The *dipendenti* form the rank and file of what is now the Democratic Party of the Left, and in some working-class areas like Turin they support the old-style Communist Party. In the rich regions of northern Italy many of the self-employed have flocked to the Northern League and Forza Italia. The League, especially, is the political voice of the hardworking, tax-dodging *autonomo* who resents the little he contributes to the national exchequer being squandered by a corrupt government in Rome. Since the civil service has traditionally been dominated by Italians from the South, it is not surprising that many *statali*, afraid of losing their privileges and their jobs in times of recession, have flocked to the neo-Fascist National Alliance, the party of white-collar paranoia in the poor South. Furthermore, the existence of a bloated civil service depends on the survival of a strong, united Italian state. The latter is a central plank of neo-Fascist thinking. It dates back to the time of Mussolini. Although Il Duce wanted to reduce the civil service in size to purge it of its non-Fascist members, he ended up by doubling it in the realization that one way of keeping the legions of overeducated, underemployed students from southern Italy quiet was to recruit them into the bureaucracy. This practice was continued during the postwar democracy.

Despite their mutual animosity, all three groups need one another much more than they think. The *statale* who belongs to the neo-Fascist party justifies his anger by pointing at the *autonomo* who votes for the Northern League. He in turn exonerates his own tax dodging by pointing at the excesses of the *statale* from southern Italy. The *dipendente* needs both in order to hoist the red union flag on the moral high ground. In November 1994 the squares of Rome filled with more than 1.5 million demonstrators protesting against the proposed pension cuts in Prime Minister Berlusconi's budget. The most impressive rally took place in the Circus Maximus, where the Romans raced their chariots. The elongated, oval-shaped basin, which once housed the Roman racetrack in the shadow of the Palatine, was awash with red flags and union banners. The one line that was repeated over and over again was: "We are the Italy that works and pays taxes."

The Italians define themselves not only by their family, their region, and their political affiliation, but also by their relationship with the state. That relationship is fraught with rivalries, jealousies, and distrust, which have been made worse by the *partitocrazia* of the last five decades. Until this relationship can be mended, there is probably little hope of real reform in Italy. Italian society will continue to lack a social contract based on individual citizens who see the rule of law as a guarantee for equal opportunities and rights and neither abhor the state as a threat nor worship it as an end in itself. However tedious it may sound, a remedy involves nothing short of a collective change of mentality that allows people to put more trust in the state and less in all the alternatives that have sprouted in its place from the political party to the Masonic lodge, to the Mafia and to the most important building block of Italian society—the family. Ousting one ruling class and replacing it with another, as the Italians have just done by exercising their democratic rights, is not enough. What's needed is fundamental constitutional reform that creates a benevolent federalist state that takes into account the country's regional differences, simplifies the tax laws, and harnesses Italy's innate humanity, which is embodied in the family, to the needs of society. It's a delicate, perhaps even impossible balancing act. For now such reform is hindered by the most popular mutual protection society in Italy: *la famiglia.* The family fills the gaps left by the state in the most mundane but important ways. This institution, which has survived despite the distractions of modern consumer society and a dramatic decline in the birthrate, is both Italy's greatest strength and its greatest weakness.

Family Values

O ur escort, a local newspaper photographer, told us to bring cream cakes "as a sign of respect." The Trimbolis of Plati were not known for their afternoon hospitality, especially when it came to entertaining foreign journalists. They had always regarded outsiders with suspicion. If they took an interest, it was more because of your value as a potential commodity. The Trimbolis are one of Calabria's notorious kidnapping families. In October 1992 Francesco Trimboli, the seventy-year-old head of the family, was in jail, accused of masterminding the kidnapping of Cesare Casella, a teenager from Pavia in the north of Italy who had been abducted in 1988. The boy had been hidden in a cave near Locri for a year and a half before the authorities managed to find him. They were spurred into action only when his mother chained herself to the railings of the courthouse in Locri, in protest against the police force's inactivity. In the case of Casella, no ransom had been paid.

Francesco Trimboli's sons, Domenico and Paolo, were also behind bars. They had been members of the local Christian Democratic Party and had sat on the town council—when Plati still had a town council. In 1991 the entire assembly, including the Trimboli brothers, was thrown into jail, accused of corruption and "Mafia-type activities." Being a town elder of Plati also meant belonging to one of the most feared crime syndicates on the Italian peninsula. The authorities had impounded $30 million worth of assets belonging to the Trimboli family and another famous local clan, or _cosche,_ the Barbaros. These were some of the revenues from years of toil and devotion in the family industries for which Plati in particular and Calabria in general have become famous: drugs, arms, and kidnapping.

That left Bruno Trimboli, the nephew, to entertain us. It was he who had invited me and Charles Richards, a friend and colleague from Britain's _The Independent_ newspaper, to visit Plati. The cakes, as it turned out, were not such a great idea. Bruno Trimboli, whose pale blue eyes stared at us through the cracks of his dry, tanned skin, was not impressed by our beautifully wrapped box of cream puffs. "There was really no need to bring them," he declared solemnly as he opened the door, leaving us in some doubt as to whether he was being polite, was angered because we had felt the need to buy his hospitality with a gift, or was simply unhappy about our choice of cake.

The Trimboli family lived in a street that had been dubbed Via Bolgetti. This was the local pronunciation of "Paul Getty." In 1973 the Getty oil dynasty had unwillingly become the biggest single benefactor that Plati and the surrounding village have ever had. The Getty family paid $730,000 in ransom to the gangs who had abducted their son Paul Getty, Jr., and held him in the dense forests and craggy hills of the Aspromonte for six months. The kidnappers hurried along the ransom by sending the Getty family's priest a part of the boy's right ear as an expression of their impatience, a gesture rooted in local tradition. Before the gangs of the Aspromonte had begun kidnapping humans, they had stolen sheep. It was usual to send a sheep's ear to the owner as a kind of calling card and as a reminder that payment was expected. With every week that went by, another part of the sheep was cut off and dispatched. It was unsettling to think that Bruno Trimboli and the members of his family who invited us into their home that afternoon were part of this gruesome, bloodthirsty tradition.

We sat in the kitchen, newly equipped with built-in "wipe-clean" Formica cupboards as well as all the modern conveniences of kitchen technology; a Bosch dishwasher, a microwave oven, a Magimix. The beige tiles were decorated with ducks flying in formation. Bruno's three daughters milled around the kitchen table. The eldest, who was cross-eyed and wore a lacy pink dress and a ponytail, made the tea and coffee. It was a picture of domestic bliss tinged with rural kitsch. We asked Bruno about the members of his family who had been incarcerated. He was adamant that no Trimboli had ever been involved in kidnapping or any other crime. "The real criminals are those people in Rome!" he snorted, crossing his arms ceremoniously. "They're the ones who steal!" Trimboli was on a roll. "Look at us here in Plati. They have just abandoned us. Let us rot. All they send us are soldiers and carabinieri." His local dialect was so strong that our photographer had to translate what he was saying into ordinary Italian. Trimboli's lament was a common refrain in Plati, which we had also heard in one of the bars near the abandoned town hall, where the carabinieri were standing guard in bulletproof vests and armed with submachine guns.

Successive governments in Rome and in the administrative capital of Calabria, Catanzaro, had indeed done little to help Plati. The Ministry of Justice had effectively declared the town a "no-go area." Since the council had been dissolved, a state administrator, appointed by Rome, traveled to Plati twice a week, staying only for a few hours to be briefed by the local carabiniere commander. Occasionally he also listened to complaints from local shopkeepers about inadequate electricity and water supplies. Plati frequently found itself cut from the Calabrian power net because the entire town had neglected to pay its bills. The families of Plati said they were being persecuted. The fact is that they were at war with the rest of Italy and with one another.

The legacy of neglect and mutual antagonism between the national authorities and Plati went back a long way. A landslide had washed away part of the town in 1953, killing eighteen. Nothing had been done to repair the damage or secure the mountain face looming above Plati. In 1973 another landslide devastated the same area. This time, luckily, no one was killed. The authorities built a canal to divert the flow of the water, but the civil engineer designed it faultily and water continues to erode the mountainside. The only thing that fills the canal is a reeking river of tins, bottles, rotting food, broken furniture, and discarded washing machines, dumped there by the locals. It was hard to believe that this was as much a part of Italy as the prosperous towns of Alba in Piedmont, Todi in Umbria, or Bergamo in Lombardy, all brimming with civic responsibility, neighborhood watch groups, and legally acquired wealth. Not that Plati was poor. The streets were full of expensive cars: black BMWs driven by young men with dark sunglasses; Mitsubishi jeeps in metallic reds parked outside the Bar Centrale; a Golf convertible parked outside the house of Bruno Trimboli. The Trimbolis, like the rest of Plati, clearly weren't lacking funds. Their house was comfortable and well equipped, a marked contrast to the street outside, which was strewn with rubbish. The asphalt had cracked as if torn apart by an earthquake, and flies were buzzing over the rotting corpse of a dog. Plati looked and smelled like the twilight zone.

"Why," we asked Bruno Trimboli in his squeaky-clean kitchen, "haven't you gotten together with your neighbors to clean up the mess, repair the roads, do some of the things the authorities have neglected for years?" "It's got nothing to do with me," came the blunt reply. As a local Calabrian saying goes, "If your neighbor's house is on fire, pour water on your own!" Not all of Plati's woes could be blamed on the government. The town had become ungovernable. In the 1980s two mayors had been gunned down in the street by a rival Mafia clan. In 1992 only 400 people out of a population of 3,800 had taken part in the municipal elections, well short of the quorum necessary to elect a new town council. In fact, the only party that had fielded a candidate was the neo-Fascist PSI. The burghers of Plati lived in fear of one another. Even if they had wanted to, they were unable to improve their lives.

The traditional solution had been to emigrate. In 1881, when Italy had done its first population census, Plati had held more than twice as many souls as today. Since then most of the inhabitants have emigrated to northern Italy, Australia, Argentina, or the United States. But emigration is no longer an option. Today the town is a ghostly ruin. The city hall had been boarded up. The door to the school was padlocked. The wall next to it had been painted with a giant mural depicting a rural scene with farmers, cows, olive trees, and carabinieri

'Ndrangheta

firing machine guns. Like much of Calabria, the town is run by the families that make up the 'Ndrangheta, the Calabrian version of the Mafia, which has recently inherited much of the expertise and trade of its Sicilian tutor and is currently fighting off the Italian authorities as never before. The 'Ndrangheta may, in fact, turn out to be less vulnerable to internal strife, betrayal, and therefore the wrath of the police thanks to its tight structure. The organization is based on families that cooperate loosely with one another. It does not have an organizational pyramid like the Mafia's cupola, which acts like a council of elders recruited from different families and regions. Pino Arlacchi, Italy's foremost expert on the sociology of organized crime and himself a Calabrian, believes that the 'Ndrangheta is far more ruthless and powerful than the Mafia, helped by the backwardness of Calabrian society and by the structure of the family. In this light the Trimbolis are a grotesque symbol of the Italian family at its worst. But they also share some of the values that have made the Italian family such a strong unit: they stick together, share resources, live under one roof, and see themselves, in the words of the late Luigi Barzini, the veteran spokesman of the Italian soul, as "the first source of power in Italy and the stronghold in a hostile land."

The negative side of Italian family values has obsessed academics for a long time. In the 1950s Italian sociologists coined the term *familismo* to explain a whole array of society's ills, from organized crime to dumping trash in the neighbor's garden. American sociologist Edward Banfield denounced "the amoral familism" of the peasants he had studied at Chiaramonte Gulfi in the poor region of Basilicata. For him the backwardness of Chiaramonte was due to the "inability of villagers to act together for their common good, or indeed for any good transcending the immediate, material interests of the nuclear family." The conclusion was that the family had become the biggest obstacle to turning Italy into a unified, modern country with law-abiding citizens. It was the family that absorbed the resourcefulness, intelligence, cunning, and energy of the ordinary Italian, which would otherwise have been invested in the *patria,* its institutions, democracy, and law and order.

Mussolini was acutely aware that the family was a hindrance to realizing the project of an obedient Fascist state. He tried to over-come the problem by becoming the Father of the Nation and turning Italy into one giant family of which he was the self-declared paterfa-milias. Silvio Berlusconi tried the same, by different means, of course. When he launched his 1995 austerity budget, he talked about "good housekeeping for the Italian family," by which he meant the whole country. It was an appeal for national solidarity that didn't work, partly because the members of the "Italian family" suspected that Berlusconi had the interests of his own family and its business empire at heart. For instance, in the budget he encouraged Italians to move from state to private life insurance as a means of slashing Italy's vast pension bill. But Berlusconi also owned three of Italy's biggest insurance companies, which sell private pensions. As a friend of mine put it, "It's not that we resent him enriching his own family. That's only to be expected. But he shouldn't do it at our expense." Berlusconi is, after all, the quintessential Italian family man. His brother, Paolo, works for the family firm. His sons and daughter sit on the company board. His children are all shareholders. And his dis-trust of the world outside his family and the small coterie of execu-tives who run his company, his political party, and much of his former government is so intense that Berlusconi has even built a fam-ily tomb in his fortresslike villa outside Milan.

The Italian family remains, at every level of society, a tightly knit, sometimes paranoid social unit. Its solidarity, which is partly volun-tary and partly enforced by the negligence of the state, becomes ap-parent in a number of important ways. The first is the sharing of resources.

Most young Italians live with their parents because the state can't provide them with a cheap apartment. A recent survey showed that almost no Italians under the age of twenty-five live away from their parental home. Even when they get married, Italian couples often stay with their parents until they can afford to find a flat of their own. The advantages are that your mother irons your shirts, prepares your meals, and looks after your baby, plus you get free use of the phone, the car and the garage. The disadvantage is that there is no privacy. Millions of Italians have lost their virginity or conceived their first child in the back of a Fiat Uno or other small cars that call for acrobatic nimbleness. From dusk till dawn car parks, highway access roads, and badly lit lanes on the outskirts of towns are full of parked but rocking cars. A telltale sign that something more serious than a kiss is taking place is the newspaper taped to the windows for privacy.*

Italian couples would, of course, prefer to live in a separate apartment from their parents but not necessarily under a separate roof. My girlfriend Penny and I live in a typical family palazzo in the historic center of Rome. The building is almost exclusively inhabited by the Pediconi family, which built it in the seventeenth century. The palazzo is still divided on a hierarchical basis. Francesco the porter lives on the ground floor with the cars and mopeds. The octogenarian widow of the head of the family resides in murky splendor on the second floor, the *piano nobile*. She and a handful of Filipino maids rattle around in a vast flat with frescoed ceilings and rococo furniture. The flat above, slightly less ornate and a little smaller, is inhabited by the brother of the deceased *capo di famiglia*. The next floor is occupied by the eldest son and heir. The two apartments above him are lived in by his younger brothers. The back of the building is reserved for a few vagrant spinster aunts, cousins, and a sad-looking professor of mathematics, a distant and destitute relative who doffs his hat to everyone. The lower your rank in the family, the higher up you live and the lower your ceilings are. We live in the top flat. One of the conditions of our moving in was that we would not insist on etching our own names into the brass plate by the front door. Hence visitors are confused by the fact that almost every one of the twelve surnames listed is a "Pediconi." Modern apartment blocks, also called palazzi, make it more difficult for families to live together under one roof. Hence many Italian families share a second house by the sea, in the mountains, or in their village of origin. In the southern province of Puglia the family stronghold becomes a veritable fortress. The traditional Puglian *masseria* is a walled, windowless complex in which all the members of the family live with their livestock like a beleaguered clan, cut off from the outside world.

*The decade when the serial killer known as "the Florence Monster" stalked the Tuscan countryside in search of mating couples did not put a stop to the practice of car-park sex, it merely encouraged scores of cars to huddle together for safety.

Family resources are also shared in other ways. One reason that the Italians have one of the highest savings rates in the world—in some areas as much as 25 percent—is that the average family spends much less money than its British or American counterpart on housing. Mortgages are almost unheard of: banks are reluctant to give them, and Italian families are even more reluctant to take them on. Nevertheless, the housing market is booming because families club together to build homes for the next generation. Parents tend to buy or build their children a house with the understanding that they will occupy one floor when they have retired. In rural areas, houses are often built by the families themselves. The hills of Umbria and Lazio are dotted with small building sites, teeming with members of the clan who have come up for the weekend to help lay bricks or tile roofs.

By saving money on housing, the Italians are free to indulge in conspicuous consumption. They spend twice as much as the European average on clothing, about $3,000 a year each. In Italy the fur coat isn't just a rare and much-maligned luxury item, it is the great social equalizer. More Italian women have real fur coats than anyone else. Walk down the Via del Corso in Rome or even down a lesser street in any small town in the weeks before Christmas, and you will be surrounded by minks, raccoons, and foxes. Cars too are a national obsession, and Italians are inordinately proud of their vehicles, even if so many of them are tiny and bruised by reckless driving. They own more cars per capita than the French, the British, or the Dutch and slightly fewer than the Swiss and the Americans. As one would expect from a country blessed with a sumptuous, varied cuisine, a lot of money also goes on food and restaurants. Italy has one establishment per 257 of the population, Britain one per 451, and France one per 795. Anyone who has been to Italy is familiar with the Sunday ritual of whole families going out for a lavish lunch with children, babies, and grandparents in tow, making a lot of noise and occupying the full attention of the waiters. Even in the age of fast food, which has also begun to blight Italy, eating is still a family affair. One Mafia turncoat recently described how, in accordance with the "godfather" cliché, his family and the other local clans would get together on Sundays and eat in one of the local restaurants near Palermo. If they wanted to keep a low profile, they would meet at one another's homes and cook. The men, he said, liked to cook and even did some of the washing up. The cult of the New Man has even reached the Italian underworld!

The key to Italian family unity is the umbilical cord between the children, especially the son, and "mamma." This is never fully severed at birth and manifests itself in the most unlikely situations. While CNN was showing U.S. paratroopers heroically clambering ashore on the beach at Mogadishu to launch Operation Restore Hope in 1993, RAI showed Italian soldiers bidding farewell to their mothers at the airport. Mother and soldier were crying into each other's arms. Men bristling with automatic machine guns, bayonets, and pistols were screaming "Mamma!" No one was embarrassed.

The mamma even occupies a central role in Italian political science. The Christian Democratic Party was commonly referred to as the *Partito mamma,* the "mama Party." Most Italians, even sober-sounding newsreaders, do not talk about *la madre,* the mother, but *la mamma:* Mommy. Italian sociology has even invented an "ism" to describe the phenomenon: *mammismo.* The children, usually sons, who suffer from it are called *mammoni.* Since a whole generation of single children is currently coming of age, Italy with its very low birth rate is in danger of being swamped by selfish brats.

If the mother-child relationship provides the emotional glue of the family, economic interests provide the financial adhesive. Italian families are run like businesses with parents, grandparents, aunts, uncles, and children all contributing to the family kitty. Family members are not only willing to bail one another out, it's expected of them. It's perhaps not surprising, then, that private businesses tend to be run by families: 90 percent of all private enterprises in Italy are family companies. This applies to the trattoria, where Mother is stuck in the kitchen, Father does the accounts, and the children rush home from school to wait tables, as well as to very large conglomerates. Silvio Berlusconi's Fininvest empire is a family business. The company isn't even listed on the stock market. The automaker Fiat is a public company, but the Agnelli family is the majority shareholder. Most of the clothing companies, from Stefanel to Missoni, are family firms. In

Benetton

1993 I went to see one of the best-known and most successful fashion families: the Benettons of Treviso, near Venice.

Today Benetton is the world's largest buyer of wool. Its colorful, well-made clothes are worn all over the world and its controversial poster campaign, depicting a patient dying of AIDS or a newborn baby splattered with blood and placenta, is celebrated or despised worldwide. The company has become a leading sponsor of sports events, and its Formula One racing team is one of the best in the world. When other Italian companies were losing money and the whole of Europe was in the clutch of recession, Benetton's sales increased by 10 percent. Its global success is reflected in the understated self-confidence of the corporate headquarters near Treviso. The firm is situated amid lush fruit orchards and vineyards. (Benetton also makes its own wine, and the company canteen serves lettuces and tomatoes from the Benetton vegetable garden.) The two thousand or so employees at the main plant, where the clothes are designed and the fabrics are dyed, don't work in a single block but in a corporate village built around an artificial lake and ponds. The roofs are made of steel coated with a liquid metal that changes color as the outside temperature changes. When I arrived in the chilly morning, they were purple; when I left in the afternoon sun, they had turned strawberry red. Underneath the village is an artificial shopping street displaying the various Benetton shops on offer. Benetton sells its clothes by selling franchises to retailers, who undertake to abide by a strict set of rules. The shops are designed and furnished by Benetton. Sales staff are taught in the Benetton school. All the clothes on sale are made by Benetton. But the shop is privately owned by the retailer. This way the company tries to guarantee a unity of product and sales philosophy. It ensures that its products are sold, but it is not burdened by the overheads and rental costs of running a store itself. The same principle is used for production. Although the clothes are designed, dyed, and packaged at company headquarters, the stitching, weaving, and sewing are farmed out to small family firms in the area.

Despite this level of sophistication and a corporate culture that can look like the mysterious rites of a religious sect, Benetton is still run like the small family firm that began making wool sweaters in the 1950s. The family remains the core of the business. While most of the employees work in the psychedelic corporate village, the family members preside over production, sales, and marketing in a sixteenth-century Palladian villa in the heart of the grounds. The offices are located in the former stables and outhouses built around a courtyard. Luciano Benetton, the chairman of the company, has his spacious frescoed offices in one corner; Giorgio, his brother and deputy chairman, is on the other side of the courtyard. The third brother, who deals with marketing, works on the *piano nobile* overlooking the courtyard. His office is next to that of his sister Giuliana, who designs the clothes. The Benetton siblings can be seen flitting across the courtyard to discuss the latest deal, corporate strategy, or design. They all meet for lunch in a common dining room. "There is nothing incestuous about our company," Luciano Benetton told me. "We are a typical Italian family business. We stick together. Decisions are made quickly. There are the occasional disagreements, but we don't quarrel too much." It would be difficult to imagine a successful business being run by a family fraught with sibling rivalries.

Italy is not so much a homogeneous country as an archipelago of families. Some of them are Benettons. Others are Trimbolis. Both are, above all, pragmatic and practical. Nepotism is regarded not as an evil but as a necessity. The fact that Bettino Craxi put his son Bobò in charge of the Socialist Party in Milan and promoted his brother-in-law Paolo Pilliteri the city's mayor would never have raised eyebrows until the family became discredited in the corruption scandal. Before becoming prime minister, Silvio Berlusconi not only divided the ownership of his empire up among the family, he also put his closest friends in top management posts. In 1994 Italy was run by a kitchen cabinet made up of the tycoon's closest advisers.

Very little has changed since Pope Pius IV made his nephew Charles Borromeo a cardinal at the age of twenty-two and gave him an annual salary of 50,000 scudi. However, in all the above cases nepotism blessed only those who were worthy of it. A relative who is an oaf would never be put into a position of power. His stupidity might jeopardize the family. It would be an unpragmatic choice.

The miracle of the Italian family is that it has survived the onslaught of modern technology, promiscuity, and mobility. Although the great majority of Italians still get married in church, the number of marriages has declined from just over 440,000 celebrated in 1947 to just over 300,000 in 1992. Since divorce was legalized after a 1974 referendum, the divorce rate has also increased. However, in Italy only 8 percent of marriages failed in 1991, compared to one in three in France and Britain. This does not mean that Italian couples are necessarily happier but that marital infidelity isn't always a reason to break up a family. A mistress, and increasingly a lover, have as little shock value in Italy today as they did three centuries ago. The pursuit of extramarital peccadilloes is frequently seen as a matter apart from marriage, which is regarded as a contract for life. Four out of five Italians who do get divorced decide to remarry, a far greater proportion than in the United States or Britain. Only 9 percent of broken marriages end in court, as opposed to 39 percent in Britain. Despite the increase in divorce, the family has remained a durable concept in what is essentially a very conservative society.

The family may have survived, even thrived, but it has not done so unaltered. One of the most significant changes is that the Italian family has shrunk. Considering their love of children, it may surprise the reader to find out that Italians have the lowest birthrate in the world. According to UNICEF figures, the average U.S. family produces 2.1 children, the average British or French family 1.8, the average German, Luxembourgian, Danish, Dutch, or Hong Kong family 1.5. But Italy, with 1.3, is at the bottom of the list. (Although 1.3 is the national average, the birthrate in the South is much higher than in the prosperous North.) The average black African woman has 7 children. For the Vatican, it's a cruel irony that Italy, the best-established home of Catholicism, heeds the Church's call to procreate less than any other industrialized nation does. The Church blames the low birthrate on artificial contraception and the excessive wealth of a consumer society that is more keen on holidays in Bali than on *bambini*. This is only part of the truth. The Italians are as fond of children as they ever have been but they can't afford to have more and maintain them in the style and comfort to which they have grown accustomed. Spoiling a child is an expensive business. Toddlers in Armani jumpsuits and babies swaddled in cashmere being chauffeured around in designer buggies are testimony to the fact that the Italians spend twice as much as any other nation on children's clothes. The birth of a child is still a reason for great, albeit increasingly rare, festivities. The day a *bambino* or *bambina* is born, his or her birth is announced by a rosette pinned to the front door or façade of the building: blue for boys, pink for girls. A British or American family looks mortified when its baby starts to scream or squeal in a restaurant or museum. In Italy it is still music to people's ears. Rich or poor, the *bambino* remains king.

Though smaller, and by and large intact, the Italian family is less and less idyllic. Judging from the thousands of calls that congest the lines of Telefono Rosa, a help line set up in 1990, Italian husbands are abusing their wives. In 1993 almost 80 percent of those who called were wives who were being beaten or put under psychological pressure by their husbands. Though there were few registered cases of sexual abuse, 82 percent of those who committed such abuse were sober when they did so. Child abuse also appears to be on the rise, although nowhere near the levels of Britain or America. And Italy registers 1,000 teenage suicides a year, a figure that is steadily rising, a fact psychologists blame on the alienation of modern society and the loneliness of only children brought up by parents who both work.

In October 1994 there was a particularly sad example. Marco Bollini, a twelve-year-boy from Padua, hanged himself in the cellar of his parents' house. The suicide took place a week after an eight-year-old American boy, Nicholas Green, had been killed by highway robbers who shot up his parents' hired car in Calabria. The parents had donated the boy's vital organs to six Italians who were waiting for organ transplants. Because Italy has very few organ donors, these people would almost certainly have died if the Greens hadn't displayed such goodwill. Italy was embarrassed and chagrined about the death of the young American and so shamed by his parents' generosity that the country went into paroxysms of guilt. The number of organ donors shot up. Marco Bollini seized the opportunity. In his suicide note he wrote that he no longer wanted to live, that his life had become worthless, but that he would like someone else to live with the help of his heart, liver, and kidneys.

The Italian family has come under siege. But it is holding out better than that of most other industrialized societies. It is Italy's secret shock absorber in times of social upheaval. It makes a lot of money and saves enough. It provides welfare, housing, and medical care when the state doesn't. Go into any Roman, Neapolitan, or Milanese hospital, and you'll find the corridors and wards congested with family members bearing food, drink, clean sheets, and sometimes even medicines. If families don't trust the state to take care of such important matters as health care, it's easy to understand why they don't see much point in paying taxes. The state's negligence has encouraged the family to think of itself as besieged, and this mentality has in turn prevented the state from encouraging civic values. With few exceptions, the community still tends to be a narrow circle based around the clan. As the next chapter shows, the Mafia, like the Trimboli family, represents the worst aspect of "familism."

The Mafia

The Other Revolution

I n the small Sicilian town of San Giuseppe Jato three carabinieri stand guard outside an empty house. The shutters are closed. It's the only house in the street with empty wash lines. On the door there is a notice: NO SEVENTH-DAY ADVENTISTS, PLEASE. But the inhabitants of Via Roma 17 now fear a visitor who offers deliverance of a different sort: the Mafia. The owner of the house, Baldassare Di Maggio, no longer lives there. The Italian police gave him and ten members of his family a new home, new names, and, for "Baldù," as his friends called him, a new face. Di Maggio was a lapsed mafioso who had broken the *omertà,* or vow of silence, and told the police where they could find the man they had been hunting for twenty-three years: Salvatore "Totò" Riina, the *capo di tutti capi,* Cosa Nostra's boss of bosses.

Di Maggio had been Riina's driver for ten years. When police captured him in October 1993, he feared that Riina would have him and his family killed to prevent them from breaking their silence. Di Maggio's chances of staying alive were better under the state's new witness protection program than at the mercy of the Mafia either inside or outside prison. If the authorities find out a *pentito* has been lying, he and his family are immediately taken out of the witness protection program and delivered into the mercy of freedom without bodyguards. As an incentive for telling the truth, it seems to have worked—so far, at least.

Di Maggio turned out to be reliable. On the morning of January 15, 1993, fifteen policemen took up positions near a busy traffic circle on the outskirts of Palermo. When a black Lancia drove past the Agip gasoline station, two officers stopped the car and asked to see the papers of the man sitting next to the driver. The last photograph of Totò Riina had been taken twenty years before. The stocky peasant features in the black-and-white photograph seemed to fit. There was no shoot-out. In fact, Riina and his driver didn't even carry guns. Their car wasn't the black stretch limo of Mafia movies with tinted windows and a minibar. It was an ordinary family car with a small plastic Madonna dangling from the rearview mirror. At first the boss of all the bosses protested that he was an ordinary farmer on his way to the supermarket to do some shopping. He was probably telling the truth. Later, however, he congratulated the carabinieri on having made such a big catch. The most wanted man in Italy was a stickler for etiquette and treated his jailors as warmly as an old, long-lost uncle would. When Riina's number two, Beneditto "Nitto" Santapaola, the boss of Cosa Nostra in eastern Sicily, was arrested six months later, he behaved the same way. Police stormed the bunker in an olive grove that he and his wife had been hiding in. There were a Bible, a crucifix, and a pistol on the bedside table. When the officers broke down the door, brandishing machine guns, Santapaola was lying in bed. He made no attempt to grab the gun. Instead he sat up, greeted his captors, and congratulated them on a job well done. As one of the carabinieri later told a newspaper reporter, "It was so easy, it was creepy. Sometimes I wish he had tried to shoot." The mafiosi have been eerily dignified in defeat.

After his arrest the police discovered that Riina had been living right under their noses for ten years. The man for whom they had combed the mountains of Colombia and for whom generations of sniffer dogs had nosed through the remote caves of Sicily had lived in what a real estate agent might call "a moderately well appointed garden condominium," near the center of Palermo, next to one of the city's busiest traffic circles, a stone's throw from a large police station.

How was it possible that the authorities didn't know about his presence? The question still hasn't been answered in a satisfactory way, but according to numerous conspiracy theories the Italian government was only too well aware of the Riina family home; it just wasn't prepared to do anything for fear of upsetting the Mafia, on whose electoral cooperation in Sicily it relied. If this was the case, the Riina family certainly obliged its protectors by keeping a relatively low profile. The Riinas' bungalow was spacious without being ostentatious. The swimming pool was small, surrounded by mushroom-shaped garden lamps and the obligatory Hollywood swing. The house, more suited to a dentist than to the head of an international crime syndicate, couldn't have been more ordinary. Rather like some of the corrupt politicians who used to rule Italy, the heads of Cosa Nostra have always cherished the power to extract money more than the money itself. The only indication that something may have been amiss about the home was the reluctance of the neighbors to acknowledge the existence of the Riina family, whom they had been living next to for ten years.

The cult of *omertà* lives on in many quarters. It is particularly healthy in Corleone, Riina's hometown. Dominated by an unseemly cone-shaped rock that protrudes from the center of town and houses the local jail, Corleone looks like a stage set for a Mafia film. The average age of the Corleonesi seems to be seventy and up. With almost the entire population sitting on stools in front of their houses or on their balconies gazing at life in the street or at one another, the town must have invented the neighborhood watch. Nothing escapes anyone. The Sicilians appreciate the subtle approach, so I asked a group of old men who sat on a bench near Riina's family home, a cramped, narrow three-story house with an illuminated Madonna above the door, whether they had heard of the following list of names: "John Major?" "Oh, yes." "Hillary Clinton?" "But of course!" "O. J. Simpson?" "Hmm, yes," they said after a little delay. "Totò Riina?" "Who?" came the chorus of feigned ignorance. "Totò Riina!" I repeated. "Your former neighbor." "Never heard of him!" said the wrinkled masters of the deadpan reply. Their lack of cooperation probably had as much to do with *omertà* as with a feeling of annoyance at being questioned by yet another foreigner about the "Mafia."

An air of disbelief also surrounds the diminutive, almost goonlike figure of Salvatore, or Totò, Riina, for twenty-three years the most wanted man in Italy. The man who was known as "il Curtu"—the Short One—to his friends and as "la Belva"—the Beast—to his enemies had been tried in absentia for five murders before he was caught and would be tried for another ten after his arrest. An alleged master in the art of liquidation, one of "the Beast's" specialities was to dissolve his victims in acid, thus extinguishing any evidence of the crime. The Mafia calls this method *la lupara bianca*—literally, "the white shotgun," in deference to Cosa Nostra's traditional weapon. During the Mafia wars of the late 1970s and early 1980s that brought Totò and his Corleonese clan to power, Riina flouted one of the oldest Mafia rules. When it was known that Tomasso Buscetta had become a turncoat, Riina had three women in Buscetta's family killed immediately: his mother, aunt, and sister. "The Beast" clearly believed in gender equality when it came to killing.

I was thus surprised to find him personally rather charming when I met him briefly in 1993 three months after his arrest. Riina was in a cage in the courtroom of Rome's high-security Rebbibio jail, on the outskirts of the city, a godforsaken place somewhere between a motorway bypass and a shantytown for north African immigrants. We had been invited to listen to a preliminary hearing in one of the many murder trials facing Riina. Both sides of the large subterranean courtroom were lined with cages. The hall was filled with journalists waiting for the judge and jury to arrive. The stifling heat and the flickering of indecisive fluorescent lights filled the room with a soporific air. I was half asleep when I turned round and saw Riina sitting alone on a stool in the last cell. Two carabinieri stood in front of the cell. The room suddenly filled with an atmosphere of near hysteria as journalists and cameramen rushed toward the cage and surveyed the "beast" inside. Riina, who was extraordinarily composed, was wearing an immaculate cashmere jacket and a smart casual open-neck shirt. His thin gray hair had been combed carefully. His tiny blue eyes twinkled brightly. He looked like the respectable owner of a hairdressing salon or perhaps the head teller at the local post office. I simply could not imagine this man controlling the most vicious and complex crime syndicate in the world, manipulating the Italian stock market, conferring with his Colombian counterparts from Medellín, or dissolving an enemy in acid. When Totò Riina stood before the judge on his first hearing, he shrugged his shoulders, lifted up his arms, and said with sad, ironic eyes, "But, sir, I am just home, church, and family." One was inclined to agree with him, despite the evidence.

Standing on the other side of the bars from Riina and looking into the lively eyes of this man whose appearance so belied his reputation and his criminal record, one was somewhat lost for words. I was about to ask him a question when the reporter next to me, a voluptuous blonde from RAI, butted in with the very issue that was on my mind. "Did you, Signor Riina," she asked, "kiss the former prime minister, Giulio Andreotti, on the cheek?" "The Beast" looked at the questioner, smiled, placed both hands on the bars flanking his face, and, gently pushing his head forward as far as he could, hissed, *"Sei bella!"* (You're beautiful!). Using familiar and in these circumstances highly patronizing "tu" form, he then asked: *"Come ti chiama?"* (What's your name?) The reporter was speechless. The mixture of myth and malice still had its effect, even on a hardened TV reporter.

The apprehension of a major underworld figure would be a major coup for any government in any country of the world. But in Italy it was all the more remarkable because of the ambiguous relationship the government and the Mafia have enjoyed since the end of World War II.

At one time, the relationship was unambiguously hostile. Indeed, the Mafia was not just at war with the Italian state but in many ways had replaced it, a process that began almost as soon as modern Italy was born. The etymological origins of the word "Mafia" are obscure, but most agree that it first appeared in the 1860s, when the Bourbon dynasty fell and Sicily was subjected to the upheavals of Italian unification. The Mafia was a product of feudal Sicilian society. As the author Guiseppe di Lampedusa described in his classic novel about the persistent feudalism of Sicily, *The Leopard,* the role of the mafiosi was to guard the vast *latifondi* of absentee landlords who lounged in the opulence of their Palermo palaces. Gradually the Mafia became an alternative authority that thrived on the neglect of government and the ruling class. The mafiosi suppressed labor unrest on the estates of their landowners, but they also protected the peasants and stole from their employers. The Mafia became the intermediary between the "palazzo" and the "piazza" in a fragmented society, loyal only to itself and motivated solely by the pursuit of power and profit.

In that sense little has changed. The modern mafiosi still look after their landlords' *latifondi*. The *latifondisti* of the 1980s cultivated not cereals or vines but votes. They were the Christian Democratic and Socialist politicians in Rome. Their *latifondi* were vast electoral estates, whose harvests yielded the deputies parliamentary majorities that enabled them to stay in power. While feudal nineteenth-century Sicily was possibly the ideal environment for such an organization to flourish in, even in the twentieth century enough alienation and suspicion of central government has remained to make the Mafia nearly impregnable.

Giovanni Falcone, the judge who was killed by the Mafia along with his wife and three of their bodyguards in 1992, was the first Italian magistrate who tried to defeat the organization by understanding it from within. To him the Mafia was "nothing but the expression of a need for order, for control by the state." He wrote, "I believe it is the lack of a sense of State, of State as an interior value, which is the root cause of the distortions of the Sicilian soul: the dichotomy between society and state, the consequent overreliance on family and on clan."

Falcone's words point to one of the most important changes that enabled the battle against the Mafia to be truly joined, which had little to do with government action. Instead, it was the battle against *mafiosità* that proved decisive. *Mafiosità,* literally "mafiosity," is a quintessentially Sicilian term invented by the writer Leonardo Sciascia, who died in 1989 and who was perhaps the most perceptive observer of the Sicilian psyche. He distinguished between "Mafia," the criminal organization, and *mafiosità,* the mentality that allowed that organization to thrive. This mentality was founded on a culture of suspicion, produced by generations of invaders and the worship of patronage, that was a holdover from feudal society. It finds expression not only in the Mafia per se but in the attitudes of ordinary Italians toward their families and the state. The battle against *mafiosità* was a fight for modernity, and it could, according to Sciascia, take place only in the mind of each individual Sicilian.

I discovered my own definition of *mafiosità* in the most unlikely place: Palermo's General Hospital. This sprawling establishment is a surreal shrine to the warped humanity that is Sicily. Enter the large central gate and walk past a flower-bedecked statue of Padre Pio, the friar turned miracle healer. Turn left, and you'll be on the lawn next to the casualty unit. A flock of ten sheep is grazing nonchalantly on tufty weeds. A street urchin selling fortune tickets for good luck and carrying a yellow canary in a box waits patiently by the helicopter pad, where patients are flown in from Sicily's outlying mountain villages. He's in luck. A helicopter lands. The sheep disperse. As the stretcher is lowered from the helicopter and disappears into an ambulance, the urchin makes for the patient's relatives. An old woman buys a ticket displaying the face of a saint. She knows her ailing husband will need all the luck money can buy to survive in Palermo's General Hospital.

In December 1993, Dr. Marco Colimberti, one of the hospital's heart surgeons, who is leading a campaign to uncover corruption and professional malpractice, put on his white coat and took me on a tour. We stopped at a building site surrounded by coils of barbed wire. "This is the new emergency ward—or rather, this *should* be the new emergency ward." Construction on the building, a concrete monstrosity in the Mafia's favorite style—square and ugly—had begun ten years before. The hospital's new wing still hadn't been completed when I visited it, but not because the money had run out. Tens of billions of lire had already been spent on it, and untold billions more would be. The doctor complained about faulty construction, which had led to an almost endless string of repairs and fresh starts and thus to a lavish flow of lire. At the time of my visit, almost half of the deputies in Sicily's regional parliament were being investigated for participation in schemes to generate bribes and contracts through faulty construction.

The emergency ward may have been incomplete, but it was being used, though not in the intended way. At night prostitutes plied a thriving trade on the mezzanine, whose rough cement floor glistened with used condoms. The first and second floors were littered with spent syringes. Dr. Colimberti hated night shifts: "It's too dangerous to walk from one pavilion to another." Fabrizio Chiodo, another heart surgeon in his early forties, was also afraid. He, on the other hand, had two bodyguards, and sometimes, when talking to me, he nervously fingered a Beretta pistol under his white coat: "Just to check it's still there."

The General Hospital is a dual homage to Federico Fellini and Mad Max. The carabinieri gave Dr. Chiodo his pistol and his armed escort after he received death threats in January 1993. The judiciary believes the threats came from the Mafia, as Dr. Chiodo had been indiscreet enough to tell Palermo's magistrates about one of the most lucrative scams in the hospital's famous cardiac surgery unit. Although the unit has three operating theaters and twenty-five surgeons, it performs only 150 operations a year. This is very little compared to a hospital in the northern city of Brescia, for instance, where eight surgeons perform 800 operations per year.

The shortfall is due to the fact that the great majority of operations take place in private clinics. The head of the unit, Dr. Renato Albiero, who was arrested in the autumn of 1993, used to pad the waiting lists for operations. Investigators found that the lists contained at least forty people who had already died and scores who had never lived. The purpose was to tell desperate patients that they would have to wait for years before they could have the necessary operation, by which time they would already have died. But if they were willing to pay an extra 8 million lire ($5,000) in fees, the good doctor knew of a way out. "There's an excellent private clinic in Palermo that performs the same operation," Dr. Albiero used to tell his patients.

Once a patient had agreed, a transfer would be quickly arranged in the hospital's ambulances to one of a chain of private clinics, where the operation would be performed in immaculate conditions by none other than Dr. Albiero himself. The average salary of a Sicilian surgeon is 7 million lire a month. For each private operation he receives another 4 million. The judiciary believes the clinics are owned

by the Mafia and are used to launder drug money. So far twelve surgeons, one owner of a private clinic, and several government health
officers have gone to jail for their involvement in the scheme.

Dr. Chiodo's bodyguards followed him everywhere. When he was
operating, they hovered outside the theater. In a hospital that employs
more than 1,000 doctors and 2,500 nurses, Dr. Chiodo had very few
friends. He had broken the *omertà,* the vow of silence, brought the
hospital into ill repute, and spoiled the extracurricular activities. The
doctor had some powerful enemies on the hospital's ruling administrative committee. All of its twelve members belonged to Palermo's
premier Masonic lodge. In fact, more doctors belong to the lodge than
to the medical branch of the CGIL, Italy's main trade-union federation. Appropriately enough, the hospital's chief administrator, Pietro
Calacione, was also the lodge's grand master. I wasn't able to see him
on my visit, but a colleague of mine from *La Repubblica* did get an
audience. When he finally emerged from his office, Calacione, an engineer by training and a slight man with thin gray hair and a high-
pitched voice, asked my colleague what zodiac sign he was. He
refused to talk about the abuses in the hospital or the Masonic lodge,
but he did leave my colleague with a parting thought. "I treat everyone well," he told him. "Those who don't like me, I treat even better.
But the funny thing is . . . all those who are against me are dead. One
died of cancer, another in a car accident . . ."

On the final stage of our tour, Dr. Colimberti took me to a special
parking lot for ambulances. A group of drivers was standing around
smoking cigarettes. "They're waiting for the dead," the doctor explained. The vehicles are in fact hearses masquerading as ambulances, waiting to pick up the deceased to take them back to their
homes, "where they can then die in peace." For many poor Sicilian
families, a faked death at home is still preferable to a real death in
hospital. And in Sicily death encourages potential beneficiaries to
flout the law in the most imaginative and ingenious way. Because a
corpse already issued with a death certificate cannot be taken back
home, the doctors are bribed by the undertakers not to certify someone as dead. Each doctor works with a group of nurses and hospital
porters who are retained by one of the rival funeral companies. They
are paid a monthly fee or retainer as well as a percentage on each liv-

ing corpse. When someone is about to die, the porter alerts the undertaker, who then gets in touch with the family. Sometimes patients are picked up from hospital when they are still alive. In most cases they are already dead.

In order to pass through the police checkpoint at the hospital gate, the dead body in the fake ambulance is fitted with an IV drip. The police don't seem to mind that the fact that the fake ambulances are traveling in the wrong direction, away from the hospital. "The system works relatively smoothly," Dr. Colimberti explained. "Different undertakers service different wards." In the interests of social peace and harmony, they have even worked out a timetable. But sometimes the system breaks down. Last February two "ambulances" from rival companies arrived to pick up the same body, and there was a shootout. Dr. Colimberti called the police, who finally arrived after twenty minutes and told him not to worry. No arrests were made.

Some of the doctors, surgeons, and administrators running the hospital's various scams have been less lucky. In 1994 twenty suspects were arrested and charged with fraud, bribery, and corruption. Palermo's General Hospital was and perhaps still is part of the Mafia's universe. Not only was it run by people who were associated with the Mafia or counted mafiosi among their patients or recycled Mafia money, it was also a monument to the way in which the Mafia corrupts civic values, creates a climate of fear and oppression, and cows people into submission or even connivance. The changes at the hospital, the arrests, the inquiries, and the new, more honest management cannot be seen in isolation. They are, like so much else in Italy today, the consequence of political upheaval.

At times the battle against the Mafia and *mafiosità* has taken on the form of a popular rebellion. In 1992 I interviewed Francesco Rovelli, a professor of sociology with a round face and a gentle smile, in the flouncy lobby of Palermo's Excelsior Palace Hotel, where he sipped a sweet coffee and ate one of the cool, sticky Sicilian cakes that testify to the mixture of cultures on this much-invaded island. Sicilian desserts are an aftertaste of occupation, a reminder that all invasions of Sicily have failed and that logic, enterprise, and initiative eventually succumb to the seductive torpor of this sensual island. "Until we start demanding our rights as citizens and stop looking for privileges or patronage, we cannot rid ourselves of our innate *mafiosità,*" said Rovelli. His face assumed the pained expression of a self-flagellating monk. "What's needed," he continued, "are not just arrests, jail sentences, and secure cells for the mafiosi but a popular revolution."

As we spoke, an extraordinary din began to invade the velvet coziness of the hotel lobby: drums, trumpets, whistles, helicopters, screeching voices on distorted loudspeakers, and the verbal avalanche of half a million people walking past our hotel. "The racket of a witch doctor driving out *mafiosità,*" said the professor. It was June 25, the day of the biggest anti-Mafia demonstration in Sicily's history. The demonstration had been organized by the Italian Trade Union Federation. Thousands of people had been bused in from all over Italy. But most of the demonstrators were ordinary Palermitani who had come to participate in this act of collective therapy. Tens of thousands of people who ten years ago would only have whispered the "M" word in private were allowed to scream "Mafia" and listen to it echo through the narrow streets of the city. In many ways the rally had the same feeling of mental liberation that had electrified the demonstrations that swept through Leipzig in October 1989 and helped to bring down the East German regime of Erich Honecker.

In Palermo people were demonstrating not just against a crime syndicate but against a whole regime of connivance in which politics had become the Mafia's shield. This regime had not only killed, stolen, smuggled, or extorted but had gagged ordinary Sicilians, ruined their landscape with ugly construction, polluted their sea, frightened off investors, and stifled their economy. A popular revolution seemed to be unfolding in Sicily at the same time as voters were turning their backs on the Socialists and Christian Democrats in northern Italy, where the judicial stampede against corruption had already begun. The Piazza Politeama, where the four columns of demonstrators converged, was a sea of flags and banners, many of which thanked Antonio Di Pietro and the Milan "clean hands" magistrates.

The demonstration had been inspired by Giovanni Falcone's murder a month before. He, his wife, and three bodyguards had been killed on May 25, 1992, by a huge bomb planted in a shallow drainage duct under a stretch of the highway near the village of Capaci between Palermo airport and the city. The explosion, which had been set off by remote control from an olive grove above the highway, had torn a crater seventeen feet wide and seven feet deep into the road. The first car, containing the three bodyguards, had been flung more than a hundred yards to the other side of the highway and landed in a vegetable garden. A group of Austrian tourists traveling in the opposite direction in their rental car were seriously injured. Falcone's car, going at ninety miles an hour, had crashed headlong into the asphalt that had buckled under the explosion like a crumpled carpet. The judge had insisted on driving the armored car himself. His driver, who was sitting in the back, survived. Falcone and his wife might have survived as well had they been wearing seat belts.

These technicalities became irrelevant as popular anger mounted. In brazenly eliminating their most formidable opponent, the bombers created a martyr whose death galvanized the protest. During the funeral in which thousands crammed into Palermo's cathedral, mourning turned to rage. The young widow of one of the three bodyguards launched a tearful attack against the political establishment in Rome and accused it of negligence in the fight against the Mafia. When they left the service, Cabinet ministers who had flown in from Rome were heckled by angry crowds. As the Mafia remained invisible, the anger was directed against those who were despised as the mob's political patrons.

The murder of Falcone was intended as a spectacular display of the Mafia's power and its ability to eliminate its enemies, however well protected. This turned out to be a grave miscalculation. The bomb had shown that Cosa Nostra was on the defensive, forced to resort to dramatic displays of violence that were completely out of character. In 1991 Falcone himself had written, "Newspapers, books, and films all concentrate on the cruelty of the Mafia. Certainly it exists, but not as an end in itself. Men who commit gratuitous atrocities provoke disgust within the organization. Participation in an act of violence is usually rigorously logical, and it is this logic that makes Cosa Nostra the feared organization it is."

By the Mafia's own standards the bomb at Capaci was a display of unnecessary violence. Moreover, police search teams discovered cigarette butts around a small cluster of olive trees on a hill over-looking the motorway. It emerged that the men who had set off the bomb by remote control had waited for Falcone's motorcade for several days. Traces of saliva on discarded cigarette butts enabled the police to acquire a DNA print of the smokers. A year later eighteen people were arrested in connection with the killing of Falcone. The murder had been sloppy work.

Two months later the Mafia compounded its problems by killing another leading anti-Mafia judge. On Sunday, July 19, Paolo Borsellino, who had been one of Falcone's closest colleagues and had inherited his mantle, went to visit his mother in the center of Palermo for afternoon coffee and cakes. When he left her apartment, a car bomb exploded on the street outside, killing Borsellino and four of his bodyguards. Instead of intimidating the public, the second killing brought even more people out onto the streets. The popular revolt gathered momentum. As the Mafia's mystique began to crumble, the *omertà,* the notorious code of silence that had protected the organization since its inception and had undermined the search for witnesses, began to be breached not just in Palermo but in more remote areas as well.

In the town of Capo D'Orlando on the northern coast of Sicily, local businessmen formed a commercial association, a kind of anti-Mafia Rotary Club. Its purpose was to resist paying the *pizzo,* literally "bird's beak," Sicilian dialect for the extortion money the Mafia demanded in return for protection. Of course, the only thing the money offered protection from was the Mafia itself. The association included businessmen, grocers, jewellers, bookshop owners, and real estate agents, each of whom was represented by a lightbulb that was hung from a kind of Christmas tree of defiance on the hill above Capo D'Orlando. The Mafia had tried to stamp out the roots of this revolt by burning down one or two shops, but the intimidation hadn't worked. The silent protest continued. I asked the head of the association, the avuncular owner of a toy shop in the central square, why he had taken this courageous step. "The recession," he replied. "I can't afford to pay the *pizzo* of 800,000 lire [about $500] a month anymore. And the Mafia doesn't take market forces or a decline in sales figures into account." Dozens of shopkeepers in Capo

D'Orlando were clearly still prepared to pay the *pizzo*. But just as the recession had undermined the system of *tangente* in Milan, where businesses could no longer afford to pay the 10 to 15 percent bribe on contracts that had virtually become a corporate tax, the shop owners of Capo D'Orlando were being forced to stand up to the Mafia for economic reasons.

They were especially encouraged to do so by the recent political climate of revolt and by the newfound readiness of the authorities to protect them. Capo D'Orlando bristled with carabinieri. We were staying in the "Turtle Hotel," a kitsch palace on the waterfront where the windows had been fitted with security bars in the shape of wrought-iron turtles. Five carabinieri were permanently on guard, because the hotel owner was about to go to court and give evidence against the local Mafia family.

By 1994 the Italian government was beating its drum over a new wave of arrests ushered in by the refreshingly accommodating climate. Every week another prominent mafioso ended up behind bars or decided to "repent," threatening to burst Italy's already overcrowded jails. In two years the Italian authorities had arrested more than 4,000 Mafia suspects, more than Mussolini's notorious Mafia-basher, Cesare Mori, had done in the 1930s. Without the *pentiti,* the government would have remained impotent in the battle against organized crime. But the willingness of the *pentiti* to come forward was above all due to new legislation giving more state protection to informers. This was a political fact that reflected the new will of the parties in Rome to fight organized crime.

The "Men of Honor" may not be aware of it, but their demise also started with the collapse of the Berlin Wall and the consequences for Italy's four-party regime. The end of the Christian Democrats and their allies as the dominant force in Italian politics meant that the Mafia lost its principal political protectors in Rome. The business relationship between Palermo and Rome had ended. The Mafia was no longer able to deliver enough votes to stem the electoral hemorrhage, and the Christian Democrats and their allies were no longer in a position to deliver favors. One incident illustrated this change more than any other.

On March 12, 1992, a silver-haired gentleman in a dark blue pinstriped suit left his spacious villa in Mondello, Palermo's elegant sea-side suburb, and got into his car. Salvatore Lima, "Salvò" to his friends, was a Christian Democratic member of the European Parliament in Strasbourg at the time. He had held many illustrious offices, including mayor of Palermo in 1987. He was a long-standing member of the Italian Parliament. Most important, indeed most fatally, he was Prime Minister Giulio Andreotti's nuncio on the island of Sicily who ensured that the "Old Fox" would receive a sufficient number of votes from Sicily to ensure his power and the influence of his faction within the amorphous Christian Democratic Party. As he got into his unarmored car—since Salvò Lima's protection came from the Mafia itself, there was no need, or so he thought, for bulletproof metal casing—two men approached on a moped and started spraying him with bullets. One shot hit Lima in the shoulder, another in the left arm. The honorable member for Sicily in the European Parliament got out of the car and crawled down the street, which was wet thanks to the morning drizzle. The two men rode slowly after him on their moped and fired another volley of shots. When the police arrived, minutes later, Lima was lying dead in a pool of his own blood.

Lima's murder, a Mafia turncoat later explained to the police, was a signal of disapproval. The "Commissione," the ruling council of the Mafia, was disappointed that Lima had been unable to get a number of court convictions quashed for mafiosi who had appeared in the famous Maxitrial of 1987. Whether Lima had lost his clout with the judges or the Christian Democrats had already lost their once-divine right to rule, something in the chain of command between politics and organized crime had collapsed. By killing Lima in March, a month before Italy's 1992 general elections, the Men of Honor had entered the election campaign with a bloody reminder that their interests after all these years of vote-buying and ballot-stuffing could not be ignored. Unfortunately for them, Andreotti and his party could not reverse the tide of history.

In the summer of 1994 Andreotti was charged by magistrates in Sicily with actually being a member of the Mafia. Part of the evidence on which the charges are based comes from Baldassare Di Maggio, the same informer who had turned in Totò Riina. What he told the investigators was that the relationship between the Christian

Democrats and the Mafia had been sealed, like so many other political relationships in Italy, with a kiss on the cheek. According to Di Maggio, Andreotti had been kissed by Totò Riina during a meeting that had allegedly taken place in 1987, while Andreotti was on a visit to Palermo. The *bacio di mafia* is more than just a peck on the cheek. It is a highly symbolic gesture indicating the power of the kisser over the kissed. Andreotti has vociferously denied that the meeting, let alone the kiss, ever took place. He has said he was in no position to slip away for an encounter with a senior mafioso in hiding while on a visit to Sicily without the fact being noticed by his bodyguards or the dozen TV cameras following him around. Pino Arlacchi, who is now a member of the Italian Parliament and perhaps Italy's most respected expert on Cosa Nostra, believes the meeting was only too plausible. "At that time," he told me, "the Christian Democrats thought they were invincible. They did what they liked. Theirs was the absolute arrogance of absolute power."

If Giulio Andreotti has maintained a polite silence about the Mafia, another Christian Democrat has embodied the attitude that you can exorcise the Devil only by pronouncing his name. The role of the Mafia's chief exorcist fell to Leoluca Orlando, a former mayor of Palermo, who defected from the Christian Democratic Party in 1987 because of its links to the Mafia. He set up his own political movement called "the Network." Perhaps the choice of name was unfortunate for a party that was devoted to fighting organized crime, but the Network became the political voice against the Mafia. It articulated in middle-class Sicily a sense of civic responsibility and civil courage that many thought had been lost forever. During the election campaign for mayor of Palmero, which Orlando won with an astounding 75 percent of the vote, his supporters described him as "Orlando Furioso," comparing him to the swashbuckling hero from the Renaissance epic. Leoluca Orlando may not be the most subtle, articulate, or cunning politician, but his uninhibited anger at the state of politics in Sicily was a welcome contrast to the previous rulers, who had masked their hypocrisy and lies with verbal garlands. Orlando was refreshingly blunt. He hammered home his message with dogged determination, not only in Italian but in English for the benefit of foreign news organizations like the BBC. Every month Orlando would discover a new sound bite with which to feed the rapacious maw of Western television. "We are a *normal* people. We want to live in a *normal* city," he would repeat, mantralike; or "The Mafia has entered the Italian state like a Trojan horse."

Dismissed by his opponents as hotheaded and rhetorical, Orlando was one of the few politicians at the time who seemed truly to understand that the paradigm had shifted. He recognized that ordinary Sicilians were sick and tired of living under the shadow of organized crime. Second, Orlando believed that the Mafia was merely the most malignant manifestation of the *mafiosità* that existed all over Italy. In its mildest form, this was called the *cultura dell'appartenenza,* in which individuals seek security and protection from a hostile world and an indifferent state by belonging to a group that protects their interests. This mentality evolves into the *cultura della raccomandazione,* where nothing, from the purchase of a pair of jeans to the awarding of a construction contract, is achieved without the recommendation or patronage of a powerful person. The logical next step, according to Orlando, is the Mafia, a mutual-aid society based on blood vendettas, violence, and illicit earnings. Orlando's accomplishment was to turn these understandings into a political philosophy.

Leoluca Orlando is not universally admired. His small party has almost splintered over accusations that he behaved in an autocratic manner. And he has never really managed to give a convincing answer as to how he, as a former Christian Democrat and mayor of the capital of Sicily, had been able to avoid dealing with the Mafia. Hardbitten cynics point out that no one in Palermo can receive 75 percent of the vote without being backed by the mob.

Indeed, early in 1994 Orlando's brief honeymoon ended. He had just been accused by a *pentiti* of conniving with the Mafia when he held the office of mayor in the 1980s. The Network had been crushed at the polls by Silvio Berlusconi's brand-new Forza Italia. The voters of Sicily had shown an extraordinary degree of fickleness. Five months after the left-wing parties like the Network and the Democratic Party of the Left had triumphed in scores of Sicilian cities during municipal elections, they were already being abandoned by the voters.

I interviewed the mayor in April at the Villa Niscemi, a seventeenth-century summer palace on the outskirts of Palermo. Orlando uses the villa, which was sold to the city of Palermo in 1987, as a temporary daytime office. He arrives in his screeching motorcade of armored cars, jumps out, pursued by his eight permanent bodyguards, and disappears into the marbled entrance hall of the villa. The mayor of Palermo is forever running away from an enemy he cannot see, whose movements he cannot predict, but whose intentions toward him are by now clear.

"We *were* witnessing a Sicilian Spring!" he told me. "Now the Spring is in danger of being snuffed out!" The waiting room at the villa was full of people looking for help, advice, and probably also personal favors. Outside, the heat was intense. Inside, the stuffy air was aflutter with women fanning themselves. Orlando, who has always been known for his bounding energy and enthusiasm, looked drawn and tired. His usually swarthy face was pale. His eyes were red with lack of sleep, the bags under them the size of walnuts. He was sweating profusely in the midday heat. The *vita blindata,* the "armored life" of bodyguards and armored cars, was clearly beginning to take its toll.

Why had his movement failed to thrive? Some blamed the Mafia for infiltrating Berlusconi's Forza Italia and buying votes by the bucketful for the tycoon. Others blamed the demise of the Left on the fact that after four months in office it hadn't achieved much. Another explanation was that the bourgeois revolution against the Mafia, the battle against *mafiosità,* had simply run out of steam. Orlando believed that his revolution had been hijacked by Silvio Berlusconi and the Right with its "empty promises of instant prosperity." Perhaps it was a combination of all these factors. The fact is, though, that in the middle of 1994 the tide seemed to be turning back in the Mafia's favor.

The victory of the Right coincided with a consistent campaign of intimidation against a number of left-wing mayors in Sicily who had been elected on a vow to fight the Mafia. In Piana degli Albanesi the office of the Democratic Party of the Left, the former Communist Party, was burnt down. In San Guiseppe Jato the Democratic Party of the Left mayor, a woman, woke up one night to find her car in flames. Altogether, there were more than a dozen incidents of intimidation.

But I found one of the most vivid examples of the Mafia's resurgence, oddly enough, in Corleone.

Paolo Cippriano, the mayor of Corleone, was the first holder of that office not to belong to either the Christian Democrats or the Socialists. Born in Corleone, he had worked for a students' cooperative doing community work before going into politics. He walked out of his house one morning in February 1994 to find a calf's head on his doorstep, a traditional Mafia warning usually followed up by another warning and then death.

"One shouldn't exaggerate these antics," said the thirty-two-year-old mayor. Wearing jeans and a checked shirt without a tie, he looked like the foreman of a radical workers' committee that has occupied the town hall after the revolution. "What *is* worrying to me and my colleagues is that we can feel the ground disappear from under our feet. We feel increasingly isolated here, and we don't think we're getting the right moral support from the new government in Rome." In 1994 this became a common complaint, especially among mayors and municipal councillors all over Sicily who had been elected during the heyday of the anti-Mafia parties. Although Prime Minister Berlusconi said he was intent on fighting the Mafia, coming from him the message didn't carry the same conviction as it had from his immediate predecessors. A large number of former politicians who had been in Parliament for the now-discredited Socialists or Christian Democrats had found a new and easy home in Forza Italia. Hundreds of Forza Italia clubs, which had been hastily set up to orchestrate the media tycoon's lighting-fast election campaign, were also suspected of having been infiltrated by people associated with the Mafia. When Forza Italia swept the board at the national elections in 1994 coincidentally with a wave of attacks against left-wing parties, it's not surprising that mayors like Cippriano felt exposed. No one suggested that the bomb and arson attacks had actually been organized by Forza Italia, only that the Mafia had seen its opportunity to scare those who had openly campaigned against it.

What impressed me most about the mayor of Corleone was his accessibility despite the tenuous position he found himself in. He occupied a vast office in the town's gloomy municipal building that had clearly been designed to keep people out, not invite them in. But his door was open, and every two minutes someone came in for a quick chat. The room was filled with trophies of power collected by his predecessors: a large moth-eaten banner made of red velvet displaying the city's emblem, a lion clutching a bloody heart in its left paw. The same emblem appeared also in the form of a cast-iron sculpture, a wood carving, and a bronze statue. It was as though the Lord Mayor of London had filled his office with statues of the Tower. A vast, sooty canvas entitled *Temptation* depicting a corpulent nude as white as a mozzarella hung over the old leather sofa in front of the mayor's desk. Another wall was decorated with the portraits of previous mayors. One stood out. The caption read BERNARDINO VERRO 1866–1915. A dedication had been added: "The farmers of Corleone remember that from him they received the first light of thinking about the dignity of the world. He was killed for his beliefs on November 3, 1915." One couldn't help but wonder whether a similar dedication would one day be written under the portrait of the present mayor.

"The reason why we haven't been able to follow up last year's successes, why the so-called revolution has suddenly fizzled out, is the economy," Cippriano continued. "Unless we can get the economy sorted out, the Mafia will always find fertile ground for recruitment." In many ways Sicily faces the same Catch-22 situation as a former communist country like Russia does. The aim of social reform is to make individuals responsible for their own prosperity within the boundaries of the law, to break the long tradition of relying on someone else to deliver prosperity, protection, and patronage. This involves starving Sicily of the subsidies that have fed straight into the Mafia economy. But a climate of increasing unemployment and hopelessness is tailor-made for the Mafia. Subsidies have already been cut in Rome, and there are signs that the vicious cycle is continuing. Again there are no statistics to underpin this theory, just individual examples.

A notable one occurred in February 1994 in the eastern Sicilian city of Messina. Police arrested Janos Ferrara, one of the local Mafia bosses, and the news spread rapidly through the neighborhood he controlled. When the boss emerged from the local courthouse, where he had been questioned by magistrates, to be transferred to jail, he was greeted by an angry crowd of two hundred people. Young men, old men, women, children, entire families were shouting from behind a metal barrier that had been set up to separate them from the court-house's entrance. The crowd was demanding the release of their local mafioso. FERRARA GIVES US JOBS AND FOOD, read one banner. In this case at least, *mafiosità* seemed to have triumphed.

The persistence of the Mafia and *mafiosità* are chilling and dis-maying and may be one of the most profound challenges facing Italy as it seeks to renew its political culture and social contract. Nowhere is this clearer than in the town of Gela.

Twenty-five hundred years ago Gela was a thriving colony of Graeco-Roman culture on the southern coast of the island, where the bougainvillea bushes grow as tall as trees, the air is scented with jas-mine and orange blossom, and a stiflingly hot wind called the *afa* blows up from the Libyan Sahara and creates the leaden mood of an eternal siesta. Gela is just about thirty miles to the north of Tunis, but such geographical references are irrelevant in a place that hails from Dante's *Inferno*. Nowhere is the contrast between the stunning beauty of the Sicilian landscape and the jaw-dropping ugliness of its towns greater than here. Set along a spectacular coastline that sweeps up the hills behind it, Gela once boasted a seafront lined with palm trees and one of Europe's broadest, cleanest, and whitest beaches. Now the city plays host to a disused oil refinery and some of Sicily's most vicious crime families, whose local version of the Mafia is called the "Stiddha."

Today Gela is under military occupation. It hasn't had a mayor in years. The only public service is the army. The customary carabinieri are outnumbered by soldiers from the Alpine Regiment, who patrol the city in armored vehicles and trucks fitted with machine guns on tripods. Army helicopters hover above like menacing insects. Judging from the expression of fear on the faces of the soldiers I saw, the Ital-ian army had not won the campaign for the hearts and minds of Gela. The Alpine uniform of a peaked Tyrolean hat with a long drooping feather simply confirmed the soldiers' status as unwanted aliens. I had been taken to Gela by Carlo Averna, the owner of a factory at nearby Caltanissetta that produces Sicily's famous Amaro, a bitter-sweet digestive drink made from a secret herbal recipe. I had met Averna while he was taking part in a special course sponsored by the

Italian government to teach Sicilian businessmen how to resist *mafiosità*. In a pink castle built at the end of the last century on the Monte Pellegrino in Palermo, businessmen like Averna were being brought together with officials from Sicily's public administration and taught the rules of the free market and private enterprise. The object of the classes, which were held once a month, was to combat the climate of distrust that had helped to create the Mafia in the first place and that the Men of Honor knew how to exploit for their advantage. Averna gave me a simple but telling example. "It's almost impossible," he said, "to get the fax number of another company in Sicily over the phone without personally knowing the person you are talking to. We are a very closed society. Our instinct tells us to trust only those who belong to our family, our clan, our village." Averna was in his forties and had inherited the company from his father. Sixty percent of his sales were on the domestic market, the rest mainly in Germany, where the brown digestive treacle had become very popular. Although Averna was run like any other modern European business, its owner felt completely isolated in Caltanissetta. Since the sulfur mines had been closed, his was the only factory in a town with more than 30 percent unemployment. Averna told me he had been approached by the local Mafia but had refused to pay the protection fee of 5 million lire a month. Now he was waiting for the next visit.

Averna was one of the founders of the Gela business association. On the day I visited Gela, the association was burying one of its members. Gaetano Giordano had owned a small chain of perfume shops. One day he had been driving his son to school when his car was sprayed with bullets. He had known he was in danger. That January, he had opened another perfumery on Gela's main street. Two weeks later, he had received a visit from a stranger who had demanded 4 million lire "as a contribution to the neighborhood watch group." In March Giordano still hadn't contributed, and the tires of his car were shot up. In April the Mafia tried to burn down his house. In May they killed him. Death was the price he paid for his stubbornness. The funeral procession of more than three thousand people, headed by the son who had survived the attack, wound its way solemnly through the cement maze of Gela. Many of the streets had not been paved. Piles of rubbish bulged out of the overflowing gullies, scrutinized by dogs and cats. The mourners included most of the eight hundred members of the local business association carrying the club's coat of arms. But they were outnumbered by those who stood on the pavement or sat on their balconies and just watched in silence. There was none of the jubilant defiance that had marked the funeral rallies of the judges in Palermo. Gela was the Mafia's natural habitat. The only employer with a future here is the Mafia. For a town with more than 30 percent overall unemployment and 50 percent of young people out of work, Gela had a disproportionate number of young men driving around in BMWs or open-top sports cars. It reminded me of the destitute town of Bovalino on the Calabrian coast, where the local Alitalia agent told me she did a roaring trade in day-return tickets to Milan and Turin. The tickets were being bought by teenagers. She believed they were shipping drugs in their luggage.

As I stood in front of the perfumery watching Gaetano Giordano's son lay a wreath, I heard a thick Brooklyn accent. "This town is apocalyptic." I turned around to see a teenager wearing a baseball cap, an alien apparition. Greg Bertini was eighteen years old and was just finishing high school in Gela. His father had moved back to his birthplace after his business in New York had collapsed.

"What kind of business?" I asked.

"Import-export," Greg replied.

"What's it like living here?"

"There's no future for any of us. Most of my classmates already work for them."

I wasn't sure whether Greg was sending me up or whether he had a well-developed sense of drama. He clearly looked uneasy. I asked him a little more about his family until he finally made his excuses and disappeared into the crowd.

Since my visit in 1993, the carabinieri have arrested more than four hundred people in Gela alone. Most of the male members of the town's four top Mafia families are in jail. Gela is the twilight zone of Italy. I had to pinch myself to remember that it is part of the European Union. Since the murder of Gaetano Giordano, no member of the business association has been killed or threatened. But how long will that last?

There has been an increasing number of examples that the spirit of defiance is fizzling out. On November 14, 1994, in conjunction with a long-planned visit to Sicily, his third, Pope John Paul II arrived in the suburbs outside Catania. The first pontiff to visit the island for six centuries, Karol Wojtyla, who had lived in the smothering embrace of Polish communism, had come to tell the Mafia to convert and the Sicilians to stand up against organized crime. The seventy-four-year-old pope, grimacing with pain from a hip-replacement operation he had had earlier in the year, was angry. Waving his silver-tipped cane, he told the congregation, "It is the duty of every one of you to speak out against the arrogant minority that oppresses and intimidates. Silence is a form of complicity."

The morning after the pope's call for rebellion against the Mafia, Father Gino Saccetti woke up in his house in the district of Termini Imerese outside Palermo. He went out to buy a newspaper and discovered a calf's head nailed to his front door just beneath the brass nameplate. There was a note, too. "If you're not careful," it read, "you'll end up like this one day." The priest, an outspoken campaigner against the Mafia, was one of the many foot soldiers who had taken the pope's defiant message against organized crime to the local pulpit. The priest, the police, the newspapers, and the public all assumed the calf's head had been sent by the Mafia. COSA NOSTRA AT WAR WITH THE CHURCH, thundered a headline in the *Giornale di Sicilia*. The bloody head had been a timely message, coinciding with the pope's visit, but it had not been the first. Several priests had received threatening phone calls pressing them to tame their sermons or face the consequences. A week before the pope's visit to Sicily, a priest had been addressing a congregation in his church in Palermo. When he had told the worshippers, as he had done on many previous occasions, that they had to stand up against the Mafia, their reaction had left him dumbfounded. The entire congregation of about a hundred people had stood up and left the church.

But the most dramatic strike against the Church had taken place in October 1993. Father Guiseppe Puglisi, another ordinary priest who had spoken out against organized crime, was shot in the back of the head as he walked home one night from the community center in his parish in Palermo. The assumption that Cosa Nostra was behind it was confirmed by a Mafia turncoat a year later. He told investigators that the organization had wanted to send a strong warning signal to the religious community by killing the priest. This was the first time the Mafia had assassinated a member of the clergy because he was preaching against it. It was an indication of Cosa Nostra's desperation. The Mafia, which Judge Giovanni Falcone once described as "enjoying the same strict unity of faith and command as an established religion," was afraid of losing the battle against the Catholic Church, a battle over the minds of ordinary Sicilians.

The Conspiracy
of Truth

L eonardo da Vinci gazed gloomily at the scene of destruction around him. Michelangelo had been hit by some shrapnel in the foot, and Vasari's left ear was chipped. Botticelli was lucky to be unscathed. The statues of Italy's Renaissance artists stood in the courtyard of the Uffizi Gallery in Florence like stunned spectators after the outrage. The ground was covered with a crunchy carpet of broken glass and fragments of masonry. The air was thick with hot dust. Rescue workers wearing face masks were carrying some of the damaged pictures to safety. Bewildered tourists who had stayed in hotels nearby were moving out and wheeling their suitcases through the mayhem. On May 27, 1993, someone had parked a large car bomb in a Fiat 500 outside the Academy of Giorgiophiles, the oldest agricultural institute in the world, which forms part of the Uffizi complex. The blast, which ripped through the historic center of Florence in the early hours of the morning, could be heard as far as Fiesole, about five miles from the city center. It caused one part of the five-story, sixteenth-century building to collapse like a house of cards. Fabrizio Nencioni, the caretaker, his wife, and their three daughters lived on the top floor. It took all night to dig their mangled bodies out of the rubble.

Parts of the devastation looked like the work of an earthquake, the rest like Bosnia. Shrapnel had lacerated the façades of the honey-combed houses in the narrow Via delle Pulci, the street of Fleas. Red roof tiles had been blown off, leaving the bare wooden staves looking like fishbones. Three satellite dishes put up by the Italian network RAI were towering above the rescue operation. The blast had been turned into a media event as only the Italians know how to stage one. Every few minutes another minister arrived in a convoy of sirens and flashing blue lights to pay his respects. The prime minister's helicopter landed between the statues of David and Neptune in the Piazza della Signoria. On one of the television monitors that had been set up near the site of the blast, one could see a game-show host introducing his program with a one-minute silence in respect for the dead. Three Playboy bunnies stood with their heads bowed and tails drooping.

The Florence bomb wasn't the only one to shake Italy that summer. A car bomb in Rome's elegant Parioli suburb almost killed Maurizio Costanzo, the host of a popular television talk show. Another bomb in Rome tore off the façade of one of the city's most beautiful churches, San Giorgio in Velabro, a twelfth-century Romanesque church in the shadow of the Palatine hill that was very popular among Romans for weddings. The third bomb, which exploded at almost the same time, damaged the façade of the Basilica of St. John Lateran, the seat of the pope in his capacity as bishop of Rome. On the same night a car bomb in Milan killed four people, including two traffic wardens and a north African immigrant. The car, stuffed with explosives, had been planted near one of the city's most famous galleries.

Although some of the bombs claimed casualties, the police thought these had been accidental, as all of the devices had exploded in the middle of the night in areas that were normally deserted and their targets had primarily been cultural.

The bombings of summer 1993 became the latest in a long line of unsolved *stragi,* literally "assaults," that run through postwar Italy like a dark subplot. There have been terrorist attacks against trains, banks, military installations, government offices, ministers, and ordinary citizens, but never before had anyone bombed the "untouchable": the country's cultural soul. Perhaps the bombs were a devious attempt to destabilize society by striking the one institution that had not yet been compromised. One of the terrifying and terrorizing aspects of these attacks was that no one knew exactly why they had been planned and who was behind them.

A group calling itself the "Armed Phalange" claimed responsibility for the 1993 bombings, but the government dismissed the claim as bogus. Instead, Interior Minister Nicola Mancino blamed the Mafia. But the Mafia doesn't go in for terrorism based on fuzzy notions of destabilization: it tends to liquidate its enemies with precision. The minister's theory wasn't taken seriously by the public or many of the newspapers. Demonstrators in Florence filled the Piazza della Signoria near the Uffizi with banners declaring STATO ASSASSINO. They were accusing the state of having bombed itself. Theories proliferated and ripened into conspiracy theories. The most common one was that the bombings in Florence, Milan, and Rome signaled a return to the "strategy of tension," a specialty of the right wing in the 1960s and '70s, whose aim had been to destabilize democracy by creating panic and then to set up in its place an authoritarian military regime or a Fascist state; in other words, to create order through disorder.

To foreigners, Italy's left-wing terrorism is well known, particularly its most famous incarnation, the Red Brigades. But the scope of right-wing terrorism matched that of the left. In the 1960s more than a hundred right-wing organizations sprang up. Many of them were simply gangs of Fascist thugs espousing the cult of violence and picking fights with their opposite numbers on the left. But a dozen or so were hard-core terrorist groups that bombed both buildings and people. They shared the Fascist faith in the purifying and liberating effects of violence and were responsible for some of the worst terrorist outrages in modern Italian and European history. In December 1969 terrorists blew up a bank in Milan's Piazza Fontana, killing sixteen people. A year later a train was derailed in Calabria, killing six persons. In 1974 an anti-Fascist demonstration in the northern city of Brescia was bombed, resulting in eight deaths. Later the same year the express train *Italicus* was attacked, killing twelve. In August 1980 a bomb exploded in the waiting room of the railway station at Bologna. It killed 85 and injured 200, one of the bloodiest acts of terrorism in Europe in the postwar period. The explosion occurred one day after four suspects from an extreme-right-wing terrorist group had been indicted for the bombing of the *Italicus* train. The finger in all these bombings was pointed at right-wing terrorists. But after decades of trials, retrials, and acquittals, only a handful of people have been convicted or sent to jail.

While left-wing terrorists held people's trials, issued manifestos, and felt the need to justify their violence intellectually, right-wing terrorism has always been shrouded in mystery. The suspicion arose in the 1960s that right-wing terrorists were acting with the connivance of the Italian intelligence services and deviant elements within the Interior Ministry. For one thing, a number of intelligence agents had been linked to the Piazza Fontana bombing. They had been tried, convicted, and then acquitted on appeal. For another, in many cases the authorities had acted with much greater ferocity against left-wing terrorists than against their colleagues on the extreme right.

This impression of collusion was reinforced by other conspiracies and plots, such as the notorious P2 Masonic lodge of Licio Gelli. Uncovered in 1980, P2 was linked to the "strategy of tension." It aimed to set up an alternative power structure in Italy, and it counted among its members the heads of the intelligence services as well as senior figures from the army and the Carabinieri. Once the existence of P2 became known, the impression emerged that the state had been plotting to overthrow itself, quite apart from the aims of any right-wing groups. This briefly revived a discussion of the "strategy of tension."

Having been buried and almost forgotten for a decade, the theory resurfaced after the 1993 bombings in Florence and Rome. The theory was plausible. After all, Italy had experienced the bloodless decapitation of almost an entire political and business elite. After decades at the helm the old guard couldn't be expected to relinquish power without a fight. But in the absence of suspects and firm, clear motives, the counterrevolution remained veiled in the opaque haze of mystery. The effect was as unsettling as the sudden and inexplicable appearance of an epidemic in the Middle Ages. It found good ground in the country's fertile imagination.

The suspicion blossomed that some members of the government were trying to put a halt to Italy's "silent revolution." No suspects were ever named. No one was arrested. No evidence was found. But a few days after the Rome bombing Prime Minister Carlo Azeglio Ciampi sacked the chiefs of SISME and SISDE, the two intelligence services, and put the organizations directly under his own command. Slowly the plausible but unproven web of conspiracy began to be woven in the public mind. Perceptions were, as ever, more important than facts.

The conspiracy weavers were out in force. In October 1993 an extraordinary woman named Donatella De Rosa burst onto the national stage with allegations that a coup was being plotted in the upper echelons of the military. Diminutive, elegant, and in her mid-thirties, De Rosa appeared every night on television talk shows and thundered against the plotters, claiming that five senior generals were scheming to overthrow the government and establish a military junta. The five included the army's chief of staff, General Gofreddo Canino, the military commander of the Tuscany and Emilia-Romagna regions, General Biaggio Rizzo, and General Franco Monticone, the commander of the Rapid Reaction Force, who also happened to have been De Rosa's lover. (These allegations were only underpinned by other allegations. One was an unsubstantiated claim that De Rosa had received the equivalent of $460,000 from her former lover General Monticone to ensure that she wouldn't reveal the incriminating contents of her pillow talk with him. The second, even more flimsy, was that De Rosa, who is endowed with large blue eyes, said she had spotted a well-known right-wing terrorist named Gianni Nardi in her hometown of Udine.) Nardi was thought to have been responsible for the Brescia bombing in 1974 and had fled to Spain in the late 1970s. He had supposedly been killed in a car crash in 1980, but De Rosa now claimed that he was alive and that according to her military sources he had carried out the bombing of the Academy of Giorgiophiles.

Her allegations were outlandish, bordering on the nutty, but police took them seriously. Nardi's body was exhumed in Spain, revealing that the dead terrorist had not wandered from his grave since he had been put there in 1980. But the allegations had more serious repercussions. One of the generals implicated by De Rosa was dismissed by the then defense minister, Fabio Fabbri, because he was allegedly involved in arms trafficking. General Monticone was investigated by magistrates for plotting against the state, and General Canino resigned over the way his friends and colleagues had been treated by the government. In the absence of a single scrap of evidence or a single official charge, such actions were dramatic to say the least.

In Britain or the United States, accusations of coup plotting by the country's senior generals would have either been dismissed out of hand or taken so seriously that they would have led to a massive outcry from the public and a large-scale criminal and governmental inquiry. Hours of news and talk-show footage would have been devoted to the subject. The credibility of the democracy and its institutions would have depended on it. In Italy the episode produced little more than a collective shrug of the nation's shoulders. Donatella De Rosa mesmerized Italy for about two weeks. Then one day she suddenly disappeared from view, her performance having come to an end. She was briefly arrested for misleading the magistrates, and now she is no doubt waiting in the wings to be asked back onto the stage of conspiracies. She has become part of that neoreality of attempted coups, Masonic lodges, secret societies, and "illustrious" corpses that envelops Italy like an ether, often too fantastic to be proven, always too plausible to be dismissed.

Karl Marx said the Russians would be unable to stage a revolution because they were illiterate. Stalin said that communism would fit the Germans like a saddle fits a cow. The biggest obstacle to collective social change in Italy is not the features normally attributed to the Italians. As we have seen, Italian society is less chaotic than outsiders would like to think, less individualistic, and much more conservative. The real problem is that dogma will always be undermined by the Italians' inborn need to complicate matters. Dialectic will always be diluted by mystery. The Italians have an instinctive aversion for the obvious. To take events at face value is an admission of stupidity. Everything has a hidden reason, which only the most intelligent people will be aware of. Again, there is even a word for it: *dietrologia,* literally "behindology."

Dietrologia is not just an intellectual sport. Seven-time former prime minister Giulio Andreotti has been accused of collaborating with the Mafia. Mr. Andreotti's lawyers have a different theory: the Cold War is over. Communism has collapsed in the Soviet Union, and the Italian Communist Party, once the biggest in the West, no longer poses a threat to NATO and the stability of Europe. The Clinton administration, more puritanical and thrifty than its predecessors, is loath to support the political system masterminded by Giulio Andreotti and friends now that the justification for it has ceased to exist. The United States wants to get rid of Andreotti and plants a Mafia turncoat on the Italian judiciary to discredit the statesman. The proof of "this destabilizing conspiracy hatched in foreign circles," as one of the former prime minister's associates called it, is obvious: the day Andreotti was forced to defend his reputation before his peers in the Senate, the then head of the CIA, R. James Woolsey, flew to Rome to meet with his Italian counterparts. It was widely assumed that he had come to plot the downfall of Don Giulio. In fact, this theory was so plausible that even Andreotti's detractors started to believe in it.

As conspiracy theories go, this one contained all the right ingredients for a great vintage: the Mafia, a statesman who prays every day, a foreign power, the CIA. The frenzy was deflated when the Information Service of the U.S. Embassy told reporters that Mr. Woolsey's trip had been planned well in advance and that, "in any case, with all due respect," the CIA had more pressing problems to consider, such as the instability of the Soviet Union, the clandestine traffic of nuclear materials to the Middle East, and the war in Bosnia.

Another example: A right-wing landowner from Puglia in southern Italy, whom I met at a dinner party in Rome, patiently explained to me the real reason why the former Communist Party had adopted the policy of privatization. "Achille Occhetto [the former head of the party], who never stopped being a Communist apparatchik despite the end of the Cold War, was blackmailed into accepting the principle of privatization for Italy's slumbering state industries by a Jewish lawyer in New York." "I beg your pardon?" "This lawyer," the acquaintance continued, "was acting on behalf of President Boris Yeltsin of Russia. Yeltsin used him to get some of the money back that the old Soviet Union had lent to its Communist satellites around the world. The Kremlin gave billions to the Italian Communist Party. Its successor, the PDS, was of course in no position to pay back the money, let alone to admit publicly that it had ever received it. A compromise was brokered by the lawyer. Yeltsin would get some of the money back. It would be supplied by big Italian business. Why? Because in

1993 the Italian business community was desperately casting around for a new political ally. The Christian Democrats, Socialists, and Republicans had all disappeared or become unelectable thanks to the corruption scandal. Silvio Berlusconi had not yet appeared on the political stage. Converting the former Communists to capitalism was the only option." According to my acquaintance, Fiat, the computer giant Olivetti, and other companies had paid off some of the Communists' debt in return for a commitment to continuing the privatization program. This would allow them to purchase shares and buy up the family silver sold off by the Italian state. My head was spinning.

Dietrologia is not confined to the political arena. I may be accused of peddling a worn-out cliché, but no day goes by without some reminder of Italy's enchantment with the Mysterious. The novelty is not that the Italians believe in superstition, witchcraft, or magic, it is that they treat them in a such a matter-of-fact way. An example: after returning from a holiday last year my friend Tamara was watering her plants outside her flat in Rome's Trastevere quarter. It was summer, and many of the plants had withered. Suddenly her next-door neighbor appeared at the window and shouted, "Your plants are dry because your period is too strong!"

Tamara has become my contact to the netherworld of healing, yoga, pranotherapy (the laying on of hands), and general quackery. First she joined a siddha yoga class in Rome, then a healing course. Her school used to organize national healing congresses in Milan that were attended by hundreds of Italians from every region, social background, and age group. On a return journey from one of these weekend "heal-ins," she was sitting on a train to Rome. Suddenly the woman sitting across from her said she had a sharp pain in her arm. Tamara set about healing her, which involved "purifying her aura" with gentle strokes. Instead of moving to the next railway carriage or hiding in acute embarrassment behind their newspapers—as they would have done in Britain, for example—her fellow passengers lined up. They, too, wanted to be healed.

Italy's faith healers appeal to the supernatural and superstitious while using the tools of modern technology or electronic media. There are scores of tiny commercial television channels offering phone-in exorcisms, death curses, or just run-of-the-mill recipes to ward off the evil eye. Advice columnists have been replaced by television sorcerers and soothsayers. For emotional problems, for example, try Signora Francesca on Palermo's Tarot Card and Horoscope Channel: (091) 580 570. From the comfort of your own living room you can watch Signora Francesca deal out and read your tarot cards. Her gaze into the future will cost you 2,540 lire per minute, plus VAT.

For those who are too embarrassed to purchase in person crystal balls, black hoods, chains, or the tools necessary for a home exorcism such as squirting plastic Madonnas that can be filled with holy water like toy pistols, there is always the European Center for Superior Experimental Magic, a mail-order company dealing in the occult.

It is impossible to put a precise figure on the total number of self-professed wizards, clairvoyants, and fortune tellers in Italy. There are hundreds of small regional black magic circles: the Association for Parapsychological and Esoteric Research in the Adriatic holiday resort of Riccione has about 120 members, and according to the Italian National Institute for Magicians, there are 6,000 registered *maghi*— magicians or wise men—working in Italy. There are also 20,000 registered *pranoterapisti,* or pranotherapists, producing an annual turnover of 250 billion lire worth of business. Devil worship has become one of Italy's most vibrant growth industries. There are more registered magicians per capita in Italy than in Haiti, the home of voodoo.

The occult has increasingly become an urban phenomenon. Turin, the city of Fiat, "northern" productivity, and Germanic efficiency, is reputed to be the black magic capital of Italy. Perhaps the climate of almost perpetual mist and the city's mysterious covered arcades have helped the occult to prosper here. Perhaps the Turinese just need a reprieve from the never-ending quest for profit. Perhaps they are simply rich enough to afford a weekly dose of black magic. But Turin is not alone. The yellow pages of Rome, Milan, and Bologna are stuffed with the telephone and fax numbers of wizards and witches. Example: "Tiziana—Specialist in curses—Defeat your rivals in business and love forever. Call (06) 653 5060 or (for emergencies) cell phone (0336 74) 40 82." Much of this activity is, however, clandestine and advertised by word of mouth. Therefore it has been impossible to determine the growth of the occult industry. A report entitled *The Devil's Cash,* published by the Italian research institute Eurispes, states, "Magic is today a business with a vertiginous turnover." It estimates the number of *maghi* at 12,000 to 120,000, most of them men. Meanwhile, twelve million Italians, most of them women, are estimated to seek their services every year. The report concludes: "Italy's vast and ongoing modernization has not swept away the age-old superstitions and eccentric beliefs that have their roots in ancient history." Professor Luigi Satriani, an anthropologist from the University of Rome, believes that the occult has filled the vacuum left by the Catholic Church. Writer Umberto Eco believes the obsession with the occult, the supernatural, and certain forms of designer Buddhism expresses the yearnings of an urban society that has rejected one creed after another. In his novel *Foucault's Pendulum* the writer describes a generation that left its Catholic faith in the 1950s, its political idealism in the 1970s, and its pure consumer culture in the 1980s. The 1990s seem to be open season for any mystic, soothsayer, or quack who can supply the meaning of life—for a price.

This manifestation of decadence isn't, of course, confined to frustrated city dwellers. It also feeds off a rich rural tradition in the South, where religion, the worship of saints, and faith healing have always gone hand in hand. In the Calabrian village of Guarda Sanframondi, for instance, young men parade through town at Easter wearing crowns of thorn. They run along a path of the imaginary twelve stations of the cross. At every station they stop and beat themselves with stones until they are covered in blood, delirious with pain, and half dead. This ritual has survived since the Middle Ages, although the Vatican frowns on such exaltation through self-inflicted pain. Near the town of Nola, a sprawling industrial satellite city creeping up the slopes of Mount Vesuvius—against the flow of lava—there is a small forest of oak trees. Here within the range of the autostrada's roar the forester and his wife heal hernias and enhance fertility once a year. They take their "patients," mostly adolescent boys, to the forest and choose one of the young trees. The forester slits open the trunk, pries it apart, and inserts two wooden staves about sixteen inches long, thus creating the shape of a vagina. The patient gets undressed, and the forester and his wife then pass him like a sack of potatoes to each other through the tree trunk. They do this six times. Every time a pass has been completed, the forester mutters a quick prayer and crosses himself three times. When the ceremony is complete, the staves are taken out of the trunk and a picture of the Madonna is inserted in their place. The trunk is then closed and tied together with waxed string. If the tree continues to grow, the patient's hernia will be cured and he or she will become more fertile. If the tree dies, the cure dies with it.

The supernatural feels most natural in Naples. Life in Italy's southern metropolis, located in the shadow of a live volcano and perched uneasily on a geological fault line prone to earthquakes, has always been a bit of a lottery. The city has often been prey to natural disasters, the last one being the 1980 earthquake in the suburb of Pozzuoli, as well as to centuries of poverty, disease, and crime. In the dank urban maze of Naples the luxuriating piles of uncollected trash amass, the traffic lights rarely work, the city has one of the highest population densities in the world, and the city council has even seen fit to appoint an "assessor for normality." His job is to see that the lifelines of the city, from transport to trash collection, maintain a semblance of normality. It is not clear whether this is normality by the standards of Cologne or Calcutta. Nevertheless, he seems to have had some success. At least Naples no longer suffers the once-regular alarms about milk being poisoned and water supplies tampered with by the Camorra.

Not surprisingly, Naples has always been at the crossroads of devout Catholicism and superstition. Thousands of Neapolitan houses are decorated with luminous shrines to the Madonna flashing in garish pinks and fluorescent greens. The Church of Gesù Nuovo, one of the most beautiful in the city, contains a shrine to Giuseppe Moscati, the "holy doctor." Beatified by Pope John Paul II in 1987, Professor Moscati achieved near-sainthood thanks to his healing methods and his humility. Death has not halted his good works. One room near the church's apse contains a replica of the professor's surgery and study, with all the original furniture. The walls of another room are covered with hundreds of small frames. Each one contains a replica of a body part in thin molded silver, a photo of the donor, and a dedication.

"Dear Professor Moscati, my right leg has been giving me too much pain for three years now. Please help me!" The dedication, in an almost illegible scrawl, is written underneath a four-inch silver relief of a leg wearing stockings and what looks like an old-fashioned shoe. Judging from the silver body parts that adorn the wall, the saintly doctor has been asked to heal arms, ears, hearts, fingers, toes, stomachs, noses, eyes, foreheads, buttocks, lungs, chests, and in many cases a composite of several. One "patient" had almost his entire body in silver parts displayed in a large frame. "That would have cost him about 450,000 lire," the dispenser of body parts, a small Neapolitan housewife wearing a housecoat, explained helpfully. From behind her counter she produced a box full of silver lungs, chests, ears, arms . . . the only organs she didn't have were sexual ones. "That wasn't really Saint Moscati's department," she said.

Neapolitans are much happier entrusting their lives and health to the supernatural health service than to the one subsidized by the state. This is not altogether surprising. The Carderelli Hospital in the center of Naples has more in common with Bedlam than with modern health care. And some of the city's most lurid corruption scandals have been nurtured in the health service. It was in Naples that Professor Poggiolini and his erstwhile boss, Francesco De Lorenzo, the former minister of health, began collecting millions of dollars to bump up the prices of medicines.

So the Neapolitans have learned to rely on miracles; nothing else really works for them. The most obvious example is the biennial liquefication of the blood of San Gennaro the martyr in Naples Cathedral. In 305 San Gennaro, the patron saint of Naples, was thrown to the lions in the Pozzuoli amphitheater, after which, being rejected by them, he was beheaded by Roman soldiers. A solid trickle of his blood is preserved in a vial kept in a reliquary behind the altar. Twice a year the vial is taken out of its casing. On those days the crystals of blood turns into a dark brown liquid. Skeptics believe that the liquefication occurs when the weather is hot enough for the crystals to turn to liquid in the hands of the bishop clutching the phial, but no one really asks for a scientific explanation. What's important is to believe, putting skepticism to one side, and thousands of Neapolitans still do. If the liquefication doesn't occur, disaster is bound to strike, as it did in 1944, when San Gennaro's crystallized blood refused to liquefy and Mount Vesuvius erupted. In 1993 the liquefication was two weeks late, and there were scenes of mass hysteria around the cathedral as a crowd of four thousand men and women sobbed and screamed. "Tangentopoli," it was widely believed, had intervened.

With such important miracle shrines, it is not surprising that the occult profession has flocked to Naples in unusually large numbers. Above the central bus station in Naples there is a large, luminous billboard advertising the services of Professional Magician Gardelio. "Expert in communication with the dead, hypnotist, exorcist, pranotherapist, and legal adviser." His office is located behind the central bus station on the second floor of a seedy block of flats. An assistant in her twenties opened the door. I should have made an appointment. The waiting room was packed with visitors, mostly women, many of them with children. Two policemen were sitting in the corner, nervously playing with their caps. Some clients leafed lazily through magazines, which had been laid out in a neat fan shape on the coffee table. One of them was a mail-order catalogue for the black magic trade. The stifling heat was redistributed by a swiveling fan. For a moment I thought I had entered a dentist's waiting room, but the walls were decorated with the *mago*'s trophies. A newspaper article explained how he had liberated a thirty-year-old carabiniere from the Devil. The picture showed the carabiniere dressed in a T-shirt and looking exhausted, as well as his father, his mother, and the magician. They were shaking hands and smiling as if they had just won the lottery. Next to the framed newspaper clipping was an elegant certificate, according to which Gardelio had taken part in a European Community workshop for small-scale entrepreneurs.

"Signor Frei," the secretary called. Gardelio's office was bathed in red light thanks to a red lampshade and red plastic sheeting taped over the window. Feeling faintly embarrassed, I was led inside. My embarrassment turned into a mixture of bemusement and awe. The magician who could drive out demons, cast evil spells, and give legal advice stood behind his desk. A small, portly man with long black hair tied in a ponytail, he wore a yellow silk shirt and black trousers with razor-sharp pleats. A large, gleaming gold medallion nestled on his hairy chest. Miniature skulls and various items of clothing were assembled on one table. The other displayed a collection of half-melted candles in human shapes. On the shelves I could see a piece of twisted aluminum foil that looked disturbingly like a human shape. "What's that for?" I asked. There was a slight pause. The *mago* looked irritated. "That," he said in an almost inaudible voice, "was the wrapper of my lunch sandwich." For a moment the spell was broken; then the *mago* resumed the session. I had, after all, paid my 100,000 lire ($60) an hour for a basic consultation.

I asked about prices. The magician's fees ranged from 800,000 lire ($500) to ward off the evil eye to 2 million lire ($1,200) for an exorcism and 20 million lire ($12,000) for casting a deadly curse. I asked him what proof he could give me of his magical abilities. He showed me a stigma on his right hand, a thumb-sized scab that he said had started bleeding when he was ten. Magic mixed with Catholicism: the classic Neapolitan recipe. His healing power, he told me, emanated from his hands. By way of demonstration, he stood up, threw back his head, spread his arms, clenched his fists, closed his eyes, and, breathing heavily, crunched his knuckles. They made a terrifying sound. More bruiser than healer, I thought. Ten years ago most of the magician's clients had come to him because of "matters of passion"—warding off rival suitors, preparing love potions, a little spiritual detective work for suspicious spouses, or simple crystal ball matchmaking. "But," said the magician, "the recession and the political crisis have ended all that. I get lots of people worried about money, about losing their jobs. I have even had a politician who was afraid of losing his seat in Parliament." "Did the spell work?" I asked. "Not in his case," the magician admitted. Italian politicians are not embarrassed to admit that they go to faith healers. Prominent public figures such as Gianni Agnelli, the head of Fiat, are open about consulting a *mago*. Bettino Craxi used to pay regular visits to a society sorcerer. His brother went one step further: he joined an ashram in India. It is perhaps surprising that so many Italians are prepared to waste their money on phony magicians, especially in times of recession. But then, the paranormal often defies orthodox economic theory.

Some of the self-appointed healers and exorcists are absurd; others are dangerous. Several tragic incidents have focused the attention of

Italians on their obsession with evil spirits and the paranormal. In August 1994 a Sicilian fisherman was tortured to death by his brother and father, who suspected him of being possessed by the Devil. Another Sicilian fisherman died after drinking a potion prescribed by a sorcerer that was supposed to bring good luck to his boats. In 1988 two young men killed themselves in an occult ceremony that was interrupted by a police raid. The authorities fear that scores of incidents are unreported. Of those that are known, the case of two-month-old Maria Ilenia in September 1994 was without doubt the most tragic.

Maria Ilenia was the only daughter of Michele Politanò and Laura Lumicisi. The couple were both farmers in their early twenties. They lived on the outskirts of Polistena, a dusty, desolate town in Calabria. The family occupied a half-built four-story house, one of the typical dwellings of raw cement and steel girders. On every floor a small effigy of Saint Francis twinkled under a neon light in a glass box. The Politanòs were devout Catholics. In fact, when the police came to search their house they discovered numerous articles of their devotion. On the blood-splattered table in Maria Ilenia's bedroom there was a picture of Christ on the cross, a map with charts and demonic emblems, and a bucket filled with about five quarts of holy water from Lourdes. There was a small wooden crucifix and a transparent plastic Madonna filled with holy water. The police also found two photocopied pages of a manual on exorcism. They were there to remind Maria Ilenia's great-uncle Vincenzo Fortini, who was leading the ceremony, of his lines: "O Jesus, free her from the torment and corruption of this evil spirit, illuminate her with your grace and goodness."

Two years before, the Politanòs had become convinced that their house had been possessed by the Devil. They had told neighbors that they were being tormented by shadows and strange noises. They had said that the temperature in the house frequently dropped to freezing, even in the sweltering summer. Laura had attributed the death of her father to the Devil, rather than to the lung cancer diagnosed by the doctors. The couple had already spent hundreds of thousands of lire on attempts to cleanse their house of evil spirits. Uncle Vincenzo, who was in his forties and lived near Rome, had already been summoned to help several times. He had taken courses in spiritual healing and considered himself to be an expert on the Devil and a qualified exorcist. But even he couldn't stop the noises and the fluctuations in temperature.

In 1993 the Politanòs decided to have a baby. Laura had been told that the presence of an innocent child in the house might ward off the evil spirits. But as soon as Maria Ilenia was born she started screaming. What other parents would regard as natural was seen by the young couple as proof that the Devil had now also possessed their daughter. They despaired, and in August they asked a local exorcist to help. They found the number in the Reggio di Calabria yellow pages. The exorcist, Francesca Giananti, spent two weeks in the house burning incense and praying. The couple paid her a million lire. Nothing changed. In fact, the more incense filled the baby's room, the more she screamed. Finally, on September 14 the Politanòs decided to call their uncle in Rome. Two days later, on Sunday night, eight members of the Politanò family, including the uncle and the girl's parents, began the ceremony to exorcise the child. It lasted until seven in the morning. At one stage, Maria Ilenia's twenty-three-year-old father, moved by the sight of his daughter screaming and being beaten, tried to stop the torture, but he was prevented by his wife and brother-in-law.

In the early hours of the morning the uncle became ever more desperate as the child refused to stop crying. He told the police that he had tried—literally—to kick the Devil out of Maria Ilenia. Shortly after dawn the infant was dead. On Monday morning the family was arrested; neighbors had alerted the police. The Politanòs were devastated, consumed by remorse for the death of their daughter. But they were still convinced that the child had been possessed by the Devil. Asked what proof they had, the uncle told investigators that Maria Ilenia had continued to cry even when she was doused with holy water. The doctor at the local hospital who performed the autopsy said that Maria Ilenia's face had been badly scratched and she was bleeding from the mouth and from the anus. Apart from that, her tiny body looked unbruised. But when the doctor opened her up, he discovered that her internal organs had been mashed "as if someone had thrashed a wall with her body, like a wet towel."

Maria Ilenia's death was particularly gruesome. She was killed by her own family, the victim of her parents' ignorance and obsession. How was such a thing possible? A survey conducted by *La Repubblica* at the time showed that one in three Italians feared the Devil. This was a substantial increase over 1991, the last time such a survey had been conducted. Furthermore, a growing number of people believed that the Devil was not just an abstract evil but the incarnation of *male,* the bad. Professor Luigi Satriani blames the Catholic Church. Under Pope John Paul II, he says, the Catholic hierarchy has emphasized the presence of evil as a physical being. The Pope speaks frequently about *il Maligno,* the Evil One. This, the professor believes, has led some people to think of evil in the form of a person. The word *Maligno* is frequently used during the exorcism ceremony.

The Church is naturally shocked by accusations that it has anything to do with the rise in black magic. Don Gabriele Amorth, president of the World Council of Exorcists and one of the scores of official exorcists recently appointed by the Vatican, said that if the Calabrian family had suspected the presence of *il Maligno,* they should have gone to the church and not sought what he called "an instant solution through an unqualified exorcist." The Catholic Church does not regard exorcisms as a weird aberration but as a spiritual service to the community. It is an integral part of the ministry. Father Amorth receives on average a hundred requests for exorcisms a week. He said he can't cope with the workload, which has doubled in the last three years. He refers most of the requests to a medical doctor or a psychiatrist. But if the symptoms such as inexplicable headaches, stomach cramps, and cold sweats persist, he will deal with the case. The priest's main grievance with the exorcism of the two-month-old Maria Ilenia was not that it had taken place but that it had been done without the guidance of the Church—left to amateurs.

In times of difficulty and crisis, people have always resorted to the occult. Traditional soothsayers have now been replaced by pranotherapists, the reading of sheep's entrails by the telephone and the fax. Apparently ex–Prime Minister Berlusconi has been one of the few Italian heads of government and party not to live by his horoscope or consult a medium. But a new bimonthly magazine, *Magicamente,* gave him the benefit of its science anyway. In its first edition

(August 1994) it predicted that the tycoon—born on September 29, 1936 (Libra)—would weather the long-standing crisis in the coalition thanks to Jupiter imposing his *epidekatea* on the waxing moon. The article went on to predict a healthy trade surplus and, more alarmingly, an increase in interest rates. But taking the long-term view, the magazine predicted that Italy's economic recovery will peak in 1999, the year in which a total eclipse of the sun can be expected in the sign of Leo. By that time Mr. Berlusconi may, of course, have long since abandoned politics and returned to business. Indeed the tycoon, who likes to think of himself as a man of great logic and clarity of thought, would probably dismiss any horoscope, however glowing, as claptrap. But although he may not consult the stars, he is in fact a closet consultant of entrails and displays all the basic requirements. Silvio Berlusconi sees conspiracy theories where others see simple mistakes. He detects plots against him and his government where others suspect incompetence or just the vagaries of the market. For instance, an increase in U.S. interest rates by the Federal Reserve Board in the summer of 1994 that unleashed a wave of speculation on Wall Street and drove down the value of the lira was portrayed as an international conspiracy to discredit Italy. According to some members of the government, the conspiracy had been hatched by the "vitriolic international press," communism, and the Jewish lobby, three not necessarily obvious coconspirators. This not only betrayed an alarming degree of paranoia but revealed an inability to accept the consequences of one's own actions.

"To you we're all a bunch of superstitious eccentrics in the grip of some quack or faith healer." My friend Anna Bruna, a petite Neapolitan with fiery red hair, was angry with my theories about Italians and their predilection for conspiracy theories, plots, and the supernatural. "If you want a true view of our supposed culture of superstition, you should ring up my former teacher, Professor Dilario. He has just completed an important work on the use of sodomy in fertility festivals in the Campania." She paused. "But don't call him today. He's a Capricorn. I think he may be going through a rough patch."

The longer I live in Italy, the more I feel that this is a country of unself-conscious paradoxes: the cult of the family in a society whose negative birthrate is threatening the family with extinction. The family as a source of both strength and weakness. A country that has more laws than almost any other in the world but whose laws are constantly flouted. A society of seemingly anarchic individualists—if you look at their driving—and sticklers for etiquette and petty rules—if you consider their coffee-drinking habits and obsession with titles. On one hand, a highly active democracy, judging from its voter turnouts and lively political debate; on the other, a quasi-feudal society, judging from the stranglehold once exercised by political parties, a successful economy, thriving in a sea of systematic corruption; a country in which the omnipresent patrols of carabinieri with machine guns or—in the case of Sicily and Calabria—soldiers with armored vehicles, remind you of a police state but one fourth of whose territory is effectively under the control of organized crime. And finally a highly sophisticated society with more cell phones per capita than Germany or the United States, where Devil worship, the occult, and belief in the supernatural are on the increase. Italy is both highly pragmatic and alarmingly illogical. Some of these paradoxes are, of course, not confined to the Italian peninsula, but here they seem to manifest themselves in a more dramatic way. Perhaps this stems from the fact that Italy is both a very old culture and a very new country.

Forward to
the Past

The city of Pontida shimmered in the midday heat. The surroundings were veiled in thick smoke that rose from the bonfire in front of the fortress. The methodical, menacing beating of drums grew louder and louder. Suddenly a knight on horseback, his sword aloft, burst into the courtyard. He was followed by what could only be described as a makeshift tank, pulled by two bullocks. This machine, called a *carroccio,* was decked in the Lombard flag. The line of armored foot soldiers broke up immediately. Some ran for cover; others, more courageous, took a stand. One of the soldiers screamed as he discarded his heavy helmet and visor, revealing an ugly grimace. The drumbeat became faster, the dust thicker. The red-and-gold banner of the Holy Roman Emperor Frederick I Barbarossa was trampled into the dried mud. Cries of *"Libertà, libertà"* (Freedom, freedom) rose above the din of clashing metal. Young men draped in white flags stormed into the courtyard behind the knight. Their faces were painted white with a red cross in the middle, and their grimaces of rage must have looked terrifying to the foot soldiers, who, though better armed, seemed only half as determined. The sun was relentless. The dusty air was pungent with the smell of sweat and horse dung. The emperor's troops flagged. They were fighting someone else's war, far from home.

Suddenly everything seemed to end without a single clash of arms or blow. With groans of pain and murmurs of surrender, the armored soldiers collapsed like marionettes whose strings have been severed. Two men dressed in strange square garments that made them look like floppy model towers toppled to the ground. Someone laughed. Then someone else shouted, "Fuck you! That's my foot!" The bullocks that had been pulling the *carroccio* now took off their heads to reveal two sweaty human faces. It was a Sunday morning in June 1992, and the 1176 Battle of Legnano had been won, yet again, by the Knights of the Lombard League, founded originally in 1167 and then again in 1982.

Today Pontida is a dreary town south of Milan. In 1167 representatives from the cities of Venice, Padua, Brescia, Mantua, and Milan met there to take the oath that formed the Lombard League. Nine years later they defeated the imperial troops of Frederick I Barbarossa at Legnano. The battle is still celebrated by the zealots of the Lombard League every year. The historical pageant has become a party-political rally. The habit of dressing up in crusader uniforms to wield axes and cudgels is like the annual reenactments of the Battle of Hastings by the British Battle of Hastings Society. The difference is that the defeat of King Harold has not inspired a political party that has swept the Conservatives from power and dwarfed the Labour Party. The King Harold Party does not control the industrial heartland of England, and it does not threaten to turn Britain into a loose federation, creating fears that the country is in danger of becoming another Yugoslavia. In Italy, the Northern League does. It is one of Western Europe's more remarkable political movements, feeding on the widespread anger at corruption and a peculiarly Italian obsession with history as a living inspiration.

Dentists dressed in codpieces and reciting Lombard poetry are also, believe it or not, one of Italy's many answers to the end of the old world order. The leagues began springing up all over northern Italy in the 1980s. They remained on the outer fringe of Italian politics until 1992, when the Northern League entered Parliament with dozens of deputies. The Northern League is an umbrella organization for a number of regional leagues, principally from Lombardy, the Veneto, and Piedmont, who joined forces in 1990. Because the umbrella's movements are heavily based on the regional identity of its component leagues, it is by nature schismatic. Originally the leagues articulated a search for a new ethnically pure identity, a disillusionment with consumer society, and a return to the patchwork of independent states of pre-Risorgimento Italy. Some leagues, especially the Venetian League of the rumbustious Franco Rocchetta, developed strong ethnic overtones, or what one commentator called "a sense of ethnic ecology." Mr. Rocchetta once told me that he thought the Venetians should spearhead the league movement because they had the purest ethnic pedigree. "The Lombards [the dominant group in the Northern League]," he said, "are upstarts and newcomers. They descended from the Celts, and they only arrived on the Italian peninsula in the ninth century."

As the Northern League gained more power and eventually entered the governing coalition in April 1994, it ditched some of its zanier ethnic ideas and their exponents, including the ethnically pure Rocchetta.

The fact that a party as important as the Northern League is inspired by events that took place almost eight hundred years ago, uses the language and emblems of the twelfth century, and has managed to become the most popular party in the richest, most advanced part of Italy is not just eccentric, it is an indictment of Italian unity. The rise of the Northern League raises serious questions about the health of a nation that was born just over a hundred years ago and that never felt completely comfortable with being one nation-state.

But then, who is these days? The collapse of the old world order, the end of the Cold War and its division of the international community into two principal blocs, the global village of high technology, fiber-optic communication, high-speed travel, and mass migration—there are so many forces and events that have put a large question mark over the nation-state, the most basic political unit of the post-Enlightenment world. Recent conflicts, from the war in the former Yugoslavia to Rwanda to the pathetic attempts of Chechnya to gain independence from Russia, have all revived questions that had remained dormant during much of the Cold War. When is a state a nation? Does a state have an automatic right to be a nation? Have migration, satellite communication, and economic interdependence rendered the nation an irrelevant, old-fashioned concept? If tribe is more important than nation, why do so many national borders cross tribal divisions? If all borders are absurd, why do they exist at all, or why do we not acknowledge and respect their inherent absurdity and stop trying to move them? These questions are linked to an identity crisis that seems to have afflicted much of the planet after the end of the Cold War as it grapples for a new and not-yet-defined world order.

This identity crisis doesn't always have to lead to violence. Sometimes consternation will do. In the United States, the North Atlantic Free Trade Agreement (NAFTA) seems like a logical extension of the U.S. market to some, a threat to national identity, North American jobs, and the economy to others. The European Union is tortured by the gulf between its ambitions and its limitations. The German government wants to create a federal Europe but can't even create a genuinely united Germany. It says it wants to adopt a single European currency, but the one national symbol its people hold dear and can display with unabashed pride is the deutschmark. The British government is afraid that monetary union will mean a loss of national sovereignty, but the country's economy is already slavishly tied to Germany's. Just what does the increasing integration of Europe mean?

Italy has been afflicted by identity crisis in a peaceful, more existential way than most other Western nations have. The fault line of the Cold War ran through Italy, creating at first a rigid balance between Right and Left. Italian unity was not questioned as long as the country was firmly embedded in the Western Alliance on the front line against communism. The questions "What is Italy?" and "Who are the Italians?" were put on ice. But these are questions that have troubled Italy ever since people first started talking about it as one country. Count Metternich, the Habsburg foreign minister at the time of the Congress of Vienna in 1815, famously dismissed Italy as "a geographic expression." Count Cavour, the Piedmontese prime minister whose machinations allowed the Italian nation to be born, spoke better French than Italian and never dared travel further south than Florence. Massimo d'Azeglio, the author, painter, and philosopher of the Risorgimento, said gloomily in 1861, "We have made Italy. Now we have to make Italians."

Today one can say the opposite. Italians have been made, but Italy seems to be unravelling. More than 130 years after unification, the country has not been able to heal the genetic fault it inherited at birth: the North-South divide. If anything, the gulf between Milan and Naples, Turin and Reggio di Calabria, is getting wider. The statistics speak for themselves. Unemployment in Calabria, Campania, and Sicily currently hovers between 20 and 30 percent; in Lombardy, Veneto, and Piedmont, between 5 and 10 percent. Northern and central Italy have some of the highest productivity rates in the European Union. If the European average is 100, Lombardy has a per capita GDP of 122. By comparison, Germany has 113.8 percent and the United Kingdom 106.3 percent. However, Sicily and Calabria fall below the 70 percent mark. They are almost half as productive as the industrial heartland of the North. Eighty percent of Italy's direct taxation comes from the North, 20 percent from the South. Eighty-four percent of national social security contributions come from the North, 16 percent from the South. The gulf is as dramatic as that between eastern and western Germany. But while the two halves of Germany are gradually beginning to merge, Italy's North and South are drifting further apart.

This is surprising when one considers the history of the last five decades. Since 1945, six million "southerners" have migrated to the industrial heartland of the North. Without their labor the economic miracles of Lombardy and Piedmont would not have happened. The South provides the market for much of what is produced in the North. The division is further diluted by the center, the regions of Tuscany, Emilia-Romagna, and Umbria. The first two are the traditional fiefdom of the Italian Communist Party—a tradition that has more to do with their anticlericalism at the time of the Papal States than with the proletarian Utopia. And yet these regions have achieved a standard of living that in some cities like Siena and Bologna is higher than the northern average. But none of this seems to have had a significant effect on the North-South divide.

The rift has been accentuated by "Tangentopoli," which folded the national umbrella the ruling parties had provided for five decades. Until 1992 Christian Democrats or Socialists from opposite ends of Italy and dramatically different income brackets could still find common cause in their party. The parties maintained a high level of subsidies in the poorer South not so much to ensure an equal distribution of wealth but to woo southern voters. For instance, the agricultural sector in southern Puglia was one of the most heavily subsidized in Europe, and the local agricultural associations and their supporters rewarded the party with votes. When the Christian Democrats became discredited and the subsidies started to dry up, the agricultural community transferred its allegiance to the neo-Fascist Italian Social Movement.

Now, for the first time since the creation of the postwar republic, the economic gulf between North and South is being mirrored in the political landscape. Herein lies the novelty: the Northern League of rabble-rousing populist Umberto Bossi has become the voice of plebeian anger in the industrialized North, while the neo-Fascists have thrived on southern fears about being left behind. The League is the party of discontent for the *ceto medio,* the professional middle and lower middle classes who are fed up with Rome and its corruption and with paying their taxes into an inefficient state machine that squanders them on the South. The real issue is not whether the Northern League is separatist, regionalist, federalist, or just pro-autonomy. When speaking to a hard-line audience in Bergamo, Bossi is a separatist. When speaking to the Venetian League, he is a regionalist. When in Rome he is a federalist, and when in Sicily he becomes pro-autonomy. Behind all these adjectives lies one continuous theme: the end of national solidarity, the glue that has held Italy together as a nation-state. Supporters of the League argue that an Italy divided so dramatically between a poor South and a rich North cannot be squeezed into the straitjacket of national unity. They argue that this is unfair to the northerners who carry the financial burden and to the southerners who have come to rely on state subsidies as a crack addict relies on his drugs. The Italians call this addiction *assisten-*

zialismo, the culture of economic dependence. Alfredo Marmato, the treasurer of the Venetian League in Venice who owns a small glass factory on the island of Murano, summed up the League's grievance when he told me in November 1993, "We catch more fish than they do. But instead of giving them our fish, we should teach them how to cast their own line." This is the sort of advice that makes Sicilians or Calabrians boil with anger.

But the dwindling spirit of national solidarity caused by the collapse of the party system is not the only factor that has undermined Italian unity. The other is Europe. In the ever-closer embrace of the European Union, national borders have become increasingly irrelevant. While Britons may worry about losing their national sovereignty, the people of Bergamo can't wait to lose theirs. For them there is only one thing worse than being raped by Eurocrats in Brussels, and that is *not* being raped by Eurocrats in Brussels. The European Union offers liberation from the central government in Rome, as long as it intervenes less in people's lives than the Italian state does. Marco Formentini, the Northern League mayor of Milan, worked for the European Commission before going into Italian politics. In March 1994 I interviewed him in the spacious mayor's office in Milan's gloomy city hall. Sitting on a huge swivel chair surrounded by overpowering old master paintings, Formentini put it like this: "We believe in a united Europe of fifty regions like Lombardy, Bavaria, or Wales—not in the Europe of twelve nations." This concept may drift in the realm of wishful thinking, but the possibility of European union exerts a magnetic pull on cities like Milan—a pull away from Rome. I have made a habit of asking supporters of the League where they belong. The most common answer is: "First I'm Lombard [or Piedmontese or Venetian], then I'm European, and finally I'm Italian."

I followed one group of League supporters who came up with this common refrain to a bar in a small village in Lombardy. Umberto Bossi had just addressed a public rally, condemning the South for its laziness, *mafiosità,* and corruption. To clamorous applause he had ranted that Italy would have to become a loose federation. The scene was a frenzy of white-and-red Lombard flags. However, this was also the night Portugal was playing Italy in a qualifying game for the

World Cup soccer championship. The bar where we had gone for a drink after the rally was packed with League supporters. All cheered the Italian team as if their lives depended on it. During the World Cup similar scenes of national soccer hysteria and soccer patriotism took place in the most radical Lombard strongholds. The genius of Silvio Berlusconi and his team of advertising executives turned party managers was to realize that Italy's national identity is alive and kicking on the soccer field and that "Forza Lombardia" (Go, Lombardy!) doesn't have the same ring as "Forza Italia." Berlusconi tried to revive the concept of Italy by talking about Italy as the "Italian family," by talking about his Cabinet as the "national team."

Millions of Italians, and not just Lombards, are quite capable of cheering the national team during the World Cup while refusing to contribute taxes to the nation's coffers or place their trust in the central government in Rome. Their regionalism is one way of expressing their distrust or dislike of any central government that imposes itself upon them. For instance, I have come across a number of hard-line League supporters who will march across Italy to demonstrate against the corruption of the Italian government, call for a separate republic in the North, and tell Sicilians to go to hell. But when I, a foreigner, asked them why Italy was so corrupt, they rallied around the flag and became defensive about their nation. The key issue is not an outright rejection of Italy but how to accommodate the country's variety and regionalism in a looser-fitting national garment. But southerners, especially those who support the extreme-right-wing National Alliance, are quick to interpret northern calls for an Italian federation as betrayal of the nation.

While the Northern League uses the prospect of a closer European union to justify an Italian federation, the neo-Fascists in the South do precisely the opposite: they think only a strong, united Italy can survive in a more integrated Europe. The neo-Fascist Italian Social Movement always had a substantial following in southern cities such as Naples and Catania, partly also because of the monarchist tradition. The Italian monarchists merged with the MSI in the 1960s. But its successor, the National Alliance, together with Berlusconi's Forza Italia, now dominate most of the South, especially the regions of Puglia, Campania, and Calabria. The rebirth of neo-Fascism is a complex, fascinating phenomenon that I will deal with more fully in a later chapter, but in brief one of the important reasons for its rebirth is southern fears about being abandoned by the North. Every time Umberto Bossi lambasts the South for being lazy and corrupt, the neo-Fascists gain strength. At a neo-Fascist rally in Lecce, the baroque city on Italy's festering heel, a demonstrator wearing a black bomber jacket and sunglasses—at night—explained, "My father sacrificed his life for Italy during the war. Most of my family works in the car factories in Turin. My sister is married to a Milanese. And now they—the Northern League—want to separate. It's treachery."

Thirty miles from the Swiss border in the foothills of the Alps, a Lombard may stress the difference between North and South. In Lecce, a mere hop across the Adriatic from Albania, or in the Sicilian port of Mazara del Vallo, southeast of Tunis, Italians tell you that Italy's North can't survive without the labor and the markets of the South. All of them are right. Their misfortune is that they can't live together and they can't live apart.

One of the bizarre aspects of the feverish debate about North and South is that no one can agree about the border. Palermitani are adamant that Rome belongs to the cold-hearted North driven by efficiency and productivity, while many Milanesi regard Rome as the deep South, the embodiment of all the "southern" clichés—impenetrable thickets of bureaucracy, laziness, oriental wiliness and untrustworthiness, the Mafia. Even Umberto Bossi, whose political identity rests on the border, doesn't know for certain where it lies. Although he has proposed to split Italy up into three republics, Padana in the North, Etruria in the center, and the Republic of the South, he neglected to point out where the borders should be. Interpretations differ. The European Union's development aid program believes the border runs along the dividing line between Lazio (the region around Rome) and the Campania to the south and the Abruzzi mountains to the east. David Willey of the BBC, who has lived in Italy since the early 1970s, insists that the border between North and South lies somewhere near his holiday home in Cortona in southern Tuscany. This was the old border between the Papal States and Tuscany, and the popes were responsible for some of the worst aspects of modern Italy, especially the reluctance of individuals to take responsibility for their actions. In other words, the border between North and South exists mainly in people's minds. In one week alone in October 1993 I was given four different reasons for the divide. A baron in Naples blamed it on the Spanish Bourbons, whose occupation of the Kingdom of the Two Sicilies confined southern Italy to the dark ages and the Inquisition until the middle of the last century, by which time it was too late to catch up. A taxi driver in Palermo blamed it on the Risorgimento, which he called a capitalist exploitation by the industrial North of the agricultural South. An anthropologist in Rome remarked cynically that Italy should never have been one country anyway since it was in fact home to three completely different peoples: Celts in the North, Etruscans in the center, and Greeks in the South. An emaciated waiter in a fish restaurant in Bari thought it was a question of diet. "The northerners are too aggressive," he said. "They eat too much red meat."

Some would even argue that the division between North and South has nothing to do with geography. Italy is in fact a mishmash of northern European and southern or Mediterranean values that has produced schizophrenia in the heart of the Italian character. Since the unification of Italy in the 1860s, the Italians have been trying to diagnose and cure the North-South divide like some genetic defect. It's as if the elegant Italian boot concealed a clubfoot. American social historian Robert Putnam has tried to explain today's differences between the North and the South by looking at yesterday's civic traditions. In essence, he believes that the causes can be found in the eleventh century, when northern Italy broke up into self-governing "communes" and city-states and the South came under the control of the Holy Roman Empire. There the rule of Frederick II, the *stupor mundi,* was the most enlightened in Europe at the time. Norman Sicily already had a highly developed bureaucracy. Frederick founded Europe's first state university in Palermo. The emperor himself was a Renaissance man, three centuries before the beginning of the Renaissance. He was an accomplished poet and an amateur civil engineer who took a great interest in everything from fortress design to irrigation systems. Under him Sicily also enjoyed an unprecedented degree of religious tolerance, and the strong Moorish influence in the architecture that dates back to Sicily is testimony to the fact. The emperor's rule was indeed enlightened, but it was also highly autocratic, creating a feudal style of "vertical dependence" between the subject and his ruler.

The northern communes meanwhile developed horizontal ties between the citizens and thus a civic responsibility. In effect, what distinguished cities like Venice, Florence, and Siena from Naples or Bari was the extent to which men were allowed to govern their own lives through laws and associations. Thirteenth-century Florence was, of course, not a democracy. It was ruled by an oligarchic family, and half the Florentines lived in slums. The streets were bristling with violence and class warfare. But the principles of mutual aid and economic collaboration were established in that period. People increasingly felt that their own well-being depended on the well-being of the community, rather than on the protection of a ruler. This nascent civic responsibility expressed itself in the formation of guilds, clubs, mutual aid societies, fraternities, cooperatives, and the rule of law. Fourteenth-century Bologna, the intellectual capital of communal Italy with one of the world's oldest universities, had 50,000 inhabitants, 2,000 of them lawyers. Wealth and power in the northern communes were based less on land and more on commerce and finance. This created a bond of economic interdependence accompanied by a high degree of social mobility.

In 1303 Verona created Europe's oldest guild structure with its own charter. "A violation of the statutes," Putnam writes, "was met by boycott and social ostracism." At the same time Florence had ten guilds, seven of which dealt with export. A medieval version of the neighborhood watch group called a *vicinanza* flourished in these cities, as did "tower societies" that provided mutual security from invaders.

Siena was a paradise for the committeeman: in fourteenth-century Siena there were 860 city posts for 5,000 adult males. They dealt with everything from trash collection to banking. Banking in itself illustrated the importance of "horizontal" ties since it was based on credit. And credit, which derives from the Latin word *credere* ("to believe") relied on trust and stability. Siena became one of the banking capitals of late-medieval Europe, with the result that in 1993 the city's bank, the Monte de Piaschi di Siena, celebrated its five hundredth anniversary as the oldest surviving bank in the world. The bank is partly administered by the city authorities. The fact that Siena has had a Communist mayor since 1945 is not a weird contradiction but perfectly consistent with a tradition in which the Communist Party and now its successor, the Democratic Party of the Left, has always represented civic pride and the art of self-government. Siena's brand of communism, which stems from anticlericalism, is quintessentially bourgeois and would no doubt make Marx spin in his grave. The famous Palio horse race, which takes place every summer in the shell-shaped Piazza del Campo, is much more than a spectacle for the tourist industry. The teams of horsemen are made up of members of the city's ancient guilds, and the race is seen by the Sienesi as a ritual celebration of their independence and civic pride, as well, of course, as a good romp in the heat and an excuse for a hearty meal. Such pageants are not confined to central and northern Italy. But in southern Italy, festivals like the famous Festa dei Jii in Nola or the omnipresent Easter parades are more mystical affairs celebrating patron saints or invoking good harvest weather and fertility.

The mystery of Putnam's theory is how the civic spirit born in the late Middle Ages was able to survive centuries of wars and pestilence. In the 1656 plague half the population of Venice, Florence, and Bologna died. For centuries Tuscany and Umbria were ravaged by invasions and border disputes. The landscape now dotted with medium-sized factories and coveted by Germans rich enough to afford a small farmhouse was scarred by centuries of poverty until the 1950s. A friend of mine who was born near Siena in 1947 has said that his village was so poor, his family couldn't even afford to eat pasta. They were fed by an uncle who worked as a waiter in a Rome hotel and stole food for his Tuscan family once every two weeks. Now the family has made a small fortune selling herbs, porcini mushrooms, and extravirgin olive oil for export. In the nineteenth century Florence and Verona were picturesque but crumbling cities, stuck firmly in the preindustrial age. Naples, meanwhile, was a teeming metropolis. The city was four times the size of Florence and three times as big as Milan. It entered the industrial age full of promise. In 1818 Naples

launched the first steamboat in the Mediterranean. In 1839 it opened
the first railway on the Italian peninsula, a five-mile track from the
city center along the coast to Portici. In 1880 it had a funicular
railway and a few years later a steel plant. However, none of this
amounted to a genuine industrial revolution. The railway and steam-
boats were launched not to satisfy the needs of a rising entrepreneur-
ial class but to flatter the egos of the Bourbon rulers, who were
desperate to show off their commitment to progress.

In 1984 a Neapolitan aristocrat and his wife set up an association
called Napoli 99. The Baron and Baroness Barraco chose the number
99 because it refers to the year 1799. In that year, inspired by the
French Revolution and supported by French revolutionary forces, the
people of Naples ousted their Bourbon ruler, King Ferdinand I, and
proclaimed the Parthenopean Republic. For a brief period the city became a chaotic island of democracy. But the Neapolitan Jacobins
lacked the support of the peasantry outside the city. Their revolution
was essentially imported from France, and when Napoleon came to
power it collapsed like the French Revolution had. By 1815 Ferdinand was back on his throne as the king of the Two Sicilies.

For the Barracos, 1799 represents the great "missed opportunity"
of Italy's South. "This was *our* chance to create civic responsibility.
And we missed it." Their mission today is a modest one: to reopen
most of the cultural treasures in Naples that have been closed due to
the lack of custodians to look after them, the threat of theft, or sheer
neglect. There are more than two hundred boarded-up churches in
Naples. The city has two thousand municipal gardeners, but the 250
acres of parkland are in a pitiful state, because until recently the gardeners collected their salaries from the municipality but no one expected them to do any gardening for the city. They were too busy
running their own private enterprises, from garden centers to tree
nurseries. What appalled Baron Barraco was that most Neapolitans
don't even seem to mind that their cultural heritage had become a
no-go area. Instead of clamoring for change, they have accepted the
woeful status quo. "We suffer from a severe lack of civic pride and
responsibility," the baron told me. "We have been trapped in a vicious circle. Because the Neapolitans haven't cared enough, it has

been easy for politicians to rape the city in search of political patronage. No one stopped the unfettered construction of bridges, highways, or ugly high-rise buildings, which were essential for providing jobs and buying votes." Corruption was fueled above all by the billions of lire in emergency aid that flooded the Naples area after the 1980 earthquake. Unfortunately, only a small proportion of the money made its way to the thousands of people left homeless by the earthquake. In 1990 most of them were still living in mobile homes.

Thanks to Napoli 99, scores of churches and parks have been reopened to the public, and in May 1993 Naples invited the rest of Italy to view its artistic treasures during an "open weekend." The city's new mayor, Antonio Bassolino, a member of the Democratic Party of the Left who narrowly defeated Alessandra Mussolini, Il Duce's granddaughter, for the post, seems to be fulfilling some of his election promises. His administration discovered that one of the reasons for the city's moronic traffic chaos is that most of the 1,400 traffic wardens, who are paid by the Neapolitan authorities, rarely venture out onto the streets. As one of them put it, "There's no point. The traffic's too bad. Better to leave it alone." The traffic wardens were free to pursue another job while already receiving a salary from the state, as well as enjoying all the privileges and clout bestowed upon them by their jobs as uniformed civil servants. It is against such self-interest disguised as resignation that the baron and his wife, not to mention untold others across the country, are battling.

Italy lacks an event like the French Revolution or a document like the American Constitution or an institution like the House of Commons that enshrines the pride and the values of the entire nation. The Risorgimento, regarded as a great feat of self-determination by some and a calamity by others, does not suffice. Italy's postwar Constitution is a beautiful but much-flouted document. Unlike the deutschmark, which has become a symbol of national unity in a country where many are still reluctant to wave a German flag, the lire has too many zeros on it to be taken seriously. Today the Italians are still raiding their history in search of a national identity. Those looking for a sense of civic responsibility have scoured the more obscure corners of their past for a model. The Barracos have chosen the year 1799, which is relevant for Naples. Siena looks back to the fifteenth century, when the Monte de Piaschi bank was founded at the height of its power. In central and northern Italy outbursts of civic pride are accompanied by historical pageants.

These festivals have naturally become tourist attractions, but they are above all a historical ritual for the local population. The choice is mind-numbing, especially in the month of May. In Umbria alone there are thirty-five different festivals in cities and hundreds more in villages. You can go to Assisi to see troubadours serenading in the streets in memory of Saint Francis, the city's most famous saint, who was a playboy before he abandoned his family wealth for monastic poverty. In Narni citizens don medieval garb to commemorate their patron saint, Juvenal. Young men representing the city's three ancient guilds compete in a game that involves lancing a ring suspended from a rope in the Piazza Maggiore. Your next stop on the pageant trail could be Gubbio with its Festival of the Giant Candles, then on to Cascia to light your own candle for Saint Rita and after that to Orvieto for the Festival of the Doves. If you have any energy left, you could flit back to Gubbio for round two: the crossbow Palio. The Northern League, which looks back to twelfth-century Milan and Mantova for inspiration, must be the first example of a historical pageant turned political party.

Italians love political trinkets, and Lombard history has provided the League with a booming kitsch industry. Every League rally is accompanied by a curious array of vendors who do a roaring trade in the movement's paraphernalia: Lombard League badges displaying the party's twelfth-century mascot, the mercenary general Alberto da Guissano. Legs akimbo and sword held high, the figure graces boxer shorts, tea towels, handkerchiefs, watch faces, and even lingerie. There are also toy models of the *carroccio* ("il Carroccio" has also become a nickname for the Northern League in Italian newspapers). For the wishful thinkers there are blue hardback passports for the imaginary Republic of the North, as well as fake postage stamps in denominations of a currency that doesn't legally exist—the lece—but that can in fact be traded at an exchange rate of one to one with the deutschmark, Europe's hardest currency. The passport vendor, who clearly hopes to be border guard between Lombardy and Tuscany one day, was attached to the party's bellicose symbol. He rolled up his sleeve to reveal a string of tattoos of Lombard knights fighting their way up to his hairy armpit. But despite its barbarian growl, the League is also very petit bourgeois. Other items on sale included a video of the Bossis' wedding, a complete set of League dinnerware, and League doilies. The League has built its own personality cult around the raucous Mr. Bossi. At one party congress I saw someone selling cigarette butts that had been smoked and stubbed out by the party leader, a bargain at 1,000 lire (about 60 cents) apiece. These curious additions to the relics of political hero worship can only gain in value, because Mr. Bossi gave up smoking two years ago. (He took it up again during the feverish period that led to the collapse of the Berlusconi government in December 1994.)

In 1993 the Northern League became the most popular party in Italy's rich industrial North. In Milan, the country's business capital and once the powerhouse of the Socialist Party and its leader Bettino Craxi, the League won 42 percent of the vote in the summer elections. Not since Mussolini's Fascists has a party been so popular here. The League's genius was that it combined a political revolt against corruption with a much more ancient rebellion against the capital. Party members, known as *leghisti,* "Leaguers," despise Rome both as the incubator of political corruption and as a central power that siphons off northern taxes and dilutes northern identity. In a country in which history has always been recruited to legitimize new political movements, the League's historical pageants are more than just fun and games. They are to Umberto Bossi what Rome's imperial past was to Benito Mussolini: an ideal from a distant era, as inspiring as it is inaccurate. An exhibition in Milan's town hall, timed to coincide with the election for a new mayor in 1993, hammered home the point. The period of the city's commune in the twelfth century was depicted as the flowering of Milan, when civic culture produced flourishing guilds, a sewage system, and stunning Gothic churches. The spirit of the commune had been unleashed when the Lombard League had produced a series of military victories, such as the one at Legnano, and forced the Holy Roman emperor to make a number of important concessions. He guaranteed the city of Milan and its allies the right to govern their own affairs, to collect and spend their own taxes, and to be subject to their own laws. Ironically, the exhibition also proved how the same historical event can be manipulated by different people for precisely opposite ends. In 1865 Verdi composed an opera entitled *The Battle of Legnano*. The music was piped through the exhibition rooms on crackly loudspeakers. But the opera, composed at the height of the Risorgimento, when Italy was being unified by force, had been composed to celebrate Italian unity in the face of outside aggression by the Austrians and the ability of the fledgling nation to stand up to foreign invaders. Today the same music is used to symbolize the struggle of Milan, Brescia, Mantova, and Venice to resist the compromises of nationality.

Much of the League's success as a protest movement is also due to its leader, Umberto Bossi. The fifty-three-year-old senator is a scruffy rake with unkempt hair and a crumpled suit who looks like a seedy encyclopedia salesman and sounds like a cattle auctioneer. He is a rabble-rouser and street fighter who would be shunned in more polite times, but during the upheaval of recent years he has come into his own. On stage he grabs the microphone as if he wants to throttle it. His voice is gravelly, his chin brutal, his thick, bulging lips look bruised, and his statements wander from insult to libelous injury. Bossi is proud to be gruff. It comes naturally, but it is also politically calculated. In a country in which the ruling parties have masked their abuse of power with an abstract, abstruse vocabulary, Bossi's blunt indiscretions have been refreshingly irreverent, if not always subtle or funny. He has called former Prime Minister Ciriaco De Mita "pig ugly," compared Massimo D'Alema, the moustachioed leader of the former Communist Party, to a "truffle pig," and described Silvio Berlusconi, his putative coalition partner, as "Berluskaiser," the self-appointed emperor who didn't know the meaning of democracy. He has also slammed the neo-Fascists as "unreconstructed blackshirts and liars." His style of rhetoric is perhaps best encapsulated by the Northern League's rallying cry: *"C'e l'ho duro!"* ("I've got a hard-on!"). A slogan emblazoned on the front of one of the League's more popular souvenirs, pairs of Jockey shorts, it is presumably meant to instill a sense of euphoria into the wearer. Some have pointed out the connection between the League's imaginary erection and the un-sheathed sword of its mascot, Alberto da Guissano. "The intention," one of the party's supporters once told me, "is to create the impression of a party thrusting ahead."

Rage is the lifeblood of Bossi's politics. Born in 1941 in a village near Varese in Lombardy, he was brought up in a family that struggled to stay above the poverty line. His father was a textile worker and sold the milk produced by two cows that he owned. His mother, who came from a poor peasant family, found a job as a concierge when the family moved to Milan. Umberto was one of the first of his generation to go to university on a state grant. "I had a difficult, tedious childhood," he told journalist Giorgio Bocca. "I saw the cosy world of my parents collapse around me. And I couldn't digest the new things around me." In a country that was transformed in a few decades from a predominantly agricultural society to an industrial one, this admission of culture shock could have come from millions of Italians, many of whom now support the leagues.

In his teens Bossi drifted from one casual job to the next, trying his hand at everything from teaching to playing electric guitar in a rock band. While many of Bossi's contemporaries were turning to either the extreme left or right, he became a born-again Lombard. At the instigation of a friend who ran the students' league for Valdotaine, the largely French-speaking region around Val d'Aosta, Bossi rediscovered his Lombard roots. He took night classes in the Lombard dialect, which must be one of Italy's ugliest, and wrote Lombard poetry, turgid ballads extolling the virtues of the hardy Lombard spirit. In the late 1970s he founded a journal entitled *Lombard Autonomy,* which folded soon afterward, saddling him with debt. In 1981 Bossi met the man who has become the League's ideologue and with whom he would form one of the more unlikely couples in modern Italian politics. A law professor in his late seventies, Gianfranco Miglio was one of the first to desert the Christian Democrats for the League. His imposingly bald head is covered by a Bavarian-style feathered hat, and he carries a cane and wears thick tweeds, giving the impression of a Habsburg landowner preserved in aspic.

Professor Miglio belongs to that rarest of modern breeds: a Germanophile. He adores Germans and is a great believer in German myths from punctuality to efficiency. He also thinks that the German federation should be the role model for a future Italy. In fact, according to Miglio, Italy in its present state defies nature. Sicily and the South should, in the professor's own words, "be abandoned to their destiny." Italian unification, he says, was a historical error. His argument goes as follows: The Risorgimento was imposed on the people of the Italian peninsula from above by "a war of conquest." Unlike German unification, which started with the Zollverein, the customs union of Germany's many principalities and kingdoms, and was driven from below by an increasingly assertive bourgeoisie, Italy had unification thrust upon it by Piedmont. Garibaldi and his redshirts were cheered in Sicily not because the peasants wanted unification but because they were promised bread and land. In 1861 most Italians were farm laborers who lived on pittance wages and a diet of bread, water, and vegetables. They had little idea of what was meant by "Italy." Some Sicilians thought that "l'Italia" was in fact "la Talia," the wife of King Victor Emmanuel II. Massimo d'Azeglio, the elder statesman of Italy at the time of unification, thought that the annexation of Naples amounted to sharing a bed with someone who had smallpox. In 1861 he wrote, "In Naples we drove out a king in order to establish a government based on universal consent. But we need sixty battalions to hold southern Italy down, and even they seem inadequate. Between the brigands and the nonbrigands, it is obvious that nobody wants us there." The Risorgimento had little to do with the romantic nationalism and spirit of liberation cherished by philosopher Giuseppe Mazzini. These issues still haunt Italy 134 years after unification.

The League's supporters are a mixture of zealots, protest voters left homeless by the collapse of the Christian Democrats and Socialists, and opportunists. It's a fluid following, and many people who voted for the League in 1993 probably defected to Berlusconi's Forza Italia in 1994. But a large number of voters are fiercely loyal to Umberto Bossi. I met some of them last March in the foothills of the Alps. Gardone Val Trompia, about an hour's drive northeast of Milan, is the home of Beretta, Europe's oldest arms factory. Beretta is still the biggest local employer. Thousands of League supporters had packed into the small square festooned with geraniums and the League's red and white colors. Mr. Bossi was two hours late as usual, but his bedrock supporters were not going to desert him even at 11 o'clock on a cold March night. Those who didn't crowd into the main piazza watched from balconies and windows, wrapped in blankets. The people of Gardone cared about two issues above all: they wanted to separate from the South, and they wanted to block a proposed ban on hunting in Italy, because this would curtail their favorite hobby and reduce the demand for hunting rifles and thus threaten their jobs. Who better to address these fears than their local candidate, Vito Gnutti? Gnutti, who was appointed minister of industry in 1994, comes from an old family of arms manufacturers and today owns one of Italy's biggest trigger factories. We asked one of the supporters, a teenager, why she had come to the rally and what she felt about separation from the South. "We want a separate republic," she said. "In the schools here, we want northern teachers, not southern teachers. There are too many southern teachers now. This is not right." "What's wrong with southerners?" I asked. "I don't hate them," she said, "but they're lazy. They're corrupt. They bring Mafia here." Her sentiments were echoed by the graffiti all over Lombardy: SOUTHERN-ERS OUT; CALABRIANS, SICILIANS GO HOME.

During the floods that devastated large parts of Piedmont in November 1994, I visited the city of Alba, which had been covered by a thick film of muddy slime after torrential rains had caused the Tanaro River to burst its banks. Ten people had been killed in Alba alone, another fifty in the rest of Piedmont. Thirty thousand cattle had drowned, and thousands of acres of farmland had been destroyed. The material damage had gone into the billions of dollars. One part of Alba, home of Italy's famed white truffle and one of the richest communities in the country, had been completely cut off by the floods. We approached a group of pensioners who were busy sweeping the mud out of their homes with brooms. They were still fuming with anger. "Do you realize," one of them told us, "that we waited to be rescued for a whole day? And then all they could send us, those bastards, were two soldiers from Naples!" The pensioners were supporters of the Northern League. Their strident "antisouthern" attitudes were all the more surprising because many of their neighbors were in fact Sicilian and Calabrian immigrants. Prejudice knows no logic.

Such sentiments characterize the lunatic fringe of the Northern League, Bossi's most loyal supporters but also the ones who will marginalize him in national politics unless he can distance himself from them. What distinguishes the Northern League from Jean-Marie Le Pen's National Front in France or Schoenhuber's Republicans in Germany is that it is as concerned about internal immigration from the poorer areas as about immigration from the third world. "They treat us like Moroccans," Gianni Carrelli, a taxi driver in Milan, told me. "Bossi is a racist. That's why I voted for Berlusconi." The driver was a second-generation immigrant from Puglia in the south. He spoke with a Milanese accent. He had never lived in southern Italy. But the rhetoric of the League had brought out the southerner in him. It had also cost Bossi another vote. The localism of the Northern League, with its racist, antisouthern overtones, is both its strength and its weakness. It has given the movement a well-defined regional identity that goes hand in hand with a "northern" reluctance to pay taxes to the central government in Rome. However, it has also limited the League's appeal. In 1992 Umberto Bossi stood for election in Sicily and Rome as well as in Lombardy. His percentage of the vote outside his turf was tiny. Bossi and the League are loathed south of Rome, where they have rekindled traditional southern fears about being neglected, disdained, and browbeaten by the North. Yet elsewhere their support is strong enough to have won them the seats to form one third of the ruling coalition's strength.

Bossi's revolution has been hijacked by Silvio Berlusconi. A fellow Lombard, Berlusconi has all the credentials of a rich northerner that are necessary to impress right-wing voters in Turin or Venice, but his appeal stretches far south, well beyond the reach of Lombard regionalism. The greatest danger Bossi faces is that he will be marginalized as the local hero of Lombardy, celebrated by zealots in crusader uniforms, but abandoned by the "Gucci revolutionaries" who have given his movement its economic clout. I went to see some of the League's fur-clad *sans-culottes* in the sedate, beautiful city of Mantova. Famous for being Virgil's birthplace as well as for producing Italy's best butter, Mantova became a member of the Lombard League in 1167 and in 1992 became the first city to be ruled by a League mayor. Luciana Poggialli was one of the original Jacobins. The owner of the Caffè Centrale, this middle-aged matron was weighed down by chunky gold jewelry and burdened by a beehive hairdo. Over a cup of Earl Grey with a twist of lemon, she explained how she was at the forefront of Italy's new revolution, how the League's victory in Mantova will be remembered like the storming of the Bastille, and how those corrupt politicians in Rome should "all rot in jail or worse." "Can I tempt you with another puff pastry?" she interrupted her own blood-curdling diatribe. "I will *not* waste my taxes on that bunch of thieves," she hissed. I didn't have the heart to ask the terrifying Robespierre of Mantova what her contributions to the national coffers were. As a self-employed caffè owner, she belonged to one of the most notorious tax-dodging brackets in Italy.

Despite her fervent support of the League in 1993, a year later she was voting for Forza Italia. She, like thousands of other voters in the North, had been scared off by the League's rabble-rousing rhetoric and found refuge in the more socially acceptable ranks of Forza Italia, where codpieces and lances have been replaced by blue blazers and cell phones.

Personally, I felt there was something endearing about the League's unorthodox array of politicians: Umberto Bossi, the street fighter; Roberto Maroni, the interior minister with designer stubble and dark Trotsky-style spectacles who used to relax by playing the piano and saxophone in a Milan jazz club; Irene Pivetti, the powerful and devoutly Catholic speaker of the Chamber of Deputies who was appointed to that illustrious position at the tender age of thirty-one and had all the pictures of nudes removed from her office; Francesco Speroni, the former Alitalia flight engineer who became Minister of Institutional Reform, responsible for drawing up legislation that would transform Italy into a loose federation of states. When I went to interview Minister Speroni in the summer of 1994, he was sitting at his vast desk flanked by Italian flags. He was playing on a flight simulator, trying to land at Chicago's O'Hare Airport. He was wearing a Harley-Davidson biker's tie, cowboy boots, and a huge silver belt buckle embossed with the sword-wielding emblem of his party.

The heart of the Northern League may reside in Lombardy, but its political ambitions have migrated to Rome. Until an Italian federation has been created that gives substantial powers to regions like Lombardy, Bossi has no interest in confining his political power to the North. He does not want to become the Italian equivalent of the late

Franz Josef Strauss, the Bavarian premier who spent the last twenty years of his life trying to persuade Germans that he was a national leader while wearing a feathered Bavarian hat and lederhosen. The Northern League is caught uneasily between its regional allegiances and its national political ambitions. The balancing act ended with the formation of the coalition government with Forza Italia and the neo-Fascists. Rivalry between Bossi and Berlusconi, two natural enemies who had decided to join forces in government, was the factor that more than any undermined Italy's ruling coalition in 1994.

By attacking his allies as he did near the end of the year, Bossi was also trying to redefine the political character of his movement. But the more he ranted, the more he frightened the mainstream voters of his movement, who have come out of the protest phase and are now looking for stability and ways of benefiting from the end of the recession. Nothing could be more damaging in this climate than the threat of tax revolt that Bossi has periodically launched. The closest anyone has come in recent years to bankrupting the Italian state was Bossi, when he called on his followers to boycott BOTs, the high-yield treasury bonds with which the Italian government finances its vast budget deficit. The Italian state borrows of its own people, which is like an airline pilot borrowing money from his passengers for fuel. This also explains why Bossi's call to boycott the BOTs could never have worked: the passengers had a vested interest in keeping the plane flying.

If Bossi is feared by the Italian mainstream voter, he is also distrusted increasingly by the Lombard puritans. One of them is his own sister, Angela. Angela Bossi and her husband were founding members of the Lombard League but became disenchanted as the movement grew more and more powerful and began to exchange the threat of separatism and secession for the gentle notion of federalism. Angela Bossi has none of the political spark of her younger brother. The picture of bucolic, round-faced simplicity, she relies heavily on her husband for even the most basic political questions. He tends to whisper the right answer into her ear. Another problem is that their movement is threatened by physical extinction. Angela Bossi has founded the Alpine/Pensioners League. Its emblem is an old man with a feathered hat and a stick walking up a very steep mountain.

Bossi may not pose a grave political threat to her brother, but she is a reminder of the inherently schismatic nature of regionalist movements.

By the end of 1994 the Northern League was in danger of splintering into a myriad of movements, ironically re-creating the fragmented map of regionalism that had originally inspired its narrow horizons. The Venetian League had split off from the parliamentary group of the Northern League, and even the stalwart Lombard deputies created a schism over the question of when and how to topple Prime Minister Berlusconi. The grand project of Italian federalism had been almost wholly forgotten in the daily political battles for survival. With the country and the economy teetering on the brink, the murky machinations of the Northern League, who threatened almost every day to topple the government, looked like the guerrilla tactics of a splinter faction in the Lombard Rotary Club. Bossi proved himself to be a masterful, ruthless political tactician, but the more he schemed, the more he was seen, to quote one newspaper, as "a political terrorist who threatens to blow up the whole country just to save his own party." You can take the man out of Lombardy, but you can't take Lombardy out of the man!

The Italians have a wonderful word for the high-pitched form of local patriotism that the Leagues came to embody. They call it *campanilismo,* literally "churchbellism." It means that one's loyalties and interests extend no further than the echo of the local church bells—that is to say, not very far at all. The word is a polite way of calling someone a parochial bigot, blinkered against the outside world. As the Italians have been reassessing the value of their nation-state, this breed of "Little Lombards" or "Little Venetians" has multiplied. "Small is beautiful" is their philosophy. They tend to dislike outsiders of all kinds, be they north African immigrants, tourists, or Italians who don't hear the chime of the same bells. Venice has become their spiritual capital. Last year the Venetians held a referendum on whether to separate from the mainland city of Mestre, thus ending a municipal marriage engineered by Mussolini in 1926. The Venetian League, which is behind the referendum, believes that the needs of Venice and Mestre would be much better served if the two cities were separate. They are indeed an odd couple. Mestre is an industrial nightmare. Instead of canals, there are slag heaps; instead of gondolas and vaporetti, buses and cargo trains. The palazzi of Mestre are highrise buildings, fuel tanks, and refinery funnels billowing black smoke into the murky sky.

Meanwhile, *la Serenissima* has become like an elegant but shriveled dowager duchess inching toward the great lagoon in the sky. Mass tourism and exorbitant housing prices have driven the majority of Venetians over the water to Mestre. Many still work in Venice during the day. At rush hour you can see them trudging along the canals like forced laborers or crowding onto the water buses heading for Piazzale Roma, the large landing station for ferries from the mainland, easily recognizable by its huge multistory car park. From here it is a mere hop to the urban hell of Mestre. Venice seems to have given itself a license to rip off everyone, even Venetians. Everything in Venice is expensive. The consequences for the city's population have been more devastating than the Black Death of 1665. From 1961 to 1993, the population dropped from 200,000 to just over 60,000. At night Venice is as deserted as a ghost town. The city that hosts one of Europe's most important film festivals has only four cinemas. Davide and Cristina, a couple who own a bookshop near the center and who were lucky enough to have inherited a house, complained that all their friends had moved away. They had no social life because it was too complicated to leave the lagoon city at night. They had become prisoners in the most beautiful city on earth. Venice, they said, wasn't dying, she was already dead. By separating her from Mestre, all hopes of bringing down housing prices and luring some of the Venetians back are likely to fade away. Venice will become a theme park for tourists. "Everyone will become a tourist," said Cristina, "even the people of Mestre. And those of us who are left will probably be forced to wear traditional Venetian costumes. For us, life will become one long historical pageant."

Fascist Hang-ups

My girlfriend and I live in the old Jewish ghetto of Rome, an area between the Tiber Island and the Capitol. The ghetto was created here in 1515 and "opened" in 1870, when Rome ceased to be under the control of the popes and became the capital of united Italy. The narrow, dank streets are patrolled by mangy cats and sweetly scented by the aromas wafting from the local bakeries clustered behind the city's synagogue. The synagogue is a large, square-domed building completed at the beginning of the century, when Rome had a Jewish mayor. It is surrounded by heavily armed policemen, a security measure introduced in 1985 after a car bomb exploded in the street behind it, killing five people. The descendents of families who moved here more than four centuries ago still live and work in the ghetto. The area still specializes in the traditional Roman Jewish trades such as laundries, textiles, mattress stuffing, and household goods and contains some of the city's best restaurants. The sense of continuity is emphasized by the ancient Roman columns that stick out of the pavement in the Via di Portico d'Ottavia and the frieze fragments from the temple complex the Emperor Augustus dedicated to his sister Octavia. They now grace the entrance to Bar Totò, my local; they were built into the wall in the fifteenth century, when most of this quarter was a lively vegetable market. The famous Medici Venus, a beautiful Roman sculpture depicting the goddess, was found underneath a pile of rubbish and vegetable compost that had accumulated over the centuries. The quarter is a testament to the fact that in Rome no aspect of the past is ever completely eradicated. Near the ancient Theater of Marcellus, an amphitheater that was turned into an apartment building in the fifteenth century, there is a memorial slab commemorating the victims of Fascism, the hundreds of Roman Jews who were shot or sent to concentration camps by the Nazis, who occupied Rome in 1943 with Benito Mussolini's support. The ghetto's backdrop of continuity is appropriate because in the last three years it has looked as if, for the neo-Fascists, history was repeating itself—this time as a farce.

In October 1992 there was a commotion in the ghetto. A group of skinheads had come to the area in the middle of the night and daubed the walls with swastikas and the invitation "JEWS GET OUT." The following day two hundred or so young Jewish men decided to retaliate by paying the skinheads a visit. They got onto their mopeds, many of them wearing their yarmulkes, drove to the Via Domodossola in a notoriously right-wing quarter of the city, and raided the offices of a small group of neo-Nazis. A few people were beaten up, some furniture was destroyed, and there was a threatening response from the skinheads, who vowed to avenge what one of them called "this violation of our political rights." Jewish community leaders denounced the Jewish raid as a dangerous provocation, and the number of policemen around the synagogue was increased. For several days the atmosphere was tense as the inhabitants of the ghetto braced themselves for retaliation. But the response never came. The skinheads seem to have been stunned by the unusually robust response of their victims. A few months later, however, graffiti started to appear again on some walls in the ghetto. This time it read ANTI-FASCISMO MAI PIU! (Anti-Fascism, never again!). The jackboot had been replaced by the open-toed Birkenstock sandal. Meanwhile, neo-Fascist members of Parliament were pleading for understanding. Mussolini, they complained, had been misunderstood. Il Duce had really been a frustrated democrat. The victimizers had become the victims. Violent thugs had become consumed by self-pity. Politicians and supporters of a movement that had once worshipped the purifying effects of violence now complained that they were being persecuted.

The bruised sensibilities of Italy's neo-Fascists have coincided with their sudden return to power after fifty years in the wilderness. The neo-Fascist Italian Social Movement has formed part of the ruling right-wing coalition under the new name of National Alliance. The architect of this conversion is Gianfranco Fini, the young, immensely popular leader of the party, who has left the margins of Italian politics to soar in the opinion polls during the last two years, eclipsing even Silvio Berlusconi in popularity. His recently declared policies of peace and harmony would have sat comfortably with any Rainbow Alliance. But in 1992 the same Fini was singing the old Fascist songs surrounded by thugs in black shirts giving the old Roman salute.

The neo-Fascists were marginalized as long as the *partitocrazia* was in power. The consensus between center Left and center Right, the solidity of the ruling coalition, and the cooperation of the Communist opposition meant that they could be ignored. Apart from a few halfhearted attempts at rapprochement, the neo-Fascists had always been excluded from power by the arithmetic of coalition government. Once the coalition evaporated, the Italian Social Movement, its image untarnished by corruption, was poised to pick up the pieces. Thanks to its marginal role, the party had never had the opportunity to be lured into "Tangentopoli." A bribe to the neo-Fascists would, on the whole, have been a bribe wasted—after all, the party had had no power on the national level. The neo-Fascist party thus managed to absorb millions of voters left homeless by the discredited Christian Democrats, especially in southern Italy, trebling its electoral base. In cities like Rome, Naples, and Bari, where it had always had a traditionally strong showing—around 8 to 10 percent—in depressed working-class areas, it has become the biggest or second-biggest party. Gianfranco Fini was nearly elected mayor of Rome in the municipal elections of November 1993, and in the first round of the elections the party emerged as the most popular in the Italian capital. The pollsters had miscalculated the final result of more than 30 percent for the neo-Fascists by around 10 points. The reason was that many of the voters who had been questioned when they had left the polling booth had been too embarrassed to admit that they had voted neo-Fascist.

It didn't take long, however, for the old taboos to be swept away. The neo-Fascists had come out of the closet. The square-jawed face and dark glare of the "Redeemer of the Heavens" began to appear on magazine covers all over the country. A rash of Mussolini publications, from 1,000-lire short biographies to cartoons, video biographies, and cassettes of his speeches, started to appear on newsstands. The book retailer Feltrinelli noted that the number of publications dealing with fascism and Mussolini had trebled to 2,300 in one year. Il Duce was back in fashion. So, too, was his voluptuous, then-thirty-year-old granddaughter, Alessandra. In 1994 she was elected to Parliament for her second term, her surname no longer an embarrassment but her main political asset.

The neo-Fascists have become socially acceptable, not to say fashionable. After the municipal elections in Rome, posters started to appear on the city's walls and billboards, advertising a Mediterranean cruise in the company of Gianfranco Fini. The cruise ship was the *Achille Lauro,* the same one that had been hijacked by Palestinian terrorists in 1984 and that later sank in November 1994 off the coast of Somalia. The ship was named after a former mayor of Naples, an extreme-right-wing populist who had also been one of Italy's wealthiest shipowners. The berths were sold out as early as February. The neo-Fascist travel bureau, next to the party's modest headquarters, was doing a roaring trade in tiepins with the party emblem, a small, almost self-effacing flame in the Italian colors of red, white, and green that flickers eternally for Il Duce. There were similarly emblazoned lighters, handkerchiefs, and watches. And for those who couldn't get onto the cruise, there was always the neo-Fascist ski weekend in the Abruzzi mountains or the hiking weekend with lectures on the fauna and flora of the mountains east of Rome. The neo-Fascists know how to enjoy themselves, and they no longer have to do so in private. In fact, all over Europe they have come out of the closet. In Germany, the extreme-right-wing Republicans are making gains at the polls, especially in depressed inner-city areas. In France, Jean-Marie Le Pen of the National Front has managed to dictate the national agenda on immigration policy; once a fringe politician, he has become a serious candidate for the French presidency. Throughout Europe, issues such as immigration, long-term unemployment, and economic insecurity have helped the right, and in some places the extreme right, though they remain in the minority. But Italy is unique as a country that defeated Fascism five decades ago only to find its heirs democratically reelected to power.

The presence of a Mussolini in Parliament and the neo-Fascists in government has forced the Italians to reexamine their past. Previously, the Fascist era had been hidden under the blanket of postwar political consensus. Whereas the Germans had at least made some attempt to ask how the rape of democracy, human rights, and civilization under Hitler had been possible, the Italians had opted for collective amnesia. One could justifiably argue that Nazi Germany had more reason to atone for its sins than Mussolini's Italy did. Nevertheless, the Italians had spent little time after 1945 asking why their fledgling democracy had collapsed so swiftly in the early 1920s. One indication of this willful amnesia is the fact that the history taught in Italian schools barely touches on the subject of Mussolini and Fascism. While textbooks devote entire chapters to the Risorgimento, the period between 1922 and 1945 gets an almost perfunctory mention.

Initially this attitude had less to do with self-censorship or a whitewashing of history than with a desire to heal the country's internal rift. Between 1943 and 1945 Italy was torn apart by what amounted to a vicious civil war between Communist partisans and the remnants of Fascism. The situation was further aggravated by the fact that the Nazis, who had occupied northern and central Italy after the fall of Mussolini, punished Fascist Italy for deserting Germany just as the fortunes of war were turning against it. Field Marshal Albert Kesselring, the Nazi commander of occupied Italy, not only sent 18,000 Italian Jews to their deaths in German extermination camps, he also deported almost a million Italians to Germany to perform forced labor in the Reich's factories. "The German generals sought revenge for Italy's betrayal," historian Richard Lamb wrote in his book *War in Italy, 1943–45.* "They wanted to treat her like Poland and the occupied countries."

After the war, the Nazis' humiliation gave both sides a common enemy. It may even have helped to heal some of the rifts. In any case a pragmatic decision was made in 1946 by Italy's allies, the Catholic Church, the Christian Democrats, and even the Communists, to reconcile. Palmiro Togliatti, the leader of the Italian Communist Party who lived in exile in Moscow during the Mussolini years, became minister of justice in 1946 for a year, the first and the last time the Communists were to hold a ministerial post. In turn, Togliatti, who sought a modus vivendi with the Christian Democrats, signed a decree abolishing the policy of *epurazione,* or purging, which had been introduced only a year earlier and under which Fascist elements were supposed to be weeded out of the bureaucracy and brought to trial.

The decision may not have been entirely the result of considered political judgment, as *epurazione* had in fact turned out to be a resounding failure. While it was being enforced, it purged low-ranking members of the Fascist rank and file while those responsible for some of the worst abuses of Fascism were left untouched. A grotesque distinction was made between "ordinary tortures" and "tortures that were particularly atrocious." Thanks to this distinction, many appalling crimes went unpunished. One, involving electric torture of a partisan's genitals applied with a field telephone, was pardoned by Italy's highest court because "it took place only for intimidatory purposes and not through bestial insensibility." While Togliatti's general amnesty ended a policy that had become distorted and unfair, the fact that the decree to ditch it had been signed by the head of the Communist Party, who had been forced into exile by Mussolini, was a remarkably nimble act of reconciliation. Many former partisans never forgave the leader of their party, especially since the Allies and the Christian Democrats made many more efforts to exclude Communists from power than they did former Fascists.

Officials from the former Fascist administration of the Republic of Salò, Il Duce's puppet state set up by the Nazis behind German lines in 1944, benefited widely from the republic's recruitment policy. Some never even left their jobs. In 1960, sixty-two of the sixty-four prefects, the principal representatives of the central government in the provinces, had been senior officials in the Fascist regime. All of the 135 police chiefs and their 139 deputies had been functionaries under Fascism. Despite the continuity of Fascist officialdom, the Fascist

Party was outlawed. Its successor party, the Italian Social Movement, which took its name from the Italian Social Republic—the official title of Mussolini's Nazi puppet state—was tolerated but marginalized. One of its defects was that it was founded in 1946, after the Italian Constitution had been written. The Italian Social Movement was the only mainstream party in Parliament that had thus not participated in the drafting of Italy's liberal Constitution. It compounded the situation by maintaining an ambiguous stance toward democracy. Until the late 1980s the Italian Social Movement advocated an alternative to the "system." Nevertheless, because the Right and the Left had both decided to bury the country's Fascist past, the Italian Social Movement was able to linger inoffensively on the margins of Italian politics as a kind of mutual aid society for survivors from the Fascist regime.

This cozy modus vivendi disappeared with the *partitocrazia* and the return of the neo-Fascists to power after five decades of disenfranchisement. The anesthetic had worn off, and history was whitewashed or blackened, according to which side you belonged to. Essentially the Left tried to show that Gianfranco Fini's party, now called the National Alliance to attract more moderate elements of the right from the former Christian Democratic Party, was the direct heir to Mussolini's blackshirts. Meanwhile, Silvio Berlusconi and the neo-Fascists themselves wanted to prove that they were no longer Fascists, but at the same time Fini insisted that Mussolini should not be demonized. Fini's simultaneous rejection of Fascism and continued worship of Mussolini amounted to a puzzling high-wire act, necessary because he had to satisfy both the hard-liners who represented the bedrock of his party and the general public nurtured for decades on the taboo against neo-Fascists.

As Fini became more and more adept at his ideological balancing act, the Mussolini years, which had been so studiously ignored for decades, were being dissected and debated on television, in the newspapers, and in the piazzas. One historical document in particular reawakened ghosts of the past that many thought had been buried forever. In April 1994, shortly after the victory of the right in the national elections, Italian state television showed the so-called "combat film." This black-and-white film, shot by an American soldier who

had entered Milan in April 1945 with the Allied forces, had been un-
earthed at the Library of Congress in Washington, D.C. It showed
some of the most painful and gruesome moments of Italian wartime
history. One was the lynching of Mussolini. Il Duce, his mistress,
Claretta Petacci, and a dozen or so Fascists still loyal to him had been
caught by Communist partisans while trying to escape across partisan
lines into Austria disguised as retreating German soldiers. Mussolini
was wearing a German Wehrmacht coat and an ill-fitting helmet that
failed to hide his distinctive features and jutting chin. It is not certain
where or under what circumstances Mussolini and his entourage were
executed, but the combat film shows clearly what happened next. The
bodies were taken to the Piazzale Loreto in the center of Milan. A
huge, angry mob had gathered. The bodies were kicked and spat at.
A collection was organized to pay for the funeral. Then a group of
partisans hung Mussolini and the others by the feet from the metal
awning of a gas station in the square. As Petacci dangled head-down,
her skirt fell over her bruised, bloodstained face to reveal her underwear. A priest pinned the skirt back up. The name of each person executed was scrawled on the awning with an arrow pointing to the
corresponding pair of feet. Mussolini's name was in large capital letters. Later the cameraman found the bodies abandoned on a platform
at the nearby train station. This time there were no crowds. The cameraman propped Mussolini, whose face was squashed, up against a
wall and put his dead mistress next to him, her head resting on his
shoulder. The two looked like lovers relaxing after a picnic. A name
tag with the name Mussolini and the number 168 written on it dangled by their side.

The mutilation of the bodies of Mussolini and his entourage by
the mob had been described many times in graphic detail, but its de-
piction on film made a powerful impact. To many neo-Fascists, it illustrated how one of the greatest Italian statesmen had been betrayed
and defiled by his own people. Mussolini's violent death became a
symbol for what the neo-Fascists regard as the hypocritical "anti-
Fascism" of the great majority of Italians, who had worshipped Il
Duce until 1943. Intoxicated by nostalgia, they failed to see that the
Italians were also punishing Il Duce for his gross incompetence, for
the fact that he had led Italy into a disastrous war for which it had

been ill prepared, allied with a country that had ended up humiliating it. As if to mirror the debate that had been fueled across the country, RAI invited a panel of former partisans and Fascist sympathizers to see the film with a studio audience. The debate became more and more heated, the participants squirming as the gruesome past was dredged up before their eyes once again. The hatred between Left and Right that had been dormant for decades flared up once more.

Any attempts by the neo-Fascists to revise history with the "combat film" were soon undermined by the second installment. This showed the aftermath of the massacre of 335 civilians, Communists, partisans, and Jews by the Gestapo and the SS in Rome in March 1944. The massacre in the Ardeatine caves outside Rome was organized to avenge the killing of thirty-two SS soldiers in the center of Rome on March 23, when Italian partisans had detonated a bomb in the Via Rasella while a company of SS soldiers marched past. Hitler was so angered by the attack that he originally wanted fifty Italians killed for every dead SS soldier. But Field Marshal Kesselring persuaded Hitler that the ratio of revenge should be brought down to ten Italians for every dead German. The head of the Gestapo in Rome, Major Herbert Kappler, had told Kesselring that he could find 320 Italian prisoners who had already been condemned to death. When he examined his records, he found there were only three.

Working all night on the list, Kappler could find only 270 Italians in German custody in all of Rome. He asked the Italian Fascist police chief in the capital, Pietro Caruso, to make up the shortfall of fifty. With the permission of Buffarini Guidi, Mussolini's interior minister, Caruso obliged the Gestapo. A raid was organized on the Jewish ghetto, where fifty innocent civilians and another twenty-five "for good measure" were rounded up and taken with the other prisoners to the Ardeatine caves. There they were led into the caves in groups of five, listening to the screams of the group in front of them, then shot in the back of the head by SS officers. The Wehrmacht had refused to take part in the operation. The shooting lasted six hours. In an affidavit to Field Marshal Kesselring's trial at Nuremberg, Major Kappler, who had been in charge of the operation, described how he had ordered his men to get drunk on brandy after the massacre. In a matter-of-fact manner he recalled how he had led one reluctant German private into the cave "in a companionable way" and how they had shot a group of prisoners in the head. Six hours later, when the shooting had ended, German army engineers blew up the cave in an attempt to bury the evidence. When the Allies liberated Rome later that year, the cave was opened and the decomposed bodies were retrieved. This is the scene shown in the documentary film: hundreds of wives, girlfriends, and mothers being led to the Ardeatine caves to identify corpses. Mass was celebrated outside the caves, and then the women were led inside one by one. Ten minutes later they emerged into daylight crying and screaming, devastated by the sight of their relatives reduced to bones. Despite the resentment felt by the Italian Fascists for their German occupiers, the film was a reminder that the Nazi atrocities in Italy had been committed with the connivance or tacit cooperation of the Fascist authorities. Before the Germans marched into Rome, Mussolini himself had urged Hitler not to spare the city's palaces and ancient ruins, if their destruction was the price of occupation.

The film elicited a powerful response on both sides of the old ideological divide. Newspaper headlines warned about a creeping revisionism. History had become politicized, the past had once again merged with the present. A country that five minutes after the fall of Mussolini began to pretend that Fascism had never existed now found itself divided by history. On April 25, 1994—Liberation Day—the Democratic Party of the Left, which had just lost in the elections, was determined to win the moral high ground by organizing a massive demonstration in Milan, ostensibly "for national reconciliation and against Fascism." The real target of the rally was, of course, the right-wing government that had just been elected. Never before had such a large rally been organized on Liberation Day. More than 200,000 people streamed into the streets in torrential rain. The Italians are masters at organizing rallies, and they weren't going to be daunted by the wet weather. A colorful carnival of union banners, brass bands, party leaders, party hacks with red flags, hooded anarchists, reformed Communists, unreconstructed Marxists, and tens of thousands of ordinary umbrella carriers made their way to the Piazza del Duomo in front of the cathedral. It was an extraordinary turnout. One housewife told me she had been driven into the streets by the neo-Fascists: "We must not let them forget the past." A taxi driver said he was "marching for democracy"; another man said he was frightened by "the return of ghosts from the past." The only right-wing leader to take part in the procession was Umberto Bossi and the Northern League mayor of Milan, Marco Formentini. Both were heckled as they arrived. Some demonstrators shouted, "Racists, traitors, Fascists!"

Meanwhile, in Rome, Gianfranco Fini went to a remembrance Mass and later preached reconciliation to the press. A spokesman for Silvio Berlusconi announced that the tycoon was staying at home with his family in their villa at Arcore outside Milan. He followed the events of the day on television and later went to his private chapel to pray for social harmony in the company of his family and a few close friends. Two weeks later he finally announced the lineup of his Cabinet, which included five ministers from the National Alliance. None of them was a hard-liner from the former Italian Social Movement. Nevertheless, they belonged to the neo-Fascist camp. The left-wing *Manifesto* newspaper greeted the announcement with a solid-black front page, representing the neo-Fascists' victory as a kind of coup staged by ghosts from the past. The fact was that five million Italians had voted for the National Alliance. Under the agreement reached with Forza Italia and the Northern League, it had fielded no candidates in the North of Italy, but it had become the dominant party in the South. And as time went on, Gianfranco Fini, who knew how to look on in dignified silence while his coalition partners squabbled in public, rose steadily in the opinion polls. By the summer of 1994, he had become the country's most popular politician.

With him a new breed of very old politicians burst out of the closet. Although Fini himself was born seven years after the death of Mussolini, some of his associates had not only been alive when Il Duce was in power, they had ruled with him. Ajmone Finestra was one of them. Diminutive and feisty, the seventy-three-year-old neo-Fascist mayor of Latina was elected in December 1994 with a resounding majority. His party had received 57 percent of the votes, an unprecedented amount for any list in Latina. The voters had rallied to the neo-Fascists' call for order and clean government, as they had done in scores of other cities. Finestra invited me to lunch at the local tennis club to celebrate his victory. The freckled terra-cotta walls were decorated with art deco lights and stylish photographs of Mussolini and of Latina's Fascist architecture, which the mayor had commissioned. Twirls of nouvelle cuisine pasta—black spaghetti with pink salmon sauce—were served on large plates, accompanied by white wine or the "lightly fizzy" mineral water that has become fashionable in Italy. The murmur of *sotto voce* small talk was drowned out now and again when Finestra raised his voice to hammer home a point to the city's new cultural officer, a frail-looking woman seated on his left. Slim-line cell phones rang with great regularity.

The mayor is a former sports coach and local businessman. Despite his age, he still does fifty push-ups a day and rides a horse named Charlie. He owns the local fitness club and opened the first physiotherapy center in the region, which he believes may account for the fact that so many handicapped people voted for him. Finestra seems like a thoroughly good chap. Why, I asked the mayor, had he won? He put his hand on my shoulder and said, "A winning smile? People think I'm a nice guy." Then he smiled winningly, displaying two rows of small but perfect teeth. His gold-rimmed half-moon spectacles gave him the air of an eminent surgeon. "And," he continued, "people respect me as an honest man." Thanks to the corruption scandal and decades of festering lies, half-truths, and empty promises, the Italian voters rate honesty very high. And Ajmone Finestra is disarmingly honest, even about his past. He was proud to have been a Fascist, he told me. But he abhors the term "neo-Fascist." "This sounds like neo-Nazi. We are not Nazis. Mussolini was never a Nazi." The voice crescendoed. The rest of the table fell silent. "Not *neo*-Fascist," the mayor corrected me, "*post*-Fascist." Okay, I thought, post-Fascist. Neo, post, crypto, quasi . . . the fact is that the party that was founded in 1948 to carry the torch of Fascism into the future still clings to the man who inspired it.

In 1946 the mayor with the winning smile was tried for ordering the execution of a dozen Communist partisans. Finestra had served as a lieutenant in Mussolini's army and as a government official in the Republic of Salò. He was found guilty and received a sixteen-year prison sentence. Shortly afterward, he and 36,000 other Fascists were released from jail under the general amnesty signed by Palmiro Togliatti. In the climate of forgiveness, Finestra went on to prosper first as a businessman and then as a politician. Before becoming mayor, he was also a parliamentary deputy for the Italian Social Movement.

Latina provided the perfect setting for Finestra's comeback. The city of 120,000 people is Fascism preserved in cement. Originally called Littoria, it was founded by Mussolini in 1932 as a Fascist model city and as part of Il Duce's settlement program for the Pontine marshes, a vast flat expanse south of Rome. The marshes had been drained by Mussolini in the late 1920s and were one of the dictator's few successful economic projects, revered by neo-Fascists as much as those famously punctual trains. Littoria was populated with destitute families from all over Italy, poor peasants from the Veneto and Calabria, unemployed blue-collar workers from Lombardy, dispossessed Italians from Istria on the Dalmatian coast of the former Yugoslavia. As elsewhere in Italy, most of Latina's former Fascists switched their allegiance to the Christian Democrats. Nevertheless, the city always harbored a quiet adoration for Il Duce, whose monumental architecture still serves as a powerful reminder of the city's founder. In fact, Latina must be one of the few Italian cities whose Fascist architecture is conspicuous by its beauty. The square-jawed Palazzo di Giustizia, the jackbooted cathedral straddling the square between the skulllike dome of the House of Youth—the inscription is as legible as it was fifty years ago—and the boxlike Veterans' Home are Latina's architectural highlights.

The rest is a monument to postwar *abusivismo* and the excesses of the *partitocrazia*. Latina has been scarred by a particularly virulent bout of unfettered construction. The brutalist church spire competes for ugliness with a vast water tower that rises out of the urban sprawl like a cement mushroom. The maze of red brick and gray cement tower blocks, worthy of any Eastern European satellite town, are the fruits of four decades of clientelism that further strengthened the Christian Democrats' hold over the city and its electorate. Votes were shamelessly bought and sold for political favors, and, according to the editor of the local newspaper, *Latina Oggi,* more than 30 percent of all jobs in Latina's medium-sized industries depended on the Christian Democratic Party. This accounts for the fact that some 34 percent of the electorate still voted for the Christian Democrats in the municipal elections of 1993, despite the corruption probes. It takes more than a trial and public disgrace to break the bonds between client and protector.

Inevitably Latina too became engulfed in the corruption scandal. Twenty-one of the city's forty town councillors were arrested for bribery. The mayor was put under investigation. The city government was dissolved, and the affairs of Latina were run by a state prefect, a Pisan dispatched from Rome. The Christian Democrats had not only left a cement nightmare, they had also bankrupted the city by pouring billions of lire into a fleet of buses that never ran and a trash collection network that remains mostly idle. The exact size of the city's debt is still a mystery; on their way to jail, the outgoing Christian Democrats were careful to shred some of the more incriminating files. As in so many other cities, the neo-Fascist candidate—Ajmone Finestra—emerged as the only "Mr. Clean," probably by dint of never having been in power. Honesty and a clean record may not be the only requirements for running a city with a huge deficit and social problems, but for now they are a prerequisite for getting elected. What the mayor's program lacks in detail, it makes up for in presentation. Addressing an audience of citizens and journalists, he began his acceptance speech in the marble chamber of Latina's town hall in a dulcet tenor only to be swept up by a dramatic crecendo in which the words *ordine, disciplina, onestà,* and *virtù* fizzed and popped like fireworks flares. Much like the Fascist movement itself, its successor, the Italian Social Movement, promised everything to everyone, often in self-contradiction. It adopted the spirit of vagueness that Mussolini had fostered for pragmatic reasons: "Fascism," he once said, "is the synthesis of every negation and every affirmation. Ideologies are a luxury for intellectuals."

The National Alliance now preaches the free-market philosophy but has also pledged to protect the jobs of government clerks in smokestack ministries and workers in some of the country's wasteful state enterprises like the much-hated SIP, the national telephone company. Italy's legions of clerks and state employees, now more beleaguered than ever, have always been the neo-Fascists' most fertile recruiting ground. The party appeals to rich and poor, to monarchists and republicans. It incorporated the old Italian Monarchist Party in

1960, even though it favors a strong presidential system along Gaullist lines. At one election rally in a vast circus tent on the outskirts of Rome, Gianfranco Fini was applauded by both skinheads in black shirts and ladies in fur. As thousands of young supporters jumped up and down like soccer fans, the aging Prince Ruspoli, a well-known salon post-Fascist, sat serenely in his chair clutching a wooden cane tipped with a golden helmet—a replica of Mussolini's helmet—and stared up at the podium with a tear rolling down his cheek.

This motley alliance of followers doesn't always see eye to eye. At a church service commemorating the anniversary of Mussolini's march on Rome in Predappio, Il Duce's birthplace in the hills of Emilia-Romagna, I was standing between a skinhead with a Mohawk cut and an elderly woman in a green hat with feathers. As the fur-lined Fascist sang along to one of the old songs, the representative of the younger generation merely hummed. He obviously didn't know the words. Outraged, the old woman leaned over to me and, pointing to the young man, whispered, "Is *he* one of us?" with a note of disgust in her voice. She was appalled to learn that he was.

The party's basic stance is that of right-wing movements everywhere: it is tough on law and order; it wants to restrict immigration; despite being a lay movement, it has a high esteem for church and family; it abhors unconventionality in whatever form; it has traditionally been suspicious of social and sexual minorities, divorce, abortion, every form of social permissiveness, and—oddly enough—vivisection. It worships the Italian nation and believes in a strong centralized state and a presidential form of government, as in France or the United States. If it hasn't been able to restore the vanished era of Fascism, it has at least been able to keep the memory of Fascism alive. Before the party took its place in the ruling coalition, one of its main functions was to organize Fascist festivities on important anniversaries such as the march on Rome. These pageants tended to be colorful, harmless, and often absurd events. The only neo-Fascist torchlight parade I have ever seen involved fruit salads. At a large dinner for more than a thousand party faithful, the chef revealed his political affiliation in the dessert. Out of each bowl of sliced kiwis, apples, and oranges rose a clenched silver fist holding a small gas flame. The lights were dimmed, and the bowls were carried in by a procession of strutting waiters. Verdi's *Aïda* blared out of the loudspeakers. The faithful stood up and saluted the fruit salads.

That's the innocent side of the party. The key question mark is its commitment to the Italian Constitution and democracy. In the past it has been ambiguous on this sensitive subject. At its congress in 1973 it adopted "an alternative to the system": it condemned the use of force to change society but never explicitly recognized the Italian Constitution. The party also has a more shadowy tradition to live down. Some of its deputies and high-ranking officials have been implicated in coup plots and other acts of subversion fostered by Italy's murky secret services. One Italian Social Movement deputy with a shadowy past was Sandro Sanducci. Like Ajmeno Finestra a former official in the Republic of Salò, he took part in the farcical coup attempt led by Prince Valerio Borghese in 1970. During the time of the Republic of Salò the prince had headed one of the most ferocious armed groups, the Decima Mas, which had been virtually independent of the Fascist government and had worked closely with the Nazi occupation forces. At one time Borghese had even threatened to imprison Mussolini, who was increasingly concerned about the independence of these gangs of thugs. On December 7, 1970, the prince assembled two hundred of his armed followers from the National Forestry Service on the outskirts of Rome. The plan was to occupy the television station and the Interior Ministry. But the coup soon descended into black farce with key commanders disagreeing and fighting among themselves. Most of the forestry workers abandoned the coup and went home for dinner. But some, it was later admitted by Giulio Andreotti, who was defense minister at the time, did manage to enter the Interior Ministry. The government also had information that a right-wing terrorist group possessed plans to poison water supplies with radioactive material, which was to be stolen from a nuclear reactor in northern Italy. Even more worrying was the fact that the investigations into the coup had implicated the head of the intelligence services, General Vito Miceli. Miceli was arrested on suspicion of subversion, accused of knowing about the plot, and charged with conspiracy. In 1974 he was acquitted for lack of evidence. In 1976 he was elected to Parliament as a deputy for the Italian Social Movement. In 1980 his name was discovered on the membership list of the notorious P2 Masonic lodge of Licio Gelli. Described as a "creeping coup" because it tried to set up an alternative power structure, the lodge, a parliamentary investigation discovered, was also familiar with the Borghese plot.

Another man who casts a black shadow on the National Alliance is Pino Rauti. This former hothead was elected the party's secretary in 1990. Three decades earlier he had founded an extreme-right-wing terrorist organization named New Order. As the defense correspondent of the right-wing newspaper *Il Tempo,* he had often given lectures in the United States on military affairs, including one paper entitled "Techniques and Possibilities of a Coup d'État in Europe" delivered at the U.S. Naval Academy in Annapolis in 1961.

The list of unsavory relics was long. Guido Leto, head of Mussolini's secret service in the Republic of Salò, was cleared of all war crimes and then promoted in 1946 to director of Italy's police schools. Giuseppe Pieche had been a general in the Fascist carabinieri and had helped coordinate Italian military assistance to Spain's Francisco Franco and to Croatia's Ustashe dictator, Ante Pavelić. Freed by the amnesty, he had later been put in charge of the Interior Ministry's fire department, a front for his real job in police intelligence. General Pieche's main task had been to oversee the retirement policy of the police force, under which former members of the pro-Communist resistance were retired at the tender age of forty and former Fascist policemen not until sixty. With such a cast of characters, it's not surprising that the Italian Social Movement's loyalty to the Italian Constitution has been called into question again and again. The party is only now trying to emerge from the twilight of illegality. Its former leader Giorgio Almirante fostered a dual tactic of overt democratic respectability and covert encouragement of the "strategy of tension." Under Gianfranco Fini the National Alliance has ditched its rejection of the "system" and has bent over backward to be accepted by the political mainstream.

Fini is without doubt the party's biggest attraction, especially for those supporters who are not motivated by nostalgia for the prewar brand of fascism. Fini has an unlikely background for a neo-Fascist. He was born seven years after Mussolini's death in Bologna, the capital of Italian communism. His family was wealthy, professional, and middle-class and—typical for this city—voted Communist. When I interviewed him, he told me that he had turned to the Italian Social Movement in 1968 because it was the only party that represented a real opposition to the Communists. "Even then I was branded a Fascist for my anti-communism." With his boyish good looks, his smooth, tanned skin, and his round professorial spectacles, Fini stands out among the pitted, cowed grimaces that are more usual in the ranks of the Italian Social Movement. The party, often the home of Italy's political and social outcasts, has always borne the mark of insecurity. Its members have usually radiated resentment against just about everything: the rich, the poor, foreigners, northern Italians. . . . In such company the tall, handsome, supremely confident Fini is an implausible figure.

While the rest of Europe was commemorating D-day, Fini told *Panorama* magazine that "the liberation of Europe by the Americans meant the loss of Europe's identity." What, one wondered, was Fini thinking of? Was he shedding a tear for the identity represented by Hitler and Mussolini? The fact that Fini, who is an extremely shrewd politician, has been able to make one public relations gaffe after another has raised the suspicion that he still worships at Il Duce's shrine, even though, when pressed, he plays down his allegiance to Mussolini. "So what *do* you stand for?" I asked him. He sat back, smiled, and said, listing the points on his fingers, "Democracy—the only system for governing a people—social solidarity, the environment, and of course peace." As he finished the list, he grinned. The question is whether his entry into the government and the political mainstream has exorcised his adoration for Mussolini and whether he can afford to leave behind those members of his party who still cling to the past.

Gianfranco Fini has attracted many center-right voters who would never have touched the Italian Social Movement with a barge pole but were driven right by the collapse of the center. Fini has become socially acceptable. He is at pains to describe his party as right wing, conservative, nationalist—anything but neo-Fascist. In December 1993 he launched the campaign to change the party's name to National Alliance with a visit to the Ardeatine caves. In 1994 he went on a goodwill tour to the United States to reassure the Jewish community and U.S. legislators that they had nothing to fear from his movement. Back in Italy, he laid wreaths in memory of the victims of Fascism, sounding as reasonable and mild mannered as a Swedish Social Democrat.

Fini has clearly distanced himself from the worst outrages of Fascism and Nazism. But does he truly represent his party? Although he may have replaced black shirts with (dark) gray suits and the Fascists' Roman salutes with (firm) handshakes, he has not been able to change the source of his party's appeal. Mussolini still has a magnetic attraction for the party's members, as well as for Fini himself. On one level there is a pragmatic explanation for the Mussolini cult. The National Alliance clung to Il Duce in the same way that the Northern League reveres Alberto da Guissano. These are the figures and the traditions that distinguished their parties from Prime Minister Berlusconi's Forza Italia.

But by the end of 1994 the need for the neo-Fascist party to distinguish itself with nostalgia gradually faded away. Fini had skillfully engineered the MSI's metamorphosis into the broader and more mainstream church of the National Alliance. This purifying ritual culminated in a special congress in the mountain spa resort of Fiuggi south of Rome. Famous for healing gout and stomach disorders, the waters of Fiuggi were now called upon to turn neo-Fascists into post-Fascists. To achieve a credible conversion, Fini needed the conference to adopt a new charter that stated that democracy was the only acceptable form of government, denounced all forms of totalitarianism, and ditched any dewy-eyed adherence to Mussolini. He also needed a small group of extremist dissidents with which to contrast the new moderate party. In the end, the number of dissidents was almost embarrassingly small. Only Pino Rauti and a handful of delegates boycotted the new charter and formed their own "Fascist Refoundation." As the MSI's hymn was played for the last time, I counted no more than three Fascist salutes. Fini had persuaded the party that the compromise of power was preferable to the chastity of ideologically pure but permanent opposition.

The conversion of the MSI was also helped by the decline of Forza Italia and by the behavior of Silvio Berlusconi, especially after he was ousted from power in December 1994. The media tycoon tried to provoke early elections, which he was convinced would bring him back to power by torpedoeing the crucial minibudget in March 1995 and thus removing Prime Minister Lamberto Dini's government of unelected technocrats from office. Had he succeeded, it would probably have sent the lira, which had already reached an all-time low of 1,200 to the deutschmark, through the floor. While Berlusconi tampered with the stability of the country for the sake of getting back into power, Fini maintained his dignified silence and his consistently high ratings in the opinion polls. It was Berlusconi who had become the extremist, and at the end of March 1995 the Italian media were talking openly about a leadership battle on the right, tipping Fini as the future head of a new center-right party comprising the National Alliance and the remnants of Forza Italia.

But the National Alliance has also occupied another important role as the southern answer to the Northern League. Its support is concentrated in regions stretching from Rome and Lazio south to the tip of Puglia, where it has become the voice of discontent. Its nationalism and its worship of a strong, united Italy are a cry for help from millions of Italians who fear that a Federation of Italy will force Campania, Calabria, Puglia, and Sicily to drift toward Tunisia and away from the European Union. The fears of the traditional supporters of the former Italian Social Movement—the white-collar workers and clerks of the vast southern bureaucracy as well as blue-collar workers in large cities like Bari and Naples—have now become the fears of a much wider part of the population. Their feistiest champion is the honorable Alessandra Mussolini, Il Duce's Neapolitan granddaughter, who has become a neo-Fascist Joan of Arc for the Mezzogiorno, Italy's southern half.

The rise of Alessandra is a Neapolitan family saga. When she entered politics in February 1992, she was "presented" to the press by her father, Romero Mussolini, a well-known jazz pianist and Il Duce's youngest son. Mr. Mussolini stood up and in a moving introduction praised his daughter's intelligence and beauty and described her as "my little songbird." At this stage a phalanx of octogenarian Fascists seated in the back row got carried away and stood up, shouting "Duce! Duce! Duce!" with their fists in the air.

Nowadays such public eruptions of nostalgic fervor wouldn't be allowed by the party leadership. Had Alessandra not been a Mussolini, she might never have entered politics. The Italian Social Movement discovered her in the same way someone comes across a precious family heirloom while rummaging through the attic. Il Duce's granddaughter abandoned a flagging career as a part-time actress for politics. In a country more puritanical than Italy, her past would have created a public relations nightmare and would probably have doomed her to political failure. In 1983 she posed nude for *Playboy* magazine. In 1986 she undressed—completely, no panties, no gauze—for the German soft-porn weekly *Quick.* All of this is potentially embarrassing. Oddly enough, it was never used by the opposition—perhaps because the pictures would have boosted her support. It was also discovered that Ms. Mussolini, who describes herself as a mature student of medicine, had cheated at exams and tried to buy her degree. This too didn't create a scandal. "Good for her, she tried to beat the system" was the common response. Ms. Mussolini may be new to politics, but she is not a wallflower. "The Mouth from the South," as the journalist Fiammetta Rocco described her, cajoles, caresses, and prods her audiences like a Neapolitan housewife. The Black Madonna, as her foes call her, wags her finger at voters and rolls her big eyeballs like an actress in a cheap Chinese opera. She clearly feels the family's rhetorical calling. Being shouted at by La Mussolini is a terrifying experience. When I asked her on one occasion whether she would still describe herself as a Fascist, she screeched, "You foreign journalists are all stupid. Stupid!" She almost spat the word. But for many there is something deeply reassuring about this fiery, pouting matron. The anxieties, fears, hang-ups, and inferiority complexes of both men and women seem to melt away in her presence.

Aging party hacks with gray tired faces feed off her young blood like political vampires. She embodies the Italian Social Movement's spirit of rejuvenation, as if the party's prayers had been answered. As one old Neapolitan woman put it to me, "Il Duce has sent us a granddaughter!" La Mussolini is unashamedly proud of her grandfather and calls herself a "Mussolinista." As she weaves her way through the dank urban maze of old Naples, she is hugged, squeezed, and kissed by fat mamas and gawped at by men. She is not embarrassed. "Go on, look! Have a good long look!" she seems to be saying.

In the picturesque squalor of Naples, La Mussolini offers a vague hope of improvement for people who have lost all faith in government. In the dark teeming maze of old Naples, some buildings are still propped up by scaffolding after the 1980 earthquake. Nothing has been done to repair them, despite millions of dollars in aid from Rome and the European Union. Most of the money has been squandered by the city's politicians shopping for votes. I went into one shop where an old man and his surly daughter were making Christmas cribs. "I'm a Fascist," said the man. "I've always been a Fascist, and I'm proud to be able to vote for Il Duce's granddaughter." "What will she do to improve your life?" I asked. The man paused, thought for a moment, and then said, "What can she do that's worse?" he replied. His daughter nodded in agreement.

Everyone in Naples hopes for a miracle. In the mayoral elections of 1993, just under half the city voters thought it might come from the neo-Fascists and Mussolini, and just over half turned to the Democratic Party of the Left and the incumbent mayor, Antonio Bassolino. He was elected mayor, but Alessandra Mussolini received more than 50 percent of the vote in the simultaneous parliamentary elections, a huge proportion by Italian standards. The other family connection in Mussolini's life is her aunt Sophia Loren, who was born in Pozzuoli on the outskirts of the city. This counts for a lot in Naples. The fact that Loren has publicly criticized her niece's politics has caused some bitterness in the Mussolini camp.

The future of the National Alliance and its attempts to become a moderate party of the right depend largely on the economic plight of the Mezzogiorno and big cities like Naples, Bari, and Rome, where the party is now the most popular political force. Rising unemployment, mass layoffs, and concerns over immigration are all likely to fuel the extremist elements that are trying to find a home in the party. Although deputies like Alessandra Mussolini and Pino Rauti are currently being marginalized, their hour of glory may still lie ahead. Like so much else in Italian politics at the moment, the National Alliance is in the middle of a delicate conversion process whose path has not been fixed. It does not represent a rebirth of old-style Fascism or totalitarianism. Democracy is firmly rooted in Italy, and will not be sacrificed as it was in 1922. Like Fascism, neo-Fascism is too woolly, contradictory, and incoherent to provide the magnetic attraction of a genuine ideology. To be magnetic, it needs a charismatic leader, and though intelligent, telegenic, and articulate, Fini is no political messiah. First and foremost, he is a man seeking recognition rather than upheaval. Decades on the sideline have made his once-ostracized party yearn for acceptance and a share of power. Furthermore, the party was only one of three coalition partners that invested their energies mostly in fighting one another rather than in shaping society.

But doubts remain. If the neo-Fascists can be so blinkered about the past and overlook Mussolini's worst outrages and blunders, can one trust them to run anything more serious than a march to commemorate Il Duce's birthday? So far Gianfranco Fini has thrived in the opinion polls, largely because he has maintained a serene silence while his partners have thrown mud at one another. His grasp of many practical issues from the economy to foreign policy is distinctly tenuous. But the most worrying aspect of the National Alliance is not the dewy-eyed nostalgia of some of its members for Mussolini, it is the fact that the party's appeal is still based on grudges, resentments, and inferiority complexes. The self-confident, suave Fini gives a misleading impression. Visiting any of the constituent organizations of the National Alliance in Rome, Bari, or Naples, one is struck by an atmosphere of restrained menace. In the National Alliance office in Rome's San Lorenzo district, young men lounge around in smoke-filled rooms declaring their love for democracy and tolerance to the cameras. Meanwhile, busts of Mussolini are stacked high in one corner and the walls outside are daubed with Fascist graffiti and slogans like ITALY FOR THE ITALIANS, WHITE ORDER WILL PREVAIL, and FUCK OFF, DARKIES, to mention but a few. An alarming increase in racist attacks in a country that has always been kinder toward its immigrants than has France or Germany indicates that Italian tolerance also has its limitations, especially as the number of illegal immigrants continues to rise. Italy has two thousand miles of open coastline, providing a relatively easy port of call for any Albanian or north African immigrant in search of a job picking olives or grapes. The National Alliance has indeed been trying to introduce tougher legislation on illegal immigrants, currently thought to number about 450,000. A draft law introduced in October 1994 proposed that all illegal immigrants who were under investigation for any crime, however petty, should immediately be expelled from Italy.

Do the thugs now think they have a license to flex their muscles against anyone who arouses their resentment? Many Italians have similar questions about the Northern League and its petty localism and macho morality. Both parties represent a culture of intolerance and what a well-known Sicilian sociologist has called a "rejection of social solidarity." While graffiti in Milan tells the Calabrian factory worker "go home," graffiti in Calabria tell the Moroccan immigrant to get out of the country. Everywhere the search for a scapegoat is on. The National Alliance is unique because it represents the direct heirs of a totalitarian regime that was ousted five decades ago, but its worship of law and order, its nationalism, and its immigration policy have their counterparts in Europe and North America. They represent a growing general disenchantment with the postwar democracies that are not only unable to ensure continuing levels of employment and well-being but also unable to fill the gaping spiritual void left by a rampant consumer culture. Observers are watching Italy closely for clues as to how the disenchantment might play out in their own countries. For Italy the biggest danger lies in the combination of social resentment, represented by the National Alliance, with the television politics of media tycoon Silvio Berlusconi.

Silvio Berlusconi

The Triumph of
Television and
Soccer in Politics

Picture a man who owns three television channels attracting almost half a nation's viewers, around twenty-five million people. The same man also controls 60 percent of all television advertising. The advertisements put out by his company Publitalia sell the products of the country's biggest supermarket chain, Standa, which he also owns. Their food is eaten in tens of thousands of homes, holiday villages, and suburban satellite towns built by one of the country's biggest real estate empires, Edilnord, which is run by the man's brother. On the coffee table in front of the television set are three magazines, including *TV Sorrisi e Canzoni* (TV Smiles and Songs), the country's best-selling listings weekly. They're all published by Mondadori, a company, needless to say, owned by the man. His publishing house also own 25 percent of all copyrights on Italian authors. You have just finished watching a video from one of the biggest film libraries outside Hollywood—courtesy of the man, of course—and now you're settling down to watch the final of the national soccer championships. But before resuming your television viewing, you may just want to read a pamphlet about life insurance that has landed on your doorstep. The insurance company is named

Mediolanum, and a billboard displaying its name can be seen on the side of the stadium where AC Milan is about to be crowned the country's indisputable soccer champion. You are watching Network 4, one of the man's three national channels. And who is being carried on the shoulders of the star players after the triumphant match, cheered by tens of thousands of fans in the stadium and admired by millions in their homes? It's the owner of the team. It's the man. And in May 1994 the man also became the country's prime minister.

The rise of Silvio Berlusconi from cruise-ship crooner to tycoon to prime minister of the world's fifth-richest nation is a fairy tale of power. It could only have happened in a country in which the collapse of the previous regime had left a vacuum and the concept of professional politics had become discredited by mammoth corruption. In an age when the traditional labels of Christian Democrat, Socialist, and Liberal and the ideologies they represent have become meaningless or redundant, Berlusconi invented a new style of politics inspired by football, patriotism, and television.

The Milanese tycoon is not the first media mogul to go into politics. He was preceded by former Brazilian President Fernando Collor de Mello and Americans William Randolph Hearst and H. Ross Perot. But Berlusconi has stylized the phenomenon more than any of his predecessors did, creating a crass political language that reflects the death of orthodox postwar politics. His party was named after a soccer slogan, "Forza Italia," or "Go, Italy." His Cabinet was called the "Azzurri," the "Blues," a term normally reserved for Italy's national soccer team. Far from being ridiculed, these new labels appealed to a large portion of Italy's electorate. Demoralized by the bankrupt politics of the past, the voters behaved like adventurous consumers happy to try a new and glossy product. Berlusconi used his advertising and marketing skills for political ends, blissfully unburdened by any sense of political correctness. And he turned Forza Italia into the world's first genuine *partito d'azienda,* or company party. Its campaign was funded by Berlusconi's holding company, Fininvest, and many of its parliamentary candidates were taken from Fininvest's board of directors. In March 1994 the Italians elected not a prime minister but a chief executive of Italy, Inc.

When ancient Roman generals would return to the capital from a successful battle and ride through the city in triumph, decorated by the Senate and hailed by the people, a servant known as a *lictor* would stand behind them on the chariot and whisper into their ear, "Remember you are not a god." The first time I saw Silvio Berlusconi, it struck me that he too should employ a *lictor*. I had gone to Turin in December 1993, three months before the elections that brought him to power and one month before he had even decided to go into politics. The occasion was the opening of Italy's biggest hypermarket, a cathedral to consumer culture in a country where most of the shopping is still done in small corner stores. The shopping mall was marooned in the middle of a never-ending building site just outside the city. The streets had been cordoned off by policemen. Blue lights flashed eerily through the thick, freezing fog. And Berlusconi wasn't even coming by road. He prefers helicopters.

When he finally landed, an entourage of more than a dozen bodyguards with earpieces stepped with him out of the fog, as well as a retinue of bag carriers, advisers, and beautiful secretaries with clipboards. It was hard to believe that Berlusconi was merely opening a supermarket, albeit a very big one. The tycoon, one of the wealthiest men in Europe, is only a hair over five-foot-eight, yet he is compelling to look at. He expects you to gawp at him. He has one of the most perfect sets of teeth in modern politics. His skin is permanently tanned and has an almost orange tint that looks extraterrestrial, especially in winter. His face is round with a pointed chin, strangely reminiscent of an exceptionally well groomed, quick-witted mouse that never stops smiling. Berlusconi is unabashedly pleased with himself and has good reason to be.

Before he became a construction magnate, a media mogul, and a soccer tycoon, Mr. Berlusconi worked part time as a nightclub singer on Italian cruise ships. A black-and-white photograph from the late 1950s shows a young, handsome Berlusconi in a white tuxedo and a white trilby hat holding a microphone stand at an angle and singing to an audience of seaborne pensioners. Today when he gives a public address, he still uses a cordless microphone, like Frank Sinatra. He sways gently onstage, as if steadying himself deftly on a slippery platform during high seas. Berlusconi puts even the most skillful baby kisser and flesh presser to shame with his startling ability to schmooze with voters in the most absurd settings. In the hypermarket near Turin, as the old entertainer inspected a formation of giggling cashiers in pink uniforms standing next to a giant mortadella from the sausage stand, I thought for a moment he might even break into a song. Under the watchful eye of his entourage, Berlusconi hugged, kissed, patted, and flattered his way from frozen foods to fresh fish and ended up in confectionaries, standing beneath a ceiling dripping with heart-shaped red balloons. The spirit of Federico Fellini was with us.

Mr. Berlusconi had made a simple calculation. The Italians, he told himself, eat my food, they watch my television channels with their low-fiber diet of game shows, B movies, and very soft porn. Tens of thousands of them live in houses and flats I have built, they go on holiday to the seaside resorts I have constructed, they love my soccer team, surely they will also worship *me* if I go into politics. And he was right. According to one opinion poll, Berlusconi was more popular than Jesus Christ among nine- to thirteen-year-olds at the time he decided to go into politics. His ratings among Italians of voting age weren't bad either. Forza Italia, the party he launched at a glossy ceremony in Rome at the beginning of February 1994, improved its approval rating in the opinion polls from 6 to 30 percent in the space of two weeks. Forza Italia even beat the former Communist Party, which had triumphed in local elections the year before and was confident that after five decades in opposition its hour of power had come. In short, Forza Italia became Italy's most popular party only a month after its creation. The elections brought it to power at the head of a right-wing majority of 366 deputies out of 574 in the Chamber of Deputies and a slim working majority in the Senate. It was an extraordinary achievement that said as much about the volatile state of the Italian electorate as about the marketing skills of the tycoon's party managers.

Silvio Berlusconi is a product of what's become known as *economia spettacolo,* business as spectacle. This has created the hero worship of a small group of captains of industry, whose business exploits are celebrated like triumphs of human achievement and whose lifestyles are the subject of intense and jealous scrutiny. Demonized in the seventies as capitalist exploiters of the masses, men like Gianni Agnelli, the head of Fiat, and Carlo De Benedetti, the chairman of the computer-and-office-equipment giant Olivetti, suddenly found themselves being idolized like soccer pinups in the eighties. This change in attitude probably stemmed from the declining fortunes of left-wing ideology and the corresponding rise in enthusiasm for life's achievers. As veteran newspaper editor Indro Montanelli put it, "The literature and iconography of business and financial success have now overtaken in popularity those once dedicated to women's breasts."

While the "yuppie" cult has faded away in other countries, in Italy it seems to have persisted. In fact, it can be said to have experienced a rebirth with the rise of Silvio Berlusconi. The club of the *condottieri,* or soldiers of fortune, the term often used to describe the princes of Italian industry, is highly exclusive. The real stars are given nicknames. Agnelli, the grandest *condottiere* of them all, is "l'Avvocato," or "the Lawyer," for the rather banal reason that he has a doctorate in law. De Benedetti is known as "l'Ingegniere," or "the Engineer," for a similar reason. Raul Gardini was known as "il Contadino," "the Peasant." The Ferruzi empire, which he headed, was involved mainly in agricultural products like cereals and sugar. Berlusconi has two nicknames: "Sua Emittenza" and "il Cavaliere." The first is a pun on the title of a cardinal and the Italian word for broadcasting; the nickname translates literally as "His Broadcastingship." The second nickname refers to "Cavaliere del Lavoro" (Knight of Labor), an honorary title bestowed upon successful businessmen in Italy.

All the *condottieri* were indirectly involved in politics, as most influential businessmen are. Through the newspapers they owned and the parties they had adopted, they tried to manipulate behind the scenes. Agnelli, De Benedetti, and Luciano Benetton were members of the small but influential Republican Party. "The Lawyer" was one of the party's life senators, and Luciano Benetton had a seat for the party in the Senate. Berlusconi's conversion to full-time politics came later in life, at the age of fifty-four. In the words of former Minister of the Budget Luigi Spaventa, who ran against him in the central Rome constituency last year, "Berlusconi used to be involved in business and politics. Now he's involved in politics and business."

"The Knight" embodied upward mobility. Compared to the other *condottieri* Berlusconi had a humble background and an upbringing that was both austere and very ordinary. In the intensely snobbish world of Italian high business, which is based on family firms and dynasties, Berlusconi has always been seen as an upstart. During the election campaign, he received very little public support from his fellow captains of industry. Agnelli let it be known that he would prefer a victory of the Left, which would continue the economic policy of the government of Carlo Azeglio Ciampi, a central banker with no political affiliations. Carlo De Benedetti went even further. He published an article in *The Financial Times* in which he warned about a victory of the right in apocalyptic terms. "The Engineer" loathed "the Knight." This was animosity fired by jealousy, because De Benedetti had suffered in the corruption scandal. He had spent a brief spell in jail on charges of corruption and is still appealing a six-year prison sentence for fraudulent bankruptcy in the notorious case of the Banco Ambrosiano, the Vatican's bank, which collapsed in 1982 and which led to the death of Roberto Calvi, the banker who was found hanging underneath Blackfriars Bridge in London. De Benedetti could not understand how the media tycoon had avoided arrest. Their dislike for each other came to a head when the Italian government awarded a lucrative contract for establishing a new cell-phone net to a consortium led by Olivetti, "the Engineer's" company. Berlusconi was leading the rival consortium. The award of the contract was made hours before the 1994 election polls closed, and Fininvest claimed it had been rushed through before the tycoon's victory. But the fact is that the government was probably doing Berlusconi a favor: he hardly needed another conflict of interest as he was about to become a prime minister.

Despite his power, influence, and money, Berlusconi had always seen himself as an outsider in the exclusive *salotti*, or salons, and banking circles of Milan. He had shunned the Confindustria, the Italian employers' federation, which he regarded as the arrogant fiefdom of rivals like Agnelli and De Benedetti, and in the spring of 1994 he even attacked the federation's ruling council as elitist and damaging to the interests of the small businessman, the much-heralded backbone of Italy's export economy. During the election campaign

Berlusconi styled himself as the champion of small enterprises, despite the fact that his own empire represents Italian business at its most monopolistic. The tycoon liked to think of himself as an outsider, an attitude that may also have inspired his political affiliations before the collapse of the old parties. While Agnelli and other grandees had been patrons of the small but worthy—and powerful—Republican Party, Berlusconi had espoused the Socialist Party of his university friend Bettino Craxi. This decision had little to do with socialist ideals, more with the fact that the Socialist Party had become the political voice of the rich and powerful who, like Craxi and Berlusconi themselves, had not been born to greatness.

Berlusconi, who was born on September 29, 1936, came from a typical Milanese petit-bourgeois family. His mother, Rosa, was a housewife. His father, Luigi, worked as an official in a small Milan bank, the Banca Rasini. It was this bank that later launched Berlusconi in the construction business with his first loan. (The bank was also investigated for links with organized crime.) Berlusconi went to a monastic boarding school, where he received a rigorous classic education. It was a spartan setup, with fifty to a hundred boys to a dormitory. The emphasis was on good manners, discipline, and a sense of duty. School friends remember Berlusconi as being hyperactive, fidgety, intelligent, and cocky. The tycoon has been very loyal to his school, keeping in touch with some of his teachers and organizing annual reunions in his sumptuous villa at Arcore. Above all, he has kept his friends, involving some of them very closely in his business empire. His school friend Dr. Adalberto Spinelli became the corporate psychiatrist of the Fininvest group. Berlusconi encouraged some of his closest employees and collaborators to subject themselves to the doctor's analytical scrutiny at Sunday-morning meetings in Arcore. Such corporate therapy sessions set the tone for his whole company. Berlusconi ran Fininvest like a feudal estate in a Brave New World of Alpha people. As its benevolent dictator, he enjoyed an exceptional degree of loyalty, which proved immensely useful during the election campaign. For instance, the tycoon created awards for the best employees of the more than 100 companies that make up his empire. Each winner received a sports car and was treated to the delights of the tycoon's inner sanctum at Arcore. They swam in the pool surrounded by an aviary of exotic birds, strolled through the parks and the private zoo of llamas and pet tigers. Berlusconi showed them his magnificent library and the permanent exhibition of Renaissance art. Together they watched films in the video room, which has seven large screens. If the tycoon was particularly fond of his guests, he would entertain them with old crooners from his cruise-ship days in the underground theater at the villa. More intimate gatherings might include a special tour of the family tomb. Modeled on an Etruscan necropolis, the Berlusconi mausoleum is situated in a leafy corner of the tycoon's private park. One enters it by a narrow passage. Inside there are thirty-six burial niches for the male members of the tycoon's family and his closest friends and business associates (the women are buried elsewhere). Berlusconi clearly wants to die like an emperor. He himself will rest in peace and splendor in the center of the burial chamber under a huge granite slab resembling a cheesecake. The mausoleum is decorated, if that's the right word, by an abstract sculpture depicting what looks like twisted torsos and heads.

This is the Never-Never Land of Italian business and politics. The Berlusconi villa is as mysterious as the secretive headquarters of an oriental sect and as gaudy as the palace of a Roman despot. Berlusconi has skillfully exploited the mystique of his palace for political ends. First, the public has been allowed to see only the villa's magnificent front façade, leaving the rest to the imagination. Second, Berlusconi has used it to make important appeals to the nation. He has turned one of his studies into a television studio, where interviews and announcements are filmed, lit, and directed by his own technical staff. The camera lenses are all fitted with stockings to soften the focus—apparently this is quite normal in quality filmmaking—and the studio is suffused with a soft light that is kind to wrinkles. From here Berlusconi broadcasts directly to the nation, reassuring his voters or threatening his opponents. The use of direct television appeals as a means of communicating with voters above the heads of Parliament became increasingly frequent toward the end of 1994, when Berlusconi came under fire more and more for his conflicts of interest and for the criminal inquiries into his companies that were being conducted by the Milan magistrates. But by choosing his own villa as a venue for public addresses and recruiting his employees as party officials, Berlusconi tried to remind the public that he is not part of the political apparatus but a self-made man. To his critics, however, these tactics created the impression of a corporate dynasty launching a hostile takeover bid for the entire country.

After leaving school the nineteen-year-old Silvio read law at the University of Milan, where he met Bettino Craxi, a fellow student who later became a close friend and godfather to one of his daughters, Barbara. After graduating with a thesis on the legal aspects of advertising—a useful subject considering his later interest in the media—Berlusconi became a stand-up comedian and a nightclub crooner. First he worked at the Tortuga (Turtle) nightclub in the Adriatic resort of Rimini for 40,000 lire ($24) a night. Later he founded a group called the Four Musketeers and toured the Mediterranean on cruise ships. His best friend, Fedele Confalonieri, accompanied him on the piano. Another friend, Alberto Ciciatello, played the drums. Both have been working with Berlusconi ever since. When the media tycoon went into politics, he put Confalonieri nominally in charge of the Fininvest empire, while Ciciatello became the head of Fininvest's internal security division. Both have a place reserved in Berlusconi's family mausoleum. Unlike the other nabobs of Italian business, Berlusconi didn't only have a family to run his empire, he also had a band.

Cruise-ship entertainment has provided him with a deep well of inspiration. His 1994 political campaign looked as if it had been conceived on the dance floor of the *Queen Elizabeth II,* and choreographed by George Orwell. When the veteran crooner launched Forza Italia at a glossy ceremony in Rome—televised live on his own channels—he looked up at the lights with a beatific smile. The same smile, three feet wide, also appeared on a giant video screen that dwarfed the entire auditorium. The video wall is to Silvio Berlusconi what the cross-country bus tour was to Bill Clinton. The grand finale included a rendition of the Forza Italia anthem. For those who had forgotten the lyrics, the words flashed up on the big screen, karaoke style. "It's time to grow, it's time to believe, it's time for Forza Italia!" Berlusconi used the same formula for every one of his election rallies. Another intriguing detail is that he always wore the same clothes: a dark gray double-breasted suit, a pale blue shirt, and a black-and-gray spotted tie. One day last summer, the prime minister changed his wardrobe to a blue suit, a white shirt, and a red spotted tie. This was his summer uniform. One of his advisers once told me that this uniformity of wardrobe was meant to inspire confidence through continuity. The Berlusconi suit and spotted tie became emblems of power and success.

Berlusconi made his first trillion lire in construction, building blocks of flats and then entire suburbs on the ugly outskirts of Milan. His company, Fininvest, is still one of the largest private construction firms in Italy. Its specialty is futuristic satellite towns like Milano 2, a manicured sprawl of consumer-friendly red-brick dwellings built around an artificial lake with a fountain. A forest of aerials and satellite dishes announces the headquarters of Berlusconi's three national television networks. Berlusconi came to television relatively late. In 1974 the Italian government deregulated television and allowed private local channels to be set up. By 1980 the country's ether was bristling with more than 1,300 local television stations, a higher number per capita than in the United States. Then as now the majority were cheap, homemade shopping channels that often verged on the surreal. On several occasions I have found myself transfixed by a two-hour talk show about the merits of a serrated carving knife. One Neopolitan channel seemed to be devoted to the marketing of a "sauna suit" for women, a plastic jumpsuit that makes you sweat and therefore, it was claimed by a man in a brown suit and unfashionably wide green kipper tie, lose weight. All you could see was a perfectly shaped bottom gyrating in a wet, clinging pair of plastic trousers. Every three minutes two hairy male hands appeared on the screen, peeled down the trousers, and revealed two supposedly shrinking buttocks. A telephone number flashed up on the screen with an invitation to buy.

In 1974, starting out modestly, Berlusconi bought Telemilano, a small local station that broadcast cooking recipes and horoscopes for housewives during the day and repeats of dubbed American or Brazilian soap operas in the evening. For the first five years, he treated the channel as little more than a hobby. But in 1979 the tycoon made a significant step toward expansion by buying a library of more than three hundred movies, none of which had ever been shown on television. This gave him control of the majority of Italian B movies, which most of the other local television channels were eager to get their hands on but weren't rich enough to buy. He rented the films cheaply to local television stations if they broadcast the advertisements made by his company Publitalia. Twenty years later Berlusconi would use a similar deal to promote Forza Italia. Local television stations were encouraged to air the party's election spot in return for Fininvest programs.

Despite his creative advertising scheme, Berlusconi had difficulty moving into national television. Fearful of losing their monopoly, RAI 1, 2, and 3 tried to halt Berlusconi's expansion. In July 1981 the political parties put pressure on Italy's Constitutional Court to issue a decree stating that only RAI was allowed to broadcast nationally. Berlusconi, who by now had effective control of scores of local channels up and down the country, reacted nimbly. He created a de facto national channel by distributing videocassettes of the same programs to scores of local stations that then carefully synchronized their broadcasts. For instance, at 1:00 o'clock on the dot, every station would screen the same movie, at 3:00 o'clock a cooking show, and so on. It created the impression of a national channel without breaking the law. The network became known as Channel 5, and Berlusconi faced increasing pressure from RAI. In 1984 magistrates in four cities including Rome issued a court order to stop Channel 5 from broadcasting in their area. Berlusconi responded by visiting his old friend Bettino Craxi. Two hours later Craxi issued a decree banning the court order. Channel 5 was back on the air and has stayed there ever since.

The tycoon battled the state monopoly in order to set up a private one. By 1986 he owned Italy's three national commercial stations, Channel 5, Network 4, and Italia 1. Together they captured almost half the country's television audience and more than 80 percent of the commercial TV market. RAI, which was bloated, unimaginative, and under the thumbs of the political parties, lost more and more viewers to Berlusconi's frothy diet of cheap game shows, and, most important, the big American series that became the cultural hallmarks of the 1980s—*Dallas* and *Dynasty*. In 1983 Berlusconi scored a *coup de théâtre* against RAI. He snatched the country's most famous television host and housewives' heartthrob, who rejoices in the unlikely name of Mike Bongiorno, from RAI 1, the Christian Democrats' channel. The "transfer," which cost Berlusconi billions of lire, was dramatic enough to cause a minor government crisis. Fininvest not only stole some of the best television stars and delivered a slicker, livelier, more popular form of entertainment, it also had a much better news service. Its news bulletins were free of party control. They were more informative, better written, better presented, and less accident prone than RAI's. In the 1980s it was Berlusconi's channels, not RAI, that broadcast the new images of consumption, the new styles of entertainment from Brazilian telenovellas to karaoke singalongs, that defined popular taste. Berlusconi's advertising created new standards in packaging and promotion.

In the late 1980s the tycoon consolidated his hold on commercial television by buying the listings magazine *TV Sorrisi e Canzoni*. In 1986 he expanded to France by buying the ill-fated Chaine Cinq and in 1987 to Spain, where he acquired a 25 percent stake in Telecinco, the largest possible for a foreigner under Spanish law. With his television stations, publishing houses, magazines, and advertising companies, Berlusconi now owned the second-largest commercial media empire in Europe after Germany's Bertelsmann Verlag. In 1990 he also bought Standa and Euromercato and turned them into Italy's most popular supermarket chains. The jewel in his crown became AC Milan, the Italian soccer champion, bought by Berlusconi in 1986 and retrained to become one of the best teams in Europe. Soccer teams have often been the toys of the world's superrich, like the late Robert Maxwell or singer Elton John. But in Italy soccer isn't just the nation's favorite sport, it is a secular religion, and Berlusconi has become its high priest. The soccer team is to the modern Italian tycoon what the band of *condottieri* was to the rich and powerful Tuscan *signore* in the fifteenth century: it is the most important symbol of its owner's power and glory.

Until Berlusconi turned AC Milan into the almost perpetual champion in the late 1980s, the undisputed *signore* of Italian soccer was his old nemesis Gianni Agnelli of Fiat, who owned the Turin team Juventus. Agnelli was the *grand seigneur* of Italian business. The next thing that Italy has to royalty, he enjoyed almost the same reverence as the pope. He is untouchable, one of the few names in business that has not been dragged into the corruption scandal, although Fiat has been investigated and several of its managers have been questioned by the magistrates. Agnelli's status as the icon of Italy's postwar economic success is sacred. Most Italians would probably prefer to keep it that way. But in 1989 AC Milan displaced Juventus as Italy's premier soccer team. In hindsight this also presaged the transfer of power from Agnelli, the old-style tycoon who influenced politics from behind the scene, to Berlusconi, who occupied center stage. It marked a change in style from dignified paternalism to brash self-promotion.

The difference was also obvious in the buccaneer manner in which Berlusconi expanded his business. Unlike Fiat, Italy's largest private firm, Fininvest, its second largest, is not listed on the Milan stock exchange. It is a private, family-owned firm with a highly secretive ownership structure and opaque accounts. It has raised its capital by borrowing from banks, especially from Mediobanca, Italy's most renowned merchant bank. Fininvest has debts of more than $4 billion. Financial analysts are divided about the wisdom of Berlusconi's corporate strategy. Some criticize him for overstretching his empire and jeopardizing those companies that are sound—like television and advertising—with others that have become a costly burden. If Berlusconi has run up enormous debts for his own company, what does this say about his promises to cure the Italian economy? Others point out that Fininvest's debts are still outstripped by its turnover. Italy is in a similar position: its budget deficit may be the highest in Europe, but its balance of payments is healthy.

The tycoon keeps his personal life very private. His second wife, the former actress Veronica Lario, seldom appears by his side. When she does, the effect is somewhat startling. Mrs. Berlusconi is slightly taller than her husband, a voluptuous beauty with a broad, toothy smile, a very large bust, and a face whose white, almost Japanese, makeup contrasts dramatically with her husband's perpetual tan. Although she is more than presentable, when her husband was prime minister she appeared before the cameras only during state visits, chatting with Hillary Clinton, or hand in hand with her husband at the

G-7 summit in Naples. Berlusconi was not breaking with tradition: Italian prime ministers and presidents tend to keep their wives hidden from public view. Some observers have suggested that Mrs. Berlusconi was told to keep a low profile because she is the tycoon's second wife, a fact that may jar with the former prime minister's public celebration of family values.

By all accounts, the divorce from his first wife, Carla Dall'Olio, was acrimonious. The two, who had two children together, divorced in 1985, five years after Berlusconi had started an affair with Lario and a year after she had given birth to his daughter Barbara. The affair was kept secret for a long time while Berlusconi maintained his mistress in an apartment at company headquarters in the center of Milan. The story of how the merchant prince met the actress is worthy of any treacly telenovella screened on the tycoon's own channels.

Veronica Lario, whose real name is Miriam Bartolini, was starring in Fernand Crommelynck's much-neglected comedy *The Magnificent Cuckold*. Berlusconi was sitting in the front row. The play's denouement involved Veronica Lario taking off her blouse. Her breasts almost fell into the tycoon's lap. After the curtain Berlusconi paid the actress a visit in her dressing room and told her how much he admired her acting. Soon afterward love blossomed. In one of her rare newspaper interviews Veronica Lario told the interviewer that she didn't mind taking her clothes off on stage but that she distinguished between gratuitous nudity and necessary nudity. She disrobed only when it was absolutely necessary. "Getting undressed is not my highest ambition," she continued. "Personally, I like to read, and I take a great interest in current affairs. . . . My greatest defect is that I am full of doubts." The same cannot be said of her husband. Berlusconi has carefully constructed a public image of himself as hardworking, enigmatic, charismatic, devout, and supremely confident. He has never tried to be modest—which is just as well, considering some of the things he has said about himself. Here are some extracts: "I know only one recipe for life, and that is blood, sweat, and tears." Or (repeated again and again during the election campaign): "I am above all a businessman who performs miracles." Or: "I am always right." Or: "I always win." Or: "I see everything instinctively. As my mother once said about me—I'm a kind of wizard."

Did Berlusconi follow a master plan, or did his political ambitions evolve week by week in the run-up to the 1994 election campaign? Left-wing conspiracy theorists believe that there was a master plan to put Berlusconi into Palazzo Chigi, the prime minister's residence, and that it was hatched by Italian big business in 1992 after it had become obvious that the old politicos would face the electoral guillotine. Others believe that Berlusconi had devised his own path to greatness well before the collapse of the *partitocrazia*. According to his own advisers, Berlusconi decided to get more closely involved in politics in September 1993. He did so at first for commercial reasons connected with his own company. The tycoon feared that Italy's left-wing parties would fill the vacuum left by the collapse of the Christian Democrats and their allies and pass legislation outlawing his virtual monopoly on private television. Berlusconi could not afford to lose the most important and profitable parts of his empire, the three television channels.

Naturally Berlusconi did not say that he wanted to get involved in politics in order to save his own business. His intention, he told journalists in November 1993 at a news conference in Rome's Foreign Press Club, was to save Italy from communism. This was a preposterous assertion since by 1993 Italy's hard-line Communists had shriveled down to the small Communist Refoundation, a splinter group of orthodox ideologues who had broken off from the main body of Italy's Communist Party in 1988. They hardly constituted the Red Peril evoked by Berlusconi. The main successor to the Italian Communist Party, the Democratic Party of the Left, had ditched Marx and become a social democratic party modeled on the German SPD. Nevertheless, as the elections were to prove, Berlusconi had turned the imaginary Communists into a powerful bogeyman. He had conjured up an enemy that existed in the inner recesses of the minds of millions of voters and proved that the fear of communism, however atavistic, was still a powerful undercurrent in Italian politics.

Berlusconi's original plan was to forge a center-right alliance of existing parties, such as the Popular Party, the reconstituted Christian Democrats, and the Northern League, through his Forza Italia clubs, a nationwide network of constituency support organizations modeled on the AC Milan soccer fan clubs. There were more than seven thousand such clubs, often set up in homes or small offices. They were financed by a mixture of company money from Berlusconi's Fininvest empire and members' contributions. Their task was to distribute posters, enlist volunteers, hold meetings—in short, to create a grassroots organization for whichever political movement Berlusconi decided to back. Before Berlusconi decided to enter the election campaign directly, he had intended these clubs to be his main contribution to politics. When it became obvious that indecision and bickering would prevent the creation of a center-right alliance, Berlusconi decided to enter the race himself and the "clubs" became Forza Italia. It was thus one of the quirks of the party's rushed genesis that Forza Italia had a grassroots network before it was even created.

Berlusconi's move was very bold. He joined the race only two months before the elections. Most political analysts and prime ministerial candidates would have considered this to be a dangerously short time. In hindsight, brevity may have worked in the tycoon's favor. Some even believe that was his original intention. Berlusconi the political product would be as fresh and enticing as a new brand of cream cheese. However, the only way he could win the elections under the new electoral law would be to forge an alliance with other parties on the right.

The new law was introduced after the 1993 referendum on electoral reform in which more than 85 percent of voters opted to scrap the existing system of pure proportional representation for British-style majority voting. It was hoped that this would inject a degree of accountability and honesty into Italian politics. Again, the reform campaigners had forgotten or chosen to forget that the "first-past-the-post" majority system had already been tried at the beginning of the twentieth century and had been abolished because it had given too much power to local party bosses. After months of debate Parliament finally agreed on a classically muddled compromise. Under the new system, 75 percent of the seats in the Chamber of Deputies would be allotted to single-member constituencies or electoral colleges. The rest would be elected by proportional representation. A minimum of 4 percent of the vote would be needed to get into Parliament, a threshold that later proved fatal for a number of smaller parties. Although the new system was supposed to limit the number of parties and therefore make Parliament less fragmented and government more stable, it had the opposite effect. In the end sixteen parties entered Parliament. Because even the smaller groups like the Christian Center Party thought they had a chance of getting deputies elected to Parliament, the new system discouraged the formation of large parties like the British Conservative Party or Labour Party.

The secret of winning the elections was thus to create alliances of parties that would ensure that candidates from the Right, the Left, or the Center that belonged to different parties would not tread on one another's toes. In short, Italy's agonizing experiment in electoral reform left the country with an even more convoluted system than before, giving birth to a number of brittle electoral pacts. The Left created the "Progressive Alliance" and the Center the "Pact for Italy." Berlusconi's task was less easy.

The Italian Right was ideologically divided between the neo-Fascists and the Northern League. The Northern League's federalism was diametrically opposed to the neo-Fascists' nationalism. At a pre-election congress the outspoken Umberto Bossi told delegates, "With the Fascists"—he didn't even bother with the polite "neo"—"never!" Berlusconi solved this problem by forging two separate alliances, one with the Northern League, called the "Freedom Pole," the other with the neo-Fascists called the "Alliance of Good Government." He was able to do this because the neo-Fascists' vote was concentrated in Rome and the South, while the Northern League focused on its own turf in the country's industrial North. This balance of mutual political antagonism worked only because Berlusconi became the pivot. The right-wing alliance hinged on him and his party. As for his newfound allies, they now had a partner who could offer them the things they didn't have, such as television airtime, a well-oiled publicity machine, and the respectability of associating with a successful business tycoon.

Forza Italia became Europe's most "postmodern" and innovative political movement. The party wasn't so much the political expression of a creed or a mood that had germinated in the electorate but was similar to the French Gaullist Party: a tool for winning power. The difference is that it used all the modern avenues of communication available to a media tycoon with his own television channels, advertising companies, and public relations know-how. Forza Italia was launched like a soap powder. In the words of Roberto Lasagna, one of its campaign managers, a former head of the advertising firm Saatchi and Saatchi, and now a senator for Forza Italia, "We discovered a market niche and proceeded to fill it." The market niche was created by the old corrupt system and by a nation that had grown tired of self-flagellation and mea culpas. It created a strong demand for a brand-new party with brand-new faces headed by a tycoon who was reassuringly rich and felt good about being Italian. In fact, the party's name wasn't new at all. In his excellent account of life in Naples in 1944 (*Naples 44*), Norman Lewis talks about the emergence of a "purposeful and sinister movement . . . with Fascist leanings," that he, as an officer in the Army's Intelligence Corps, had been sent to investigate. He describes the brooding faces of the supporters of Forza Italia, meeting at a rally to express their opposition to the Allied presence. The slick image of Berlusconi's Forza Italia couldn't be further removed from that of its gruff predecessor, but the muscular patriotism is a common theme.

Berlusconi's party represents the genesis of politics in reverse: first came the opinion poll, then came the political party. In his austere but elegant Rome office, Forza Italia's national administrator, Mario Valducci, explained the evolution of the party in three phases. "Phase one," he said, sitting back in his swiveling black leather armchair, "involved conducting a poll. We wanted to find out whether Italians would support a completely new party with a right-wing ideology. We asked about twenty thousand people and found that the answer was a resounding 'yes.' Then came phase two: setting up a network of Forza Italia clubs all over the country. Finally, phase three: choosing parliamentary candidates and winning the elections." Modeled on the fan clubs of Berlusconi's own soccer team, the clubs are in essence constituency support associations.

There are seven thousand of them, with more than 1 million members. To start a club you first paid about 300,000 lire ($180), which was later reimbursed by the party. This bought you a basic set of tools: posters, rattles, ties, flags, pens, and a list of the party's ideological principles, which can be summed up as low taxes, minimum bureaucracy, little government interference, a free market, and law and order. Most of the clubs had no more than a dozen members. Often they met informally in a member's home, which avoided the need to pay rent for an office. During the election campaign the clubs had a threefold task: first, to recruit potential candidates who could run for election (in the end the party auditioned more than 3,000 applicants and chose 267); second, to support the candidates during the campaign by organizing rallies and spreading Berlusconi's message of confidence and national pride; and third, to develop the party's greatest asset, the personality cult of Silvio Berlusconi. Festooned with posters of the smiling tycoon, the clubs were not so much classical grassroots organizations where citizens met to discuss politics and get their local candidates elected as units in a vast publicity machine run by the prime minister's own company executives. Once the euphoria of the Berlusconi victory had evaporated, this became a problem, as some clubs complained about the autocratic behavior of the party leadership and the lack of internal debate. Indeed, Forza Italia's biggest shortcoming is that it is not a true political party. It is quite likely to disappear whenever Berlusconi decides to return to the business world. Despite their large membership, the clubs have no ideological or social roots.

In two months Forza Italia rose from nowhere to become Italy's most popular political party. The clubs were one reason for this meteoric rise. The other was the party's message. Berlusconi used the language of soccer for political ends. When he entered politics, the media tycoon said, *"Scendo in campo,"* "I'm taking to the field." The mellifluous male voice at the end of Forza Italia's slick television election spot called on voters to *"Scendere in campo."* Berlusconi described his candidates as *"gli Azzurri,"* or "the Blues," the name he normally uses for his soccer team and that was used for Italy's 1994 World Cup team. He also called his Cabinet "the Blues" or *"la Squadra,"* "the Team." So far there has been an uncanny coincidence between his political successes and the triumphs of his soccer team. On the night Berlusconi won his first big parliamentary hurdle, a no-confidence vote in the Senate, in which his alliance did not have a majority, AC Milan beat Barcelona 4–0 in the Union of European Football Associations (UEFA) Cup. Berlusconi evoked a strong Italy with a bright future at a time when national self-esteem was low and when many Italians were growing tired of the traditional pessimism of the Left. The corruption scandal, the recession, the strains on the country's unity, the confusion unleashed by the end of the Cold War, the end of an era of complacent certainty, all these have left Italy in a mood of self-flagellation, yearning for assurance. His genius was to realize that the Italians wanted to be reassured, that all the debate about secession and federalism stimulated by the Northern League was essentially an expression of national self-doubt in the face of recent political upheavals.

Berlusconi manipulated a wave of surging national pride at precisely the right moment. The nation was already beginning to have a higher opinion of itself. Berlusconi's entry into politics coincided with a shower of gold medals for the Italian team at the Lillehammer Winter Olympics. But patriotism couched in the language of soccer was only one part of the Berlusconi appeal. The other was the promise of an economic miracle, which seemed more plausible than such promises usually do because it was made by a tycoon who clearly had the Midas touch. "If Berlusconi can do it for his company, he can do it for his country!" This was the conclusion voters were supposed to draw, and at least 25 percent of the electorate clearly did. The promise of a new miracle seems to have been particularly effective among young voters, who had suffered from unemployment the most. Berlusconi was also careful to attract female voters, who had been repelled by the male chauvinism of the Northern League. The handsome tycoon went out of his way to court the powerful Federation of Housewives. At one meeting during the election campaign, he told more than a thousand enchanted housewives that he loved to do the housecleaning and liked using a feather duster. The audience of mainly middle-aged, fur-coated women squealed with delight at the pious protestations of the former nightclub crooner. Ingratiation paid off: 55 percent of Berlusconi's votes came from women.

Berlusconi proved himself to be a magician of electoral engineering. He turned his company into a political party and tapped into the modern Italian mind like a psychiatrist. Soccer had fine-tuned his grasp of mass psychology. Above all, he was a candidate made for and by television. The electronic medium is an integral part of every modern election campaign. Every presidential candidate from Little Rock to Lima times his rallies, press conferences, and sound bites to appear on the evening news. Meetings are stage-managed to look good on the small screen. But Berlusconi has invented a new brand of politics created by TV. His election spots, broadcast at least twenty times a day on his own channels, were a brilliant compilation of all the most famous advertisements the Italian viewer would have seen, from the languid shampoo ad to the frantic and exciting car ad, to the reassuring homeliness of the insurance ad, to the escapism of a holiday video, all underscored by stirring music. It was pulp fiction, but it moved millions of people to vote for Forza Italia.

Media moguls around the world may want to imitate him and become prime minister. But they probably need a country like Italy to succeed: an electorate in the midst of a vendetta against the old political order and a public, media, and political institutions that aren't too bothered about the blatant conflicts of interest inherent in the tycoon's campaign. Berlusconi fought an American-style election campaign without any of the checks and balances of the American system.

"No, no, no! Not like that! You hold the microphone like this. Make sure you don't trip over the cord." Looking a little nervous, the Forza Italia candidate explained to the woman in the red suit with the shrill voice that he had never held a microphone before in his life, aside from once at a wedding. "Try again," the voice trainer said more softly. The candidate was an accountant from Milan being groomed to be a politician. He flicked back his fringe of graying hair, adjusted his round horn-rimmed glasses, and for the fifth time launched into his campaign speech, trying to imagine that the white wall and the video camera he was addressing were in fact thousands of voters at a rally. "As a businessman, I promise you, I can assure you, we will lower taxes, we will make Italy work again . . . we will create another Italian miracle—" "No, not like that! Please!" The voice again, shrill. "Stress 'taxes,' 'miracle.' Those are the words you want people to remember." I wondered whether this candidate would make it. But on the first day of Parliament I saw him sitting in the fourth row of the Forza Italia section of the Chamber of Deputies. The metamorphosis had been successful. In the room next door, equally bare except for a few chairs, neon strip lighting, a rubber plant, and a video camera, another candidate was learning how to breathe. "In ... out. In ... and out," intoned the teacher, her hand on his expanding and contracting abdomen. Down the corridor six people were watching a video of themselves being interviewed. None of them had ever been in politics before either.

This laboratory for creating Forza Italia candidates was in the cellar of the Diakron Public Relations building in Milan. One wing on the ground floor contained the printing presses that created the party's posters, postcards, and pamphlets. The smiling face of the party leader decked the floor of a storeroom, where posters were ready to be taken away and pasted onto the country's billboards. In another wing, eager volunteers assembled the party's gift packages. These included a tiepin, a badge with Berlusconi's smiling face, a handkerchief, and a rattle, the type given to babies. Presumably this gadget was meant for stirring up support in public. Upstairs, the party's managers sat in rooms filled more with aftershave aroma than with smoke, discussing strategy. Where charts showing the consumer target group for a particular deodorant had once hung, there were now charts showing the consumer target group of the prime minister's party. The setup was very convenient because Diakron is the public relations company that belongs to Berlusconi. It had now become a factory for the election of its owner and his party. The media tycoon chose forty managers from his company to run the election campaign. Thirty Forza Italia deputies and senators now sitting in Parliament are former Fininvest executives.

Candidates were not just groomed to look and sound as confident as their party leader, they also had to be taught the ABCs of parliamentary politics. Their teacher was a former general and defense correspondent for a national newspaper, Luigi Caligaris. Caligaris had his office in Forza Italia's Rome headquarters, a splendid palazzo near the Via del Corso in the Via della Umiltà. The penthouse had been turned into an apartment for Mr. Berlusconi. The rest of the salmon-colored palazzo was dedicated to party business. "I am here to oil the weapons of our soldiers in preparation for battle," Dr. Caligaris told me. "Inexperience is the price of political honesty that we have to pay. We do not want to be associated with the old political system. There isn't one 'old' politician in our party. That means we are untainted. Unfortunately, it also means that few of us know anything about Parliament. And we have to be ready to fight for our cause once we get elected. Our deputies have to know how Parliament works, how committees work, how legislation works. That's where I come in. . . . Together we will create a new generation of politicians." I was reminded somewhat of Peter Sellers's rendition of Dr. Strangelove.

Forza Italia found it easier to recruit voters than qualified candidates. In fact, only hours before the final lists of candidates had to be presented to the Interior Ministry, Berlusconi himself was gripped by panic. Livio Caputo, who was elected senator and became minister for European affairs, told me how he was called up at three o'clock in the morning by Berlusconi himself. "Silvio asked me whether I wanted to run for Forza Italia in a safe seat. 'Can't this wait until tomorrow?' I replied, half asleep. 'No, you must decide here and now. We need people like you, people who speak English, who know something about foreign affairs.' " Caputo, who was one of Italy's leading commentators on international relations and the deputy editor of a newspaper, *Il Giornale,* formerly owned by the media tycoon, said yes. He was given a safe seat in Bergamo near Milan, and now he is number two at the Foreign Ministry, in charge of drawing up Italy's much more assertive and independent foreign policy, especially toward Europe. Livio Caputo had at least been a seasoned observer of politics. But the lack of experience among many other Forza Italia candidates forced Berlusconi more and more to recruit help from the old political class, especially the Liberal Party. The free-market philosophy of the Liberals was close to Berlusconi's heart, and despite its being the party of former Health Minister Francesco De Lorenzo, it had been less tainted by "Tangentopoli" than the Socialists or Christian Democrats had.

During the elections Forza Italia wore its political virginity like a badge of distinction. It did this for a very good reason: opinion polls conducted by Diakron had shown that many Italians would vote only for a party that had nothing to do with the old discredited political system. Being aware of this, even the old parties did their best to change their names. Forza Italia simply applied the Orwellian mantra "Old is bad; new is good" with far greater rigor than the other parties did. The novelty message was hammered home relentlessly. And it seemed to work.

The opposition spent much of the campaign trying to convince voters that the Forza Italia product owed more to skillful recycling than to genuine novelty. They had a point. Berlusconi was linked to the past as much as any of the other *condottieri*. The era of greatest expansion of his media empire had been in the 1980s, when Bettino Craxi was prime minister. The difference was that Berlusconi himself had never been arrested or, as far as we know, investigated for the charges that had disgraced so many others. During the election campaign the magistrates attempted to make up for lost time. They questioned his brother, Paolo, for suspected bribery in a number of real estate deals. They issued arrest warrants for three senior Fininvest managers. Among the three was Marcello Dell'Utri, the head of Publitalia, arrested on suspicion of having been involved in the payment of bribes for the transfer of soccer stars to AC Milan, the so-called "clean feet" scandal.

A week before the elections, plainclothes officers from the DIGOS secret police raided Berlusconi's headquarters in Rome and Milan and demanded to see the lists of all the Forza Italia candidates and presidents of the Forza Italia clubs in the poor southern province of Calabria. The warrants had been signed by Maria Grazia Ombroni, a magistrate in the Calabrian city of Palmi who was conducting an investigation into the links among the local Mafia, Masonic lodges, and politics. Berlusconi's spokesmen pointed out that they could have done this by faxing the information department of the Interior Ministry a list of requests. A raid, they argued, was as unnecessary as it was headline grabbing. The president of Italy, Oscar Luigi Scalfaro, sensibly pointed out that the magistrates could not ignore questions of political timing. According to Berlusconi's in-house pollster, Gianni Pilo, the episode produced a last-minute swing in favour of Forza Italia.

Two days previously, Italy's Interior Minister Nicola Mancino had declared publicly that he was afraid Forza Italia clubs in Sicily had been infiltrated by the Mafia. A day later Luciano Violante, the respected head of the Parliamentary Anti-Mafia Commission and a member of the Democratic Party of the Left, resigned after leaking the names of three Fininvest managers under suspicion for links to the Mafia to the press. The investigations misfired and may have cost the Left the elections. Instead of bowing to the judiciary, the media tycoon took them on. The raid on his headquarters was the final straw. Berlusconi was incandescent. He called a special press conference in which he denounced "a conspiracy to prevent us from competing fairly in the elections, inspired by our left-wing opponents." The mask of serene confidence and the perpetual smile had now given way to a grimace of rage. "These are totalitarian tactics!" the future prime minister thundered. "This has never before happened in our democracy!" The claim as well as the response was exaggerated, of course. While being careful not to mention the name of Italy's best-loved judge, Antonio Di Pietro, Berlusconi had declared war on the magistrates, on the very heroes of Italy's "sweet revolution." At the time it was a shrewd move. The attacks on Berlusconi in the run-up to the elections had all the hallmarks of orchestrated coincidence. The media tycoon suddenly became the victim of the unreasonable forces of law and order. His outcry may have rekindled the innate fear and loathing so many Italians harbor for a state that makes up for its negligence with sporadic acts of ferocity.

The left-wing coalition never managed to dent the credibility Forza Italia had established so rapidly. They themselves had been minority shareholders in the systematic corruption, and they were constantly on the defensive, fending off accusations that they had received bribes. Furthermore, Achille Occhetto, the then leader of the Democratic Party of the Left, looked and sounded like a tired party apparatchik. He had made the mistake of assuming that he was the sole occupant of the moral high ground and of taking victory for granted after the successes in the local elections in the winter of 1993. Many Italian voters also clearly relished the seductive arias of the Berlusconi campaign. They were fed up with the grisly reality of politics. They wanted some escape from the dreary routine of "Tangentopoli." Berlusconi, described by Eugenio Scalfari, the editor of *La Repubblica,* as "the Great Seducer," provided it. Whenever and wherever I asked Forza Italia supporters why they had voted for the party, the reply was always the same. "Berlusconi's new. He's a new man. His party is new. He'll renew Italy." Few bothered to ask themselves seriously whether novelty or indeed honesty were sufficient qualities for running a country. The impression of a new class of citizen politicians was all-important.

Who better to stand for the party in the Sicilian city of Catania than Franco Zeffirelli, the outspoken film and opera director? He was one of the most illustrious citizen politicians in the Berlusconi camp, keen to prove that the business of politics should be handled by gifted amateurs rather than professional hacks. In that sense Berlusconi's party was both ahead of its time and very old fashioned, re-creating the nineteenth-century ideal of parliamentarians who first made their name and their fortune outside politics before being considered qualified to lead their community as elected representatives. We interviewed Zeffirelli in the courtyard of a crumbling baroque palazzo in the stunningly beautiful center of Catania. The walls were decorated with voluptuous stone putti, puffy-cheeked, pert-bottomed angels. There were lemon trees and a brilliant blue sky overhead. Mount Etna was still capped with snow, and as a reminder of its hidden force the live volcano exhaled a wispy plume of smoke. Zeffirelli couldn't have staged it better himself. "Infiltrated by the *who*?" Zeffirelli flicked the ash contemptuously from his long, thin cigarette and gave me an incredulous look. "Isn't there a danger," I repeated my question, "that the Mafia will try to use Forza Italia, which is a completely new political force, as its protector, now that it has lost its old friends? Furthermore," I continued, "so many Forza Italia politicians like yourself are new and simply can't know what they're up against." The Forza Italia candidate for senator in central Catania, the base of the Mafia in eastern Sicily, became strident. "Any mafioso who wants to infiltrate"—he spat the word—"my party in this city will first of all have to deal with *me*."

Although he is from Florence, Zeffirelli had decided to run in Catania because he felt the challenge was greater. He also had a great deal of affection for the city. He had made some of his best films here, and he loved the baroque town center. "The Via dei Crociferi is the most beautiful street in Europe, darling. Have you been there yet?" I hadn't. The interview was occasionally interrupted by one of the director's Jack Russell terriers. The tiny, sausage-shaped dogs were wearing leather harnesses studded with Forza Italia badges showing the smiling face of Italy's future prime minister. They pounced on their owner, affectionately licking his cheeks. Zeffirelli is very good with dogs. Finally Sabrina, his assistant, had to lead the dogs away. A charming, bubbly Roman, she had been reluctantly seconded from the film set to the election campaign. Like hundreds of other Forza Italia campaign workers and even some of its candidates, she had been "volunteered" into politics by her boss.

"Mafia . . . *Mafia,*" the director continued airily. "I can't bear that word anymore. I think Sicily has been given a bad press by films like *The Godfather*. There is crime, yes, and banditry, and of course drugs. But that's everywhere." His eyes squinted in the bright sunshine. Forza Italia had rented an apartment in a baroque palazzo. There was a bedroom for Zeffirelli, a small kitchen, and three offices. The walls were festooned with election posters showing Zeffirelli lounging in a wicker armchair wearing a blue-and-green flowered silk shirt. His blue eyes had a twinkle in them. The atmosphere in Forza Italia's Catania headquarters bubbled with the same jollity one might find backstage at a musical, completely alien to the melancholy air that hung heavily over the city. The office was run by a former Socialist with a drooping walrus mustache, to whom the others deferred when the film director wasn't there. I wanted to ask him what he felt about the accusations of Mafia infiltration, especially since he had belonged to the Socialist Party of former Defense Minister Salvo Ando, a powerful Catanese who was forced to resign in 1993 because he was under investigation for links with the Mafia. But in the friendly show-biz atmosphere of Zeffirelli's campaign headquarters, the question would have seemed too rude. It would have shattered the suspension of disbelief. I refrained and had another coffee.

Catania is one of the most exotic cities in Sicily. Ringed by the usual concrete sprawl of unfettered construction, the center is a stunning baroque honeycomb built by the Bourbon kings of Spain in the seventeenth century. The limestone façades are still translucent despite the film of grime and smog. The detail carved into the stone is voluptuous. Every Saturday there is a fish market in a sunken piazza, shaped like a triangle, between the covered market and the town hall. From the marble fountain that marks the entrance to the piazza at the top of some stairs, I looked down into a hive of activity. The stench was overpowering, the walls echoing the noisy market chorus. Fishmongers in blood-spattered aprons stood in front of buckets filled with eels, squid, and lobster, all squirming, wriggling, and wrestling against the odds. A young man was cutting a large swordfish into thick, bloody slices on a block of wood. He saw our camera, slit open the stomach, took out something raw, round, red, and disgusting, and put it into his mouth. He chewed and then laughed hysterically. At that moment Franco Zeffirelli descended the staircase into the market, his entourage in tow, including the Jack Russells.

Zeffirelli, who is clearly not put off by the fact that he is better known on the opera and cocktail circuit in Rome, Milan, and New York than in Catania's fish market, threw up his hands in delight and exclaimed, *"Carino!"* "Darling." He approached a mountain of a fishmonger who was holding up an octopus for sale and letting its slimy tentacles run through his fat fingers. The man smiled. Franco ate a prawn, lowering it into his open mouth. There was applause. A vote had been won. The opera director is a consummate campaigner, and although the fishmongers of Catania's market might not have heard of him, many were clearly intrigued by the man and his entourage. Policies were barely discussed on the hustings in the market, but Forza Italia's feel-good message of reassurance came across, and that's what counted.

Zeffirelli fervently believed in the Sicilians' native genius. "All you have to do is get rid of the old parties and all that stifling bureaucracy, and you will unleash the creativity of people here, some of the most articulate, intelligent, and sophisticated in Europe." Claudio Fava, Zeffirelli's opponent from the Network and a local Catanese, who should have been flattered by the director's appreciation of the Sicilian character, disagreed. He believed that Catania needed more than just a face-lift and deliverance from the threat of communism. It needed economic development to reduce the unemployment of almost 25 percent and youth unemployment that is twice as high. It needed a revolution of the mind.

Claudio Fava was in his mid-thirties. He and his wife lived in a modern house in the hills above Catania, surrounded by a high wall and barbed wire. They had two soldiers constantly on patrol in their yard. When Claudio Fava went to town, he traveled in one armored car with two bodyguards. The other bodyguards followed in the second armored car. They drove at a high speed. The Favas rarely went out at night, and then only with an armed escort. The couple owed their *vita blindata* to Claudio's father, Giuseppe. Like Claudio, he had been a journalist and writer. In January 1984 he was killed by the Mafia for publishing what in those days people only dared think: that the Mafia ran Catania, its construction business, its port, its drugs, its arms, its politicians, the lot.

On the wall of Fava's kitchen was a photograph. It was taken in 1983, and it showed a group of men clutching champagne glasses at a party. There were Salvatore Coco, the city's mayor; Salvatore Di Stefano, the regional head of the ruling Christian Democratic Party; Franco Guarnera, the chief doctor at the local prison; Antonello Longo, the head of the local Social Democratic Party; and Salvatore Lo Turco, a Socialist Party deputy in Parliament and a member of the Parliamentary Anti-Mafia Commission. Lo Turco had one arm intimately slung around the shoulders of another man, Benedetto "Nitto" Santapaola. He was the head of the Mafia in eastern Sicily and, after Totò Riina, considered to be the most senior mafioso in Italy. At the Maxitrial in Palermo in 1986 Judge Giovanni Falcone asked Lo Turco how he had found himself embracing the Mafia's number two. "Believe me, your Excellency," said the deputy, "I would never have imagined. . . . That Santapaola conquered me with his gentle manners and kindness."

In Catania too the Mafia thrived on a potent mixture of myth, malice, and manners. Protected by a conniving political establishment and a warped judiciary, Nitto Santapaola and his clan turned the port city into one of the centers of the international drug trade. They imported cocaine from Bolivia and Peru, heroin from the Golden Triangle, hashish from North Africa. They exported arms to Yugoslavia and Turkey. At home they created a criminal empire based on extortion, prostitution, gambling, and construction. Santapaola was arrested in 1993. Since then hundreds of other mafiosi have been arrested in the region, but few people are foolish enough to claim that the Mafia has been defeated. Its web of interests was intricately woven. Despite the fact that millions of dollars' worth of Mafia property has been seized by the state, billions are still thought to languish in Swiss bank accounts. And the conditions of unemployment and economic misery in which organized crime recruits new blood continue to exist.

Fava said his mission was to persuade ordinary Sicilians that they didn't have to be sucked into the lure of organized crime, that the Mafia was an affront to their rights as citizens, and that the Mafia offered protection only from itself. The message was popular, but it didn't win Fava the election. In fact, the Network suffered a humiliating defeat all over Sicily. Palermo, which had elected Leoluca Orlando, the head of the Network, as mayor in December 1993, suddenly turned its back on the party. Antonio Caponetto, the venerated former head of the city's anti-Mafia magistrates, who had received 40,000 votes as city councillor only three months earlier, also failed to get a majority. In almost every case the election was hijacked by Forza Italia and Silvio Berlusconi.

Why, I wondered, did the people of Catania vote for Franco Zeffirelli, a Florentine opera director who had romanticized the Mafia as a colorful band of brigands? The opposition claimed that the votes were bought by the Mafia, which was looking for new political patrons after the collapse of the Christian Democrats and the Socialists. They alleged that the Forza Italia clubs, fifty of which had been set up in notoriously sleazy parts of the city, were under the mob's influence. This was plausible, but by the end of 1994 little evidence had been brought forward to support it.

The hairdresser in the run-down district of San Cristoforo, the principal domain of the mob in Catania, had a Forza Italia sticker on his shop window. His parlor was full of giggling, cigarette-smoking young men who were having their hair cut: short at the back, long at the front. The hairdresser was a man in his forties who was wearing a yellow silk shirt and deftly held a cigarette while snipping his clients' hair. "Why Forza Italia?" I asked him. "Why not? They're new, they say they'll improve things. They're clever. I like Berlusconi. He's done well. He's a self-made man. He's not like the others!" Had he heard of Franco Zeffirelli? I asked. "Franco who?" asked the hairdresser. I explained. The hairdresser listened patiently. "If he's Forza Italia, and if you say he's a famous and intelligent man, I'll vote for him. After all, he's Berlusconi's man." For many Italians, especially on the left, the victory of Forza Italia meant that a genuine chance for reform had been missed, that the "sweet revolution" started in 1992 had been derailed, and that the transformation of Italians from individuals who seek refuge in their family, church, or party to citizens who trust a benevolent state would have to wait. They may have expected too much in the first place.

Power and
Its Limitations

I f Roberto Baggio, the Italian striker, had not missed his penalty shot in the tiebreaker of the 1994 World Cup soccer final, would the country's political development have been radically different? The question is less flippant than it sounds. Silvio Berlusconi had achieved a perfect, if crass, marriage among soccer, television, and politics in Forza Italia. For two weeks in the summer of 1994, as the entire country was gripped by World Cup fever, one couldn't be sure whether Italians shouting "Forza Italia" were egging on the national team or the prime minister's ruling party. This had been Berlusconi's precise intention when he named his movement after a rallying cry from the nation's favorite sport. It was a brilliant idea. Unfortunately, its success depended in part on the scoring ability of the national soccer team. At 11:30 P.M. on Sunday, July 17, when Italy's streets and piazzas were deserted because the nation was glued to the television, Baggio missed the shot and lost Italy the cup, albeit in a most unfair way. A collective groan of despair echoed through the country. World Cup–weary Italians, who had hoped to celebrate all night, lurched home, their heads bowed, their flags rolled up, their rattles silent. "Forza Italia" had begun to sound hollow, both in soccer and, as it turned out, in politics.

Had Italy won, some of the soccer glory would have rubbed off on the prime minister, whose club had supplied most of the players on the national team. The tycoon would have laid on a spectacular "coming-home party." His popularity rating would have shot through the roof. He would have felt confident enough to threaten his unruly coalition partners with fresh elections and might have been able to consolidate his power. But above all, if Italy had won the World Cup, the fans might have forgiven Berlusconi a series of "own goals," as *La Repubblica* put it, which revealed that the tycoon–prime minister had not yet mastered the craft of politics. It was this deficiency that eventually led to his downfall in December 1994.

Is this attaching too much importance to soccer? Perhaps. But for the Italian public soccer is a religion, and Berlusconi, the soccer and TV tycoon, regarded it as the modern equivalent of bread and circuses. Five days before the game against Brazil, in fact at the very time when Italy was rallying to defeat Bulgaria in the semifinals and the country was in the grip of a euphoria bordering on hysteria, the Berlusconi government tried to pull a fast one. It issued a decree that almost caused its own downfall barely a hundred days after taking power. The Biondi decree, named after Justice Minister Alfredo Biondi, stipulated that all suspects being held under preventive detention for crimes relating to corruption as well as a number of other minor offenses would be released from jail and put under house arrest. The government justified the decree as a necessary measure for reforming the country's judicial system.

The prime minister had taken on the Milan judges, partly out of revenge for their attempts to humiliate him during the election campaign, partly because he rightly feared that the noose of investigations into his companies would tighten. The dividing line between Italian institutions is notoriously fuzzy, but "Tangentopoli" and the election of Berlusconi further muddied the waters and produced a bizarre reversal of roles: the politicians accused the judges of behaving like politicians, and the judges attacked the government for meddling in the judiciary. Both were right. The Biondi decree was Berlusconi's first serious salvo against the judiciary. His spokesman, Giuliano Ferrara, a former journalist and talk-show host (on one of the prime minister's channels) with an acid wit and a Falstaffian girth, said the decree was an attempt to end the injustice of Italian justice. "We are one of the few democratic countries who have no habeas corpus. Our legal system is based on the principle of guilty until proven innocent, rather than the other way around." Anyone who has been subjected to the terrifying whims of an Italian judge or who has been locked up for months without being charged would agree. Unfortunately, Berlusconi, burdened by his conflicts of interest and by the criminal investigations into his companies, was not the ideal man to change the system. What should have been a legitimate question of judicial reform turned into a fierce political battle.

Indeed, reform was needed urgently. More than half of Italy's prison population of about 27,000 inmates—at present including the 2,000 or so suspects in the "Tangentopoli" affair—are routinely kept in jail without being tried or even charged. They are effectively detainees without trial, a fact Amnesty International has regularly criticized in its reports. The director of Rome's Regina Coeli jail was overjoyed by the decree. "We have released five hundred people in the last three days. There has never been so much space." Inmates who had been forced to sleep four to a cell designed for two were finally granted some breathing space. Tension in the prison declined.

Antonio Di Pietro saw the decree as a direct challenge to his authority. After all, he argued, had it not been for preventive custody, none of the suspects in the corruption scandal would have confessed. The Christian Democrats and Socialists would have continued to extract bribes from business as before. In an unprecedented move, Di Pietro and three other colleagues went on prime-time television the day after the decree was issued and said they wanted to be removed from their posts. Without the power to decree preventive custody, "their conscience did not allow them to continue working on the corruption probes." The burly Di Pietro looked ashen-faced, almost moved to tears. His somewhat sanctimonious address was a direct appeal to the Italian people to back him in his battle against Berlusconi. They did. The tycoon had underestimated Di Pietro's popularity. Even more serious was the fact that Berlusconi had failed to see the consequences of his actions. He had not bothered to ask himself what the public reaction would be to the release from jail of some of the country's most disgraced politicians. On leaving jail, Francesco De

Lorenzo, the former health minister accused of having taken bribes in return for bumping up the price of medicines, was greeted by an enraged crowd of Neapolitans spitting and throwing coins—a traditional sign of disrespect for convicted thieves, helped considerably by the fact that coins of 50 or 100 lire are worth next to nothing. Within days of the decree being issued, almost two thousand suspects were released. Most of these had in fact had little to do with the corruption scandal; they were petty thieves, drug addicts, drug dealers, and Totò Riina's doctor, who had been held on suspicion of links to the Mafia. But the impression was created that Berlusconi, who had been elected on promises to clean up the country, was freeing some of its most lurid offenders.

Berlusconi had also failed to see the suspicion that surrounded his motives for passing the decree. Newspapers and café gossip bristled with the obvious question: Had he passed the decree to protect family and friends? Bettino Craxi, for example, was languishing in self-imposed exile in Tunisia at the time. He was the main defendant in a corruption trial concerning Milan's Metro, and had sent a fax to the judges claiming to be too ill to turn up in court. However, pictures of him tossing a volleyball on a beach at Hammamet cast some doubt on his claims. Would Craxi now discover a miraculous cure and return to Italy in the secure knowledge that he would not go to jail? Another potential beneficiary of the Biondi decree would have been the prime minister's younger brother, Paolo. The forty-four-year-old head of the family's property business, Edilnord, had already been indicted on charges of bribery. Now a nationwide probe into the peccadilloes of Italy's Financial Police, the Guardia di Finanza, had cast the net of investigation over Berlusconi's business empire once again, with the finger of suspicion pointing again at Paolo.

In the face of mounting pressure from the public and from his own coalition partners, Berlusconi was forced to abandon the Biondi decree and come up with a draft law that would address the serious issue of judicial reform. The judges got their revenge by pressing ahead with the investigations into widespread tax fraud, casting their net slowly but inexorably over the prime minister himself. First, an arrest warrant was issued for Salvatore Sciascia, the head of the Fininvest tax department, as well as a handful of other executives from the prime minister's company. Under oath Sciascia confessed to having paid $200,000 to the Financial Police on two occasions to ensure a "favorable" reading of the books of three Berlusconi-owned companies. He told magistrates that the payments had been authorized by Paolo Berlusconi. Then an arrest warrant was issued for Paolo Berlusconi, stipulating that he must stay in jail because of legitimate fears that he might tamper with the evidence, thus adding insult to injury. After two days of negotiations during which Paolo had gone into hiding, a deal was finally struck between his lawyers and the magistrates. Paolo Berlusconi would not have to suffer the indignity of jail; he would be questioned in Milan's Palazzo di Giustizia. After a hearing that lasted seven hours, Paolo was smuggled out of the courthouse in the back of a florist's van while his lawyers confronted the press. The prime minister's brother admitted that his company had created a $2 million slush fund for bribing the Financial Police, "to keep those officers at bay who had become a nuisance." His lawyers put it in a familiar way: "Paolo Berlusconi," they said, "was the victim of a system of corruption from which neither he nor any other entrepreneur could escape." Here was the excuse that had become so familiar in the last two years: universal corruption neutralizes personal culpability. Meanwhile, the Guardia di Finanza, the very organization that was supposed to be enforcing the law, was still reeling from the fact that forty of its officers, including one general, had been arrested. Three officers implicated in the scandal had committed suicide in one month. When the allegations continued, the commander of the force sued the judiciary for libel. The "sweet revolution" had degenerated into farce: one branch of the police force was suing the judiciary, which was engaged in a full-scale war with the prime minister, whose brother had admitted paying bribes. Everyone blamed someone else. No one was completely above suspicion.

About this time something innocent but significant happened to me that speaks volumes about Italy's law enforcement machine. One weekend in August some friends had invited me to the Amalfi coast, the spectacular stretch of mountainous coastline south of Naples, where Moorish-looking villages and terraced lemon groves cling precariously to the cliffs. The water below is teeming with boats, small and large. Italy has more pleasure boats per capita than any other country in Europe. When the government announced a tax on yachts two years ago, a shudder went through the entire nation, not just a small part of it. My friends have a boat, a small one. It was a hot day, and we decided to set off for one of the shady bays, where smugglers used to moor their vessels and where one of their caves had been turned into a good fish restaurant. There were no tables available so we decided to wait in our boat on the bay. Suddenly we noticed that a gray Guardia di Finanza patrol boat with two uniformed men on board had entered the bay. It was sitting menacingly in the still water. "Could this be one of the routine tax checks?" my friends wondered. The oiled, tanned bodies on the boats beside us stirred in anticipation. Some disappeared to find the documents proving that they had paid their boat tax. Most probably they had no documents to find, because no tax had ever been paid. The whole scheme, my friends said, was ludicrous in any case. But they too got nervous. One of them wanted to start the engine and leave. The two uniformed men on the patrol boat were watching lazily.

Then a small, noisy motor launch made its way toward us. It was Bachis, the gnarled old man who owned the trattoria where we were planning to have lunch. He was with his son, and he was carrying two large trays. One was filled with pasta, the other with crayfish and grilled calamari. Between his legs were two bottles of wine. As Bachis passed our boat, he winked. He was heading for the patrol boat. One of the uniformed men took the trays and the wine from Bachis. The other started the engine.

This scene, harmless by national standards of bribery, seemed like an ideal way to introduce a broadcast I was doing about who in Italy corrupts whom. Had the Financial Police forced Bachis to pay the edible bribe, or had he offered them a free lunch? In fact the question is almost irrelevant, because in Italy both sides know what is expected of them. In any case, the broadcast went out on the BBC World Service. The following day I received a call from a Colonel Lisi of the Guardia di Finanza. To my horror, he told me that my anecdote had been reprinted and considerably embellished by *Il Giornale*. "And you know who's behind *Il Giornale*!" he said in a confidential voice. The newspaper was in fact owned by the same Paolo Berlusconi who was trying to prove that he had become a victim of Italy's evil Financial Police. "Will you print a denial of the story and write a letter to the newspapers?" "No," I said. "The story was true, even though it was exaggerated." Would I at least be prepared to meet the colonel and his commanding officer to discuss the situation? I agreed. Two days later I found myself being met at the gate of Guardia di Finanza headquarters in Rome.

A young officer in civilian clothes with a pistol crammed into the small of his back led me down what seemed like miles of stifling corridors. I grew increasingly nervous, convinced I had fallen into a trap, that I would be blackmailed, that the Guardia di Finanza had sifted through my records and discovered that the tax disc on my car had expired a month ago. I would be expelled from Italy. . . . My head began to spin when I suddenly heard myself say, "Colonel Lisi, nice to meet you." The colonel was wearing a Hawaiian shirt and smoking a large cigar. He wasn't what I had expected. We sat down and began to talk about the political situation in alarmingly general terms. All the time I was waiting for him to pull a document out of his drawer and confront me with an unpaid tax bill. Finally the colonel leaned forward in his large swivel chair, looked straight at me, and said, "Help us. We, the Guardia di Finanza, are getting so much bad press, we are being unfairly persecuted." I tried to imagine the Internal Revenue Service begging my colleague from *Corriere della Sera* to write a glowing article about it. The colonel went on, "Do you realize," he said, "that while all this fuss is being made about a handful of our boys indulging in some bribes, the other parts of the police force are getting away with murder? Last week forty officers of the Traffic Police in Modena were arrested for running an illegal parking scheme. Not a squeak about it in the newspapers." I had to control myself from bursting out with laughter. I had realized that Italy's Carabinieri, Cavalry Carabinieri, Municipal Police, Traffic Police, Financial Police, Forestry Police, Border Police, and numerous special squads were all competing against one another, but I hadn't expected them to reveal their dirty secrets to a foreigner. The national press clearly hadn't been interested in publishing their leaks, and the editors of the local newspapers in Modena were probably too frightened and aware to get involved in a battle between two police forces.

I told the story to an acquaintance who owns a large farm in southern Italy. He was delighted, delirious with *schadenfreude*. "I regularly supply the Financial Police with *bustarelle* [little envelopes]. I have to," he said. "Otherwise they would shut down my business." He continued, "They have more than two hundred laws at their disposal, which they can use in any way they like. Laws about the size of my cow sheds, the width of an irrigation canal, or the tax on a milking machine, laws that went out of date twenty years ago but can still be enforced because no one has bothered to erase them from the Penal Code. They can put me in jail for up to six months under preventive custody for any number of mundane trivialities. What's more, the web of laws is so complex and contradictory that when I *have* gone by the book I find that by following *one* law I'm breaking another. The situation's hopeless." He sighed. "The only way out is a gift."

There is no answer to this question of who is corrupting whom any longer. No one and no institution in this country is beyond suspicion. Perhaps corruption is like original sin: it can't be erased. The only solution may be a nationwide mea culpa, a general amnesty for everyone, and more spaghetti for the Guardia di Finanza.

Meanwhile, the shadow of suspicion had fallen on the prime minister. From the public's point of view, the arrest of Paolo Berlusconi and the Fininvest tax scandal confirmed their suspicion that the prime minister was trying to save his brother by issuing the Biondi decree. Suddenly all the questions and conflicts that had hung precariously over the prime minister's head and had been partially ignored by the public crashed down on him. His aura of invincibility was shattered, giving way to the suspicion that his political problems were exclusively of his own making. "The Great Seducer" had become his own worst enemy.

The episode gave the Italian public an alarming insight into Berlusconi's impatience with the laborious process of democracy. From their very first day in Parliament, Berlusconi's manager-deputies began complaining about the tedium of debates, voting procedures, and other parliamentary formalities. "Mr. Berlusconi," his advisers quipped at first, "feels as if he's on holiday. The workload of a prime minister is nothing compared to that of a businessman running a company with a seven-billion-dollar-a-year turnover." The eleven deputies and senators who had been employed by Fininvest before they were volunteered into politics all wore the same expression of glazed boredom when they sat in Parliament. They had a point, of course. The Italian Parliament is notoriously time consuming, ranking almost with the U.S. Congress. Its machinery is slowed down and sometimes brought to an abrupt standstill by the fact that every piece of legislation has to be approved by both chambers and will be tossed from one to the other in a kind of parliamentary Ping-Pong until the right deal can be struck and the law can be approved. The inherent fractiousness of coalition politics doesn't help either. To overcome these obstacles, Italian governments have often resorted to decrees rather than to laws. Although decrees should be invoked only in "exceptional and urgent circumstances," they have almost become the norm. Before Berlusconi's election, the government of Prime Minister Ciampi, for example, issued eighty-eight decrees, ranging from privatization of state companies to tax reform.

A government decree comes into force as soon as it has been published in the parliamentary gazette, which is usually the next day. It then has to be approved or thrown out by Parliament within sixty days. Most of the decrees announced by the Ciampi government had been widely accepted as the bitter but urgently needed medicine of economic damage control. In fact, they had made the government headed by an unelected central banker with a Cabinet of professors the most effective, resolute, and even popular administration since the era of Prime Minister Alcide De Gasperi in the 1950s. But Berlusconi issued a number of decrees, none of which were deemed essential but all of which were tinged with the suspicion that they could benefit his own business interests, in addition to the Biondi decree. A decree on legalizing unauthorized construction could theoretically have helped Berlusconi's construction company, Edilnord, which had been prevented from building a number of holiday villages in Sardinia because the local authorities had refused to grant building permits. Another decree created a virtual amnesty for water polluters. Companies that polluted rivers or lakes with waste were now allowed to pay a flat fine of 3 million lire, about $1,800. Although it was still illegal for them to pollute rivers, they would no longer be taken to court. This measure helped to clear a massive backlog of cases, but with such a low fine it also gave companies a financial incentive to pollute. A decree about copyright—hardly an issue of "exceptional and urgent circumstances"—extended the copyright Italian publishing houses have on authors from fifty to seventy-five years. Since the prime minister's publishing empire, Mondadori, owns 25 percent of all Italian copyrights, his motives naturally came under suspicion. By dint of his own policies the tycoon managed to highlight the fundamental problem bewitching his government: Silvio Berlusconi owned too much and was too rich for his own good.

Belatedly most of the Italian public, the media, Parliament, and Berlusconi himself discovered the blindingly obvious conflicts of interest. They existed on so many different levels that it was difficult to think of a single piece of legislation that would not somehow have come under suspicion. During the election campaign Berlusconi's business power had been seen as proof of his Midas touch. Only a handful of opponents from the former Communist Party had warned about the conflicts of interest. Berlusconi had already given up the management of his company in January, when he entered politics, and for most people that had been enough.

Berlusconi would probably have been able to keep his conundrum a secret had it not been for the fact that he himself gave the game away. At a time of utmost political sensitivity, when his decrees were being questioned not only by the press but by his coalition partners and the magistrates were homing in on his company, the tycoon decided to host a dinner in his villa in Arcore. Among the guests were his brother, Paolo, Minister of Defense Cesare Previti, who had once been Berlusconi's private lawyer; Under Secretary of State (effectively Berlusconi's chief of staff) Gianni Letta, a former executive manager of Fininvest; and Fedele Confalonieri, Berlusconi's oldest friend and now the chairman and chief executive of his company. Salvatore Sciascia, the head of the Fininvest tax department who had just been issued with an arrest warrant in the investigations concerning tax fiddles and bribes to the Financial Police, was represented by his lawyer. "Just old friends meeting for a chat," Confalonieri angrily told reporters who had heard about the meeting. "This country is worse than Stalin's Russia if old friends can't even meet socially!" he thundered. The kitchen cabinet, which spans business and politics, had been convened to discuss a common strategy regarding the "legal problems" of Paolo Berlusconi. It is hard to imagine an equivalent, because nothing like the Berlusconi situation has ever existed in a democracy before. Even Berlusconi's spokesman, Giuliano Ferrara, described the meeting as "foolish." Yet again the prime minister had revealed himself to be a stranger to the concept of accountability in public life. He still thought he was running a boardroom.

Berlusconi's blunders have become textbook material for any tycoon contemplating a life in politics. Another lesson the prime minister had to learn the hard way was how to use his own television and his own in-house opinion polls. The television channels, which the prime minister had used to great effect in the run-up to the elections, broadcasting his own campaign messages and covering his party rallies live, became a liability once he was in power. Afraid of being bombarded with hostile questions from journalists who were not on his payroll, Berlusconi preferred to appear on one of his own channels, fielding questions from his favorite anchorman, the oleaginous Emilio Fede.

Too smooth to be real, Fede, a Sicilian by birth, is not so much a newscaster as a master of ceremonies in the television court of Prime Minister Berlusconi. He has complete editorial control over the news on Network 4, which means the prime minister can rely on favorable coverage; he also directs the news bulletin from his chair—on air—as if he were conducting a circus. He walks around the studio impatiently if stories are late; two terrified assistants sit on either side of his chair, staring into computers and supplying their master with news updates. Fede treats them like his children. "Gianni!" he is prone to shout. "What's the latest on Reuters? . . . What do you mean, they haven't come up with the story yet?" All this is live on air. Fede's introductions to news stories are laced with opinion, delivered in a grandfatherly fashion. "The really important thing about this story is . . ." or "Look out for . . ." Emilio Fede is the anchorman the prime minister turned to in his times of trouble. At the height of the crisis caused by the Biondi decree, Berlusconi's only interview on national television was with Fede. While the newscaster asked such irreverent questions as "What's troubling you, president of the Council of Ministers?" or said, "It must be very hard to govern under these circumstances!" Berlusconi poured out his anger and indignation like a wounded animal with a bruised ego. "The Great Seducer" looked ruffled. The rigid mask of haughty composure had cracked. His voice was hoarse with anger. His hurried justifications sounded insincere. The whole spectacle produced in the viewer a most profound and delectable sense of *schadenfreude* as one of the mightiest egos in Italian politics was deflated. The prime minister had been made to look ridiculous on his own television channel. He had only himself to blame.

A few weeks later he still hadn't understood that as prime minister he would have to be more careful about how he used television. In order to regain some popularity and credibility, Berlusconi commissioned a series of advertisements that reminded the weary viewer of the government's achievements. The spots were broadcast on RAI as well as on the Fininvest channels, incurring the wrath of the opposition both inside and outside the ruling coalition. After four days Italy's media watchdog banned the advertisements apart from one on taxes, which was considered a useful public information broadcast. In the end the episode was another embarrassment for Berlusconi.

Berlusconi also relied too much on opinion polls. Like many other heads of government, the Italian prime minister makes no important move without first consulting his polls. The difference is that he owns the polling organization. It's part of his characteristic distrust of the world outside his company and his inner circle of advisers. The prime minister's chief pollster is a young executive who used to work for Network 4. Gianni Pilo was one of the thirty managers who had helped to orchestrate Berlusconi's election campaign and one of the eleven who had ended up in Parliament. In September 1993 Pilo and a partner bought Diakron, a Milan-based polling company. Nominally Diakron is independent, but almost all of its business is with Fininvest. While in office Berlusconi consulted Pilo and his polls at 6:30 every evening.

Diakron's offices, which are located in a Fininvest building on the outskirts of Milan, were used as Berlusconi's campaign headquarters. Here the symbiosis between his politics and his business was perfect.

Pilo employs a staff of 150 receptionists who each day question a sample of five hundred Italians—the number stays the same, the names vary—on the political issue or issues of the day. Although the sample is relatively small, it is carefully chosen from different regions, age groups, and professions. He assured me that the frequency of the polls produced an accurate trend of opinion. When I interviewed Pilo, whose radically short hair, boyish looks, and dark blue suits make him look like a reformed skinhead, he told me that he had conducted two polls that day. "We asked people whether they feared that the presence of the neo-Fascist National Alliance in any way threatened democracy; the answer was a resounding 'no.' We also asked them what they felt about the Northern League as a coalition partner. The majority were not happy." Pilo was quick to point out that Berlusconi doesn't follow his polls slavishly. "Sometimes he follows his instincts, even if the polls point in a different direction." But the danger, surely, is that the polls begin to blunt the instincts, especially if the surveys become a daily confirmation of the prime minister's popularity. At the height of the decree crisis Berlusconi insisted on referring to the results of his own polls, which, needless to say, endorsed his policies, even as independent opinion polls indicated that the country was turning against him.

Five hundred years ago, Berlusconi would have been consulting the stars; two thousand years ago, he would have been staring at some pig's entrails. The daily polls are nothing more than an attempt to predict the future, and sometimes they prove to be as inaccurate as more traditional modes of divination. First comes the poll, then the policy. If legislation and decrees were drafted and issued on the basis of Berlusconi's in-house polls, the nature of the questions in the surveys became an essential part of government. In the case of the Biondi decree, which allowed hundreds of corruption suspects to leave jail, Gianni Pilo had clearly asked the wrong type of question. Apparently he had asked his sample whether they were in favor of judicial reform in Italy. The answer was of course a resounding "yes." But the question should have taken into account the consequences. "Would you be in favor of judicial reform if it meant releasing the suspects in Italy's corruption scandal?" The answer to that question turned out to be a clear "no."

At the end of August 1994 Berlusconi had demonstrated two things: first, that he was better at winning elections than at governing the country; and second, that he couldn't tell the difference between the two. There were several reasons for this: his will to rule was not matched by the political means at his disposal. Although the right-wing "Freedom Pole" had an overwhelming majority in the Chamber of Deputies, it narrowly lacked one in the Senate. Thus every piece of legislation could theoretically be stalled by the opposition. In addition, Berlusconi gave the impression that he wanted to create a tyranny of the majority. Whenever he encountered a political hurdle or some sharp criticism in the newspapers or on state television, he would accuse his detractors of "going against the will of the majority." He appeared to be convinced that once he had been endorsed by a narrow majority of the Italian people, he was free to wield power as he wished. This system works in Great Britain and the United States, whose institutions are strong and independent, but not in Italy, where they have been weak and politicized. The solution here has traditionally been one in which the opposition has been encouraged to become a minority shareholder in the system of power. Compromise has been a means of taking the sting out of one's opponents. Berlusconi tried to break with this tradition. But his declared desire to establish a British-style democracy with an alternation between government and opposition was frustrated not only by Italy's fragmented political landscape but also by his own conflicts of interest.

The most alarming illustration of Berlusconi's interpretation of majority rule was his attacks against RAI. In June 1994 Berlusconi said, "The fact that state broadcasting repeatedly criticizes the government, which is after all the expression of the majority of the Italian electorate, strikes me as an anomaly." The real anomaly was of course that the prime minister already had a virtual monopoly on commercial television. A week later Berlusconi stepped up the offensive, threatening RAI with sweeping cuts and reforms. Few people doubted that these were necessary to drag the bloated, overspent, overstaffed, and underachieving excrescence that is RAI into the late twentieth century. But once again Berlusconi the media tycoon was the wrong man to launch the attack. The entire four-man board of directors at RAI resigned. Berlusconi tried to appoint his own people but was stopped by his coalition partners. After several weeks of hag-gling, RAI had a new board of directors, including a medieval histo-rian, a real estate agent, a stockbroker, and the owner of a small news agency. None of them knew anything about television or radio; they had apparently been chosen for their business and management skills. The most important fact, however, was that the directors mirrored the constellation of the right-wing majority in power. Two were ap-pointed by Forza Italia, one by the Northern League, and one by the National Alliance. Under the old regime RAI had reflected the con-sensus of the *partitocrazia*. The Christian Democrats had controlled RAI 1, the Socialists RAI 2, and the Communists RAI 3. Under Berlusconi and the new RAI management, this consensus had been sacrificed. Although the government had made some attempt to put men and women from the right-wing parties into new management positions at RAI, it had failed to satisfy the demands of the Northern League for its own TV channel. The most obvious and easiest solu-tion would have been to give the National Alliance and the League RAI 1 and 2, which had once been controlled by the Christian Dem-ocrats and the Socialists, and allow the Left to hold on to RAI 3. This way some degree of balance would have been achieved and the larg-est number of political parties would have been kept happy.

As a business tycoon who was used to getting his own way, Silvio Berlusconi did not suit the times. Italy is not yet ready for a "Thatcherite" leader, as Berlusconi likes to describe himself. It may never be. He had come up against the bitter reality of Italian coalition politics, which is the art of surviving conspiracies, a fact that he failed to recognize and that he compounded with a mixture of polit-ical incompetence and personal arrogance. Berlusconi looked like an emperor whose ship of state was no more than a rubber dinghy with a puncture. Most of the opposition to the prime minister came from his own partners, especially from Umberto Bossi, the cantankerous head of the Northern League, whose party had lost much of its sup-port to Forza Italia. Bossi's political survival depended on his ability to oppose Berlusconi within the coalition without being blamed for its demise. By attacking the tycoon, he was defining his own features as a politician. This explains the fact that he became a constant thorn in the prime minister's side. Berlusconi obliged him with his string of mistakes and miscalculations.

Gianfranco Fini, the leader of the National Alliance, pursued a similar policy, though in a much more subtle way. Fini too opposed the prime minister because that was one way of showing how his right-wing party differed from Berlusconi's. But as the streetfighter and the bruised tycoon locked horns in the parliamentary arena, the neo-Fascist leader gazed on the spectacle with princely disdain. At the height of the coalition crisis in December 1994, I interviewed Fini in his small office at party headquarters, filled with Christmas presents and cards, many of which seemed to have been sent by the Carabinieri, the Police Federation, and the armed forces. While his allies looked more and more exhausted and ashen-faced from the daily political battles they were fighting, Fini sported a winter tan and a self-satisfied smile. The jolly image was underscored by the pattern on his multicolored tie, which was of frolicking dolphins. On the table in front of him was a chessboard, and after the interview, in which Fini had produced the usual litany of bland reassurances, he challenged me to a game. I was beaten after only ten minutes. Considering how badly I play chess, this was hardly surprising. But what did strike me as unusual was that the leader of one of Italy's ruling parties found time to play games while the political establishment was collapsing around him. Fini was rewarded for his cool. In the summer of 1994, he had begun to overtake Berlusconi as the most popular Italian politician. By the end of the year every opinion poll put him at the top of the list, well ahead of his rivals.

Ideological differences over privatization, taxation, subsidies, the Constitution, the federation, abortion, and a host of other issues meant that Italy's right-wing ruling coalition was in constant danger of neutralizing itself. If all these policies automatically lead to a coalition crisis, it is better not to broach them at all or to water them down so much as to render them ineffective. This is precisely what had happened before the "sweet revolution." The difference then was that the ruling parties had enjoyed the near certainty of staying in power, however often they fell. The same government had reconstituted itself, Humpty-Dumpty style, over and over again. The system had been deeply unsatisfactory, but at least it had created an illusion of change. The present coalition was not strong enough to govern and not weak enough to be removed by the opposition. In the meantime it did what all previous ruling coalitions had done, which was to carve up, or "colonize," the state as much as possible. Italy's vast state holding conglomerate IRI is a case in point: the board of IRI, like the board of RAI, echoes the fine balance within the ruling coalition. It contains members from all of the three main parties, creating a perfect political equilibrium among the various forces of government. But when substantive issues are discussed, the board comes to blows.

The right-wing coalition that was elected in 1994 turned out to be much more fractious and paralyzed than many of its predecessors. After years of agonizing electoral reform and soul-searching about a new, more efficient political system, the coalition often seemed like little more than a cruel joke. Ideally, both the Northern League and the neo-Fascists wanted to hold fresh elections in the summer of 1994 to feast off what they thought was the rotting carcass of Forza Italia. But such thoughts of revenge turned out to be premature. Although the Northern League had cut Berlusconi down to size by opposing him on key pieces of legislation, it still could not be confident of reversing its own decline. A protest movement deprived of its principal object of protest, the Northern League degenerated into a kind of multiple psychosis. The movement became increasingly schismatic, with one wing keen to stay in power at all costs and carve out a part of the patronage cake for itself. Meanwhile, the other wing was yearning for constitutional reform to turn Italy into a federation. Eventually the two will become incompatible, and the League is likely to split.

Meanwhile, the neo-Fascists needed more time to prove that they were socially acceptable and had ditched some of their more embarrassing ideas and bedfellows. The longer they could be associated with government, the more respectable they hoped to become. They too had a vested interest in putting off fresh elections.

The result was a government in office but not in power. Like some ancient fable warning about the excesses of vanity, Berlusconi had been politically emasculated. His miracles began to sound like hollow promises.

Although the Italians like to think of themselves as great individualists, they are essentially creatures of the tribe. They like to huddle together in clusters, whether on beaches, on highways, in the piazza, or in politics. The bandwagon is their favored mode of political transport, whether in victory or in defeat. Berlusconi, who himself had done so much to nurture the consumer herd instinct with his television, his advertising, his cinema, and his publishing empire, became first its beneficiary and then its victim. In Italian politics especially, no one is indispensable. Furthermore, the Italians are ruthless with losers, especially in politics and soccer. One day Roberto Baggio, the Buddhist striker with the ponytail, was hailed as the "God of soccer," the "savior," the "magician," and the "little Buddha." The next day, after missing his World Cup penalty shot, he was called a "wet lame rabbit," "a sour disappointment," a "failure." The knives were out for Baggio in the same way that the knives were out for Berlusconi only a hundred days after he had become prime minister.

At the end of November 1994 Berlusconi received an *avviso di garanzia*—a notification that criminal proceedings had been started against him—on the very day he was hosting an international conference on organized crime in Naples. With shrewd timing the judges had dealt Berlusconi a bitter blow laced with stinging irony. The prime minister's earnest protestations in the conference chamber that Italy and his government were at the forefront of the fight against the international Mafia were deflated—to say the least—by the fact that Berlusconi himself would be interrogated by the judges. His response was emotional. In public he swore "on the heads of my five children" that he had never corrupted anyone. Almost in the same breath he admitted that illegal payments had been made to the Guardia di Finanza. But like so many before him, Berlusconi described himself as a victim of extortion. "I, like tens of thousands of other Italian businessmen, was subjected to a system of extortion"—he used the word *concussione,* meaning extortion by public officials—"that we were powerless to oppose." But this left several questions unanswered. First, why had Berlusconi not alerted the press, the judiciary, or the regular police about this extortion when his companies had made the payments in 1989 and 1991? Second, what had been the benefits in unpaid taxes for Fininvest? As his rival Carlo De Benedetti had admitted a year before, extortion was immensely profitable. The investigations reached their humiliating climax when Berlusconi was summoned to the forbidding Palazzo di Giustizia in Milan, where he was questioned by the magistrates for almost eight hours. Instead of giving a press conference, as his advisers had promised he would, Berlusconi was driven under tight security to his favorite habitat: a television studio at one of his own stations from which he launched a stinging televised attack on the judges.

It was no use. On December 22 Berlusconi was forced to resign. Rebels from the Northern League, led by Umberto Bossi, had finally pulled the plug on the ruling coalition, threatening it with a vote of no confidence supported by the left-wing opposition. Berlusconi preempted the inevitable result by resigning before the vote took place.

What finally toppled the tycoon prime minister was neither his conflicts of interest nor his legal problems nor even his humiliation at the hands of the judiciary. It was betrayal by his own allies, the rebels of the Northern League. Berlusconi's time in office had lasted barely eight months. Instead of creating an economic miracle and a million jobs, as he had promised, under his tenure the number of unemployed rose by 400,000. Between the time Berlusconi took office and gave it up, the lira had lost 13 percent of its value against the deutschmark and 8 percent against the dollar. By all accounts the tycoon's prime ministership had been a resounding failure. And yet, even before he had resigned, Berlusconi was already pressing for fresh elections as soon as possible, convinced that his trials and tribulations had created a sympathetic groundswell of support on which he could capitalize. Was this extraordinary self-confidence merely the final gasp of a deluded ego, or was it based on fact? To many commentators' surprise, independent opinion polls confirmed that if new elections were held Berlusconi would be reelected. It seemed as if the prime minister had succeeded in portraying himself as a victim. The revolution that had sought to turn the Italians into responsible citizens and make the country's rulers more accountable still had a long way to go.

The Men of Providence

A British diplomat in Rome tells the following story. In the summer of 1966 a Roman taxi driver was stuck in some appalling traffic. When he could no longer bear the heat, the noise, the chaos, and the fact that he wasn't moving, he threw up his hands and shouted, *"Duce, Duce! Dove sei?"* (Duce, Duce, where are you?) In 1513 Niccolò Machiavelli wrote in Chapter 26 of *The Prince,* "Italy waits for him who shall yet heal her wounds and put an end to the ravaging and plundering of Lombardy, to the swindling and taxing of the Kingdom of Tuscany, and cleanse those sores that for long have festered. It is seen how she entreats God to send someone who shall deliver her from these wrongs and barbarous insolencies. It is seen also that she is ready and willing to follow a banner if only someone will raise it."

The yearning for a man of providence who will deliver the people of the Italian peninsula from their torments—be they foreign invaders, internal feuds, or, for that matter, Roman traffic jams—has been a recurring theme of Italian history, starting well before the creation of the Italian nation. This constant search for unity and greatness has often been fueled by the distant memory of empire, glowing dimly amid the ruins of ancient Rome. In the fourteenth century Cola di Rienzo tried to re-create the Roman Republic in the lawless, festering city marked by disease and torn apart by feudal disputes. He failed and died a violent death when he became too powerful and irreverent for the feudal families like the Colonnas, who were the real masters of medieval Rome. The Risorgimento, the political creation of Italy in the 1860s, was part of the nineteenth-century tradition of nation building, but it was also inspired by ancient Rome and by a return to past glories. Dwarfing the Capitol and the Forum, for example, and poised majestically above them at the intersection of four of the city's major boulevards, stands the white marble monument to King Victor Emmanuel II. It was under the king's banner that unification was first accomplished. The monument is a prime example of architectural one-upmanship. But Victor Emmanuel is not buried in the monument; he lies in the Pantheon, the best preserved of all ancient Roman monuments, another demonstration that the architects of the Risorgimento tried to establish a continuity between past and present. The most brazen neo-imperialist was Mussolini. He tampered with Rome's layout by building the Avenue of the Imperial Forum, which connects the Piazza Venezia with the Coliseum. When that wasn't enough, he tried to re-create the ancient capital at EUR on the outskirts of the city. But above all Il Duce described himself as the "Man of Providence" who would restore Italy to greatness. Of course, he too failed, undermined by his own follies and excesses, by his disastrous decision to go to war on the side of Nazi Germany, and by conspiracies in his ranks.

Does Berlusconi fit into this tradition? He himself would strongly deny it. The dramatic failure of the Mussolini experiment and the establishment of Italian democracy have ruined the sex appeal of Italy's imperial past. But in a stark contrast to his predecessors in office, Berlusconi has spoken of himself as much more than just a prime minister chosen by Parliament. In December 1994, shortly before his resignation, the tycoon said he had been "spiritually anointed by the Italian people to lead them." He felt he had received a mandate that no party could break. This was not the case. Unlike in Britain, the Italian electorate does not elect its prime ministers directly. The head of government is appointed by the president on the advice of the victorious party or parties who form a majority in Parliament. During the election campaign of 1994 it was, for instance, by no means clear that Berlusconi would actually become prime minister after his coalition of right-wing parties had been elected. Though he fully expected the appointment, neither Umberto Bossi nor Gianfranco Fini would go gently into that good night. Strictly speaking, only 23 percent of the Italians had voted for Forza Italia and therefore for Berlusconi, the party's leader, a percentage that hardly amounts to a spiritual contract with the nation. Nevertheless, in his highly controversial TV addresses, which became more frequent as his troubles mounted, Berlusconi attempted to appeal directly to the voters. At one stage he even called on people "to take to the streets in silent protest" if he should lose a vote of no confidence in Parliament. Critics of Berlusconi, such as Professor Luigi Berlinguer, were outraged by the prime minister's "Peronist behavior." They feared that Italy would degenerate into a Latin American–style populist dictatorship. Some, like veteran newspaper editor Indro Montanelli, compared Berlusconi's use of television to Mussolini's use of propaganda. Montanelli, who edited Berlusconi's right-wing *Il Giornale* before he broke with the tycoon over editorial interference, had set up his own polemical newspaper, *La Voce* (The Voice), at the ripe old age of eighty-four. One of the leading campaigners against Berlusconi's attempts to control all of Italy's electronic media, Montanelli described the tycoon's use of television as "the electronic balcony," a reference to the balcony in the Palazzo Venezia favored by Mussolini for his public addresses.

"He may not know it, he may not *want* to know it, but Berlusconi is a kind of Mussolini figure." Franco Ferrarrotti, professor of sociology at the University of Rome, delivers his wisdom with all the nuances and cadences of a Lord Olivier, surrounded by towering piles of books and yellowed papers in his study. "He wants to be seen as the man of providence, the man who alone is capable of uniting the country, of giving it a fresh start and creating a miracle, as only the Italians can dream of one. A miracle to save them from the skullduggery of their daily lives. He wants to be seen as the *deus ex machina*."

Berlusconi had promised salvation, miracles, prosperity, and sweeping reform. They would have to emerge from his many contradictions and inconsistencies: champion of the free market whose fortune had sprung from a virtual monopoly on private television and advertising; Mr. Fix-it of the Italian economy whose company is drowning in a sea of debts; devout Catholic and family man who has had an acrimonious divorce; prime minister of unity who is planning to promote devolution of the regions and federalism. There is something for everyone in Forza Italia, just as there was something for everyone in Fascism.

Ideally, Berlusconi would have liked an American style presidential system; Forza Italia's entire *raison d'être* was to be a vehicle for Berlusconi's triumph. He wasn't just the leading candidate of his party, he was its chief embodiment. The party's candidates were cloned in the image of the tycoon in order to remind voters that a ballot for their local candidate was as good as a ballot for Berlusconi. In the language of advertising, which so inspired his campaign, there was total brand identification.

Berlusconi has also shown that the unabashed celebration of power still exercises its lure. While the old ruling parties were desperate to hide their cell phones, limousines, and bodyguards, the toys of power that reminded the electorate of their past excesses, Berlusconi preened like the newly crowned king of the jungle. The number of bodyguards milling around him swelled. He traveled in motorcades that dwarfed those of the president of the republic. Wherever he went he was pursued by a swarm of paparazzi and his own personal television cameramen. In Britain or Germany, Berlusconi the candidate would have tried to play down his power to appease a public and media worried about his conflicts of interests. Not in Italy. The ownership of Fininvest became a public issue only four months after the election. In Italy, power is not there to be checked and screened, it is above all to be respected and exploited as a source of patronage. As a friend of mine put it, "If they gave Olympic medals for jumping onto bandwagons, Italy would win gold every time."

Berlusconi was not an isolated phenomenon. While he lured voters on a national level, a politician in a town in the southern tip of Italy provided an uncanny mirror image. Taranto is situated on the instep of the Italian heel. Its air is thick with the stench of fish and the acrid fumes wafting from Europe's biggest steel plant. The old city, lodged on a narrow strip of land between the gulf and the lagoon, looks as if it has emerged from the bottom of the sea after decades of submersion. The once-luminous yellow stone of the stuccoed houses has become encrusted with the green moss of decay. The peeling walls are festooned with damp washing hanging out to dry in the rain. The shrill flatulence of mopeds echoes through the dank alleyways. The city's tourist industry has been reduced to one Swedish backpacker, who has taken on the shabby appearance of a street urchin, begging for his fare back to Stockholm.

While the old city is imbued with the folklore of petty crime and chaos, the steel plant on the other side of the bridge hails from a futuristic thriller film. Ilva at Taranto is Europe's biggest steel plant. A giant landscape of blast furnaces, billowing funnels, and huge metal pipes that look like gleaming intestines, it contains more than 30 miles of railway track and 120 miles of road. The pollution descends like a yellow blanket onto the nearby olive groves and fruit orchards for which the city used to be famous and in which most of its inhabitants used to be employed before the arrival of steel in 1960. Taranto's 250,000 inhabitants care little about the foul smell hanging over their homes or the continuous roar coming from the blast furnaces. For them the smoke represents jobs. But despite being one of Europe's most efficient steel producers and despite having already scaled its workforce from 24,000 in 1974 to just over 10,000 today, Ilva must cut another 5,000 jobs in the next three years to meet the European Union's productivity requirements. As they spill out of the factory's main gate at the end of a shift, the workers look particularly glum. Taranto, in short, is a depressing place. An old guidebook reminds the visitor that it was Taranto that gave its name to the tarantula, "a species of spider whose bite was the reputed cause of a peculiar contagious melancholy madness known as tarantism, which was curable only by music and violent dancing. The hysterical mania reached its height in southern Italy in the late seventeenth century and has left its memory in the tarantella, the graceful dance of the region."

Faced with rising unemployment, crime, and more decay, Taranto is once again in the grip of tarantism. This time the distraction comes not from music or violent dancing but from the city's mayor,

Giancarlo Cito. Elected to office in December 1993, he embodies all the confusions, hang-ups, and urges that have been unleashed by the collapse of Italy's old party system.

For decades Taranto had been ruled by a Christian Democratic administration. As in hundreds of other cases, the city government was disbanded at the height of the corruption scandal amid the usual flurry of investigations into bribes, rigged construction contracts, and large-scale graft, fueled by steel subsidies from Rome and Brussels. For eighteen months Taranto didn't even have a mayor, an omission that made very little difference to the running of the city. During the campaign for the municipal elections in November 1993, it was widely assumed that the left-wing alliance of reformed Communists, unreconstructed Marxists, Greens, Radicals, and the mild-mannered Democratic Alliance would win in Taranto, as elsewhere. They were running against a dinosaur coalition of the old ruling parties who had, in the words of one local newspaper, "changed their suits but not their underwear." Giancarlo Cito was the unorthodox outsider, running as an independent candidate with his own homemade party. It thus came as a shock to many when the burly proprietor of the local television station was elected in the second round with a resounding majority.

Mayor Cito was one of the first practitioners of the new style of television politics pioneered in Italy, both presaging and paralleling Berlusconi's eventual mastery of the form. In 1984 he sold his construction business and set up the local television station. In 1990 he formed his own party, the Mezzogiorno Action League. First he lured his viewers with a mixture of cheap bootleg movies and soft-focus pornography, then he bombarded them with propaganda. Both the party and the television network were created for the sole purpose of promoting Citizen Cito, as one newspaper had dubbed him, and his message of no-nonsense, table-thumping government. Crude, perhaps, but it worked. Viewers relished the way Cito harangued, insulted, and browbeat his opponents. The libel charges didn't seem to matter as long as the viewers were happy. Neither did the mayor's shady past, widely reported in the local newspapers, concern the majority of voters. It was an impressive oversight, considering the fact that Cito had been given a one-year suspended sentence for receiving stolen goods.

He was also the subject of sixteen separate judicial inquiries by the Parliamentary Anti-Mafia Commission into alleged links with organized crime, the dubious financing of his television station, and the illicit funding of his construction business. Before forming the Mezzogiorno Action League, he had also been a member of the Italian Social Movement and had once belonged to an extreme-right-wing band of thugs. The local magistrates are trying to get Mayor Cito unseated on the grounds that someone with a suspended sentence should not hold public office. But the chief of police and the city's senior traffic warden still salute him on his daily tours of inspection around the city.

He struts around Taranto like a grotesque reincarnation of the Fascist *podestà* of the 1930s. Mussolini changed the title *sindaco* (mayor) to *podestà,* an ancient Roman term that was supposed to bestow added authority on the officeholder. Mayor Cito, with his swarthy complexion and few strands of thin black hair pasted over his large bald head, is today's black farce of authority. His sense of importance can be measured by the number of bodyguards accompanying him, four at one count—quite a crowd for the mayor of a medium-sized city. When we visited the mayor in February 1994, Taranto's town hall was teeming with policemen. Some were pacing up and down the vaulted entrance hall in nervous expectation of the mayor's arrival. Others were lounging on the staircase outside his office like the retinue of a warlord. At first I thought a senior politician from Rome must be visiting. But when I was told that the mayor feared for his security in sleepy Taranto, I began to fear for his sanity.

We made ourselves comfortable in the mayor's office and examined the etchings and paintings on the wall for glimpses into Cito's soul. Psychological detective work proved unnecessary with such an outgoing subject. The doors were suddenly flung wide open, and a very large man marched in, preceded by a whirl of secretaries, deputy mayors, and bag carriers. Mayor Cito sat down underneath a crucifix. His desk was flanked by two large flags, one Italian, the other displaying the crest of Taranto. The mayor's grand entrance had been filmed by his own personal cameraman, "Mimmo," who follows the mayor like a footman. The most mundane mayoral act, from a meeting with the deputy mayor about a new set of lampposts to a meeting with the BBC, is recorded on video and then broadcast that evening on the mayor's own television channel. "Get us some coffee, Mimmo!" the mayor said in the gently menacing tone of someone who commands enough authority never to have to raise his voice. Mimmo, who was in his early twenties, sported a wispy mustache and bore the scars of a turbulent complexion, recently tamed, it seemed, with pungent antiseptic creams. He lurched to attention and left the room.

Our main purpose was to film the mayor being filmed on one of his inspection tours around the city, at which he revives that crucial contact between the "palazzo" and the "piazza." Unfortunately, we had just missed that morning's inspection round. "Don't worry!" said the mayor. "What would you like to see? The municipal cemetery, which I have had cleaned up? Garibaldi Park?" One of the mayor's flunkies, visibly embarrassed, cleared his throat and interrupted. "Sorry, Dottore, but the workers have gone home. It's raining. Have you seen how it's raining now?" The mayor's swarthy face clouded over. "Get me Girolamo!" The flunky disappeared. Two minutes later the cell phone rang. The mayor pressed the slim-line miracle of modern communication onto his jowly cheek and hollered into it. "Girolamo! It's me, Cito. Get your boys back out there . . . I don't care if it's raining. I've got the BBC in town. Let's organize something big for them." The mayor sat a little more upright. His chin jutted out a fraction.

We waited for him, as arranged, by the gates of Garibaldi Park. The police had cordoned off the street. Flashing blue lights announced the mayor's cavalcade of two cars. The five municipal gardeners, who had been dragged away from their game of cards, stepped up their pruning. Idle for decades, they were now shearing hedges, mowing grass, and raking leaves in a park that had once been a metaphor of the city's decay and neglect. The mayor's entourage included the head and deputy head of the Taranto Parks Authority, the senior local policeman and traffic warden, and, of course, Mimmo, the camera/footman. Mayor Cito stopped to admire a freshly pruned hedge. Everyone nodded approval. The municipal gardener began to snip even faster. He looked as if he were pruning for his life. Wherever the mayor strutted, he unleashed feverish activity. Four gardeners in white overalls were raking leaves so vigorously, they were in danger of digging up the lawn. None of them, apart from the foreman, looked up to greet the mayor or even catch his admiring eye. Authority, however murky, inspires respect in these parts.

The inspection was just about to end, hailed as a resounding success, when the mayor and his entourage discovered that someone had parked a rusty blue Fiat Uno between the oleander bushes. The faces of the entourage blushed visibly. "Who does this *car* belong to?" asked the mayor, casting around him with a stern look on his face. "*Who* does the car belong to?" shouted the chief traffic warden. Finally the chorus was taken up by the entire party. Curious bystanders slunk off quietly. A woman who was carrying a child and had been watching the mayor's procession from her window disappeared behind a curtain. Cito was about to throw a tantrum. Suddenly a young man appeared from behind the bushes, hastily got into the car, and drove off. The mayor smiled and glanced quickly at us, perhaps to make sure that we had filmed the lesson in authority. His own cameraman certainly had. There was relief all round. The mayor declared himself satisfied and headed back to his armored car after telling one of his flunkies to order someone to remove some rotten fruit from the pavement. The *podestà* sped off into the distance, blue lights flashing. The gardeners stopped pruning, the woman reappeared at the window, and the deputy head of the parks department looked at me pleadingly and asked, "Can we go and have lunch now?"

Taranto provided a fascinating insight into the trappings of power and the deference they produce. During our visit many people seemed to be entranced by their hyperactive mayor as he flitted from pruned hedge to swept pavement. It reminded me of the famous light in Mussolini's office that burned after midnight in the Palazzo Venezia so all Rome could see that Il Duce was toiling for his country. The light was on, but the office was often empty. Whenever lower-ranking visitors came to see him—"lower-ranking" meaning everyone else in Italy with the possible exception of the king—Mussolini made them run from the door of his office to his desk—a distance of forty-five yards. When they arrived at the desk, they had to stand. This was not only designed to humiliate his underlings, it was also meant to enhance the impression of tireless activity.

Elements of this absurd cult of activity had resurfaced after fifty years, not just in Taranto but also in Rome. Almost no press conference or television address went by without Prime Minister Berlusconi telling the Italian people how little he slept and how hard he worked for them. "I work eighteen hours a day," he once told his audience, "much harder than when I was a businessman." As the agony of his government dragged on in December 1994, the tycoon looked increasingly exhausted. The harder he worked, the more he created problems for himself.

Berlusconi has often been compared to H. Ross Perot, the U.S. presidential candidate who threw in the towel at the eleventh hour and who is his neighbor in Bermuda. Two months before he entered politics, I asked Berlusconi whether he thought of himself as Italy's H. Ross Perot. "I know and like Mr. Perot," he replied. "The man is my friend. But I would never give up the way he did." The comparison with Perot is more misleading than edifying. Perot used his millions to buy airtime and create a grassroots network, but he never turned his data-processing company into an election machine. He was less plausible as a public figure. But most important, he was competing against two established political parties with deep roots and traditions, and a capacity for renewal. Berlusconi rose out of a vacuum left by the collapse of the old system. He hijacked a revolution that had been started by others, and he was able to conduct his crusade without the checks and balances that would have tripped up someone like H. Ross Perot.

But how powerful was Berlusconi as a prime minister? Heads of Italian governments have never been strong. The tycoon led a brittle coalition of northern regionalists and neo-Fascists that was conceived as a shotgun marriage of convenience and fell apart in December 1994, forcing Berlusconi to resign after only eight months in office. He would no doubt have preferred to control one large majority party. It took him many months to learn that you can't dominate a parliamentary coalition like you can a company boardroom. Umberto Bossi and Gianfranco Fini saw themselves not as salaried managers but as majority shareholders. The cantankerous Bossi saw opposition to Berlusconi, his own coalition partner, as the only way of ensuring his own political survival.

Silvio Berlusconi followed in the tradition of Julius Caesar and Benito Mussolini, strongmen toppled by palace coups because they had become too powerful. The tycoon was forced to resign by Umberto Bossi and the rebels of the Northern League because he was too ambitious, owned too many vital enterprises, and thus upset the delicate balance of power at the heart of Italian politics, the *consociativismo* of old times. The recipe for staying in power in Italy is not to coerce but to juggle conflicting interests, be they factions within one party or different parties within one coalition. Like the ringmaster in a circus tent, one should crack the whip and wear the glittery uniform of power, but the horses, lions, and clowns are so well trained they would jump over the hurdles and through the hoops anyway. The illusion of control is more important than control itself. Crack the whip too hard or too often, and the performing beasts will turn on the ringmaster and trample him into the dust. Berlusconi failed to respect that rule.

Perhaps real change in Italy can only be imposed from outside. The end of the *partitocrazia* owed less to a popular desire for change than to the collapse of the Berlin Wall, which had ended the communist threat, the Maastricht Treaty on European integration, which established stringent standards of economic convergence, Italy's growing debt mountain, and the weakness of the lira, which made it increasingly difficult to finance the wasteful system of patronage on which party political power was based. Had Berlusconi grasped this, he would perhaps have stacked his plate of electoral promises less high. He would also have realized that the secret of power in Italy is not imposing one's will but merely maintaining the truce between a large array of interest groups from coalition partners and trade unions to pensioners, taxpayers, and tax dodgers. Mussolini, who had tried to browbeat, coerce, brainwash, and dazzle the Italians into obedience, realized his fundamental mistake toward the end of his political adventure. A brilliant if impotent analyst of his own demise, Mussolini was only too well aware of the fact. "It is not impossible to rule the Italians," the dictator once said. "It is unnecessary."

EPILOGUE

A Revolution Without Climax

The Italians take their porn queens seriously. When Moana Pozzi, the Queen of Queens, died suddenly of cancer in September 1994, she was mourned with full honors not only for her matronly looks but also for her intellect. Miss Pozzi was the thinking man's porn queen, appealing to the lecher and the intellectual snob alike. *"Addio Porno Diva, Intelligente"* sobbed the earnest *La Stampa* on the front page. *"Ciao Moana"* wailed the politically correct *Il Manifesto*. *La Repubblica* mourned "an Italian icon." But *L'Espresso* magazine upstaged everyone when it eulogized *"Santa Moana Vergine"*—Saint Moana Virgin—and pointed out that she had died at the same age as Jesus, thirty-three. Columnists earnestly discussed the de facto canonization of the author and star actress of films such as *Moana—Deep Hole, Wet Ecstasy,* and *Orgasmissima.*

But in Italy you don't have to be dressed to be an intellectual. Ms. Pozzi had received an excellent education courtesy of the Urselline Sisters. Her library had been stacked with the tomes of Italo Calvino, Primo Levi, Marguerite Yourcenar, Alexandre Dumas, and many other hard-core literati. Her deathbed literature was nothing less weighty than *The City of God* by Saint Augustine. Not surprisingly, the archbishop of Naples, Michele Giordano, was moved to speak at

Sunday Mass about "our poor daughter, Moana Pozzi," who "had demonstrated how often faith dwells in the hearts of human beings like a spark under the ashes." Italy may be the home of the Vatican and boast more saints per square mile than any other country, but it is also one of the least prudish societies in the world. Public servants may have been hounded out of office for their fiscal irregularities, but on the carnal front they are free to frolic. When he was still foreign minister, Gianni De Michelis, a divorcé, made no attempt to hide his philandering. Surrounding himself with beautiful models was a manifestation of power. Luigi Rossi, an eighty-seven-year-old deputy for the Northern League and a friend of Winston Churchill, is the leading force behind a campaign to legalize Italy's brothels and prevent the spread of AIDS through illegal roadside prostitution. "I lost my virginity in a brothel," he told me. "It did the trick, and the embarrassment was minimized by the anonymity of the act." Rossi describes himself as a practicing Catholic.

There are historical reasons for this lack of prudishness, from which men, needless to say, have benefited more than women. The Church has long ceased to be a moral authority in Italy, a fact senior clergymen would blame on the permissiveness of modern society. But in Italy the Church also has itself to blame. The experience of the Papal States, which ruled central Italy in conditions of feudal deprivation for four centuries, has left behind a deep seam of anticlericalism. As hosts to the popes, the Italians have always known the papacy as a political institution, dictated by the *realpolitik* of power as much as any Bourbon court or ruling party. Second, the very teachings of the Church, especially the comforting notion of original sin, have made the Italians remarkably tolerant toward their own and other people's temptations. Italy's ambiguous relationship with the Church helps to explain the "canonization" of a dead porn queen; but the main reason is that the Italians are living in a sumptuously decadent country, where the end of an era happens to coincide with the end of a millennium. Faced with such doom, anything goes ... even Moana Pozzi.

Two years before her death the porn queen tried to take advantage of Italy's feverish spirit of sexual tolerance and occupy what she felt was her rightful place in the Italian Parliament. After all, she was merely following in the footsteps of "la Cicciolina," "the Little Bunny Rabbit," who was elected as a deputy for the maverick Radical Party in 1987. The Partito del Amore, or Love Party, was Pozzi's contribution to Italy's political transition. It was founded in 1992 and was committed to the free market—in love. According to the party's manifesto, Italians should be allowed to relieve stress and tension by making love in their lunch hour. For those too far from home, special love parks would be opened where office workers could copulate between shifts. "La Cicciolina" was the party's guiding spirit and its honorary president. Real power was, however, concentrated in the manicured hands of Moana Pozzi, who became the party's general secretary, and Barbarella, the secretary for propaganda and external relations.

The founding congress took place in one of Rome's largest discothèques, a cluster of pink domes built around a green fountain made of cherubs in erotic embrace. The discothèque had been hired by the Love Party's secretariat for one evening in February 1992. Pink heart-shaped invitations beckoned supporters to pledge their signature and thus help legalize the party in time for the elections. Finally I managed to beat a path through the throng of reporters, supporters, and titillated teenagers to put my question to Pozzi: "What made you decide to go into politics?" Moana fixed me with her large green eyes and launched into a brilliant exegesis. "Italy is going through a profound transition. The rigid structure of party politics that prevailed in this country for four decades has been shattered by corruption and by the end of communism. The breaching of the Berlin Wall and the end of communism," the protagonist of *Moana's Wet Dreams* confided to me, "have deprived the Christian Democrats and their allies of the reason for perpetual reelection. What you are witnessing in Italy today," she concluded, "is dramatic, unique." Her bosom heaved. She took a deep breath. "The danger," she continued, "is that this so-called revolution of ours will fizzle out . . . in a coitus interruptus."

Pozzi was ahead of her time. In 1994 it did indeed seem as if Italy's ethical cleansing had stopped in its tracks and been denied a climax. The "revolution" was, after all, nothing more than foreplay. The country had opted—once again—for a typically Italian Catholic solution: collective confession, mea culpas, penitence, and absolution, woven into a soothing blanket of forgiveness and compromise. Proposals for a general amnesty, which had almost brought down the government two years before, were now being made by the very judges who had spearheaded "the revolution."

Antonio Di Pietro, the magistrate-turned-folk-hero, was so overwhelmed and exhausted by the sheer volume of corruption cases that he suggested wiping the slate clean of existing charges and imposing tougher sentences in the future. Later he resigned from the pool of magistrates he had helped to make famous, cast off his gown in anger, and complained of too much political interference. For all the high drama of arrests, subpoenas, and resignations, the Italian judiciary had very few convictions and prison sentences to show for its efforts. In October 1994 Sergio Cusani, the most famous "Tangentopoli" defendant to reach the dock, was preparing his first of two appeals trials and suing the judges for negligence. It was now the judiciary's turn to fend off a smear campaign. In June 1995 Di Pietro himself was interrogated for eighteen hours by magistrates over a number of alleged misdemeanors. The Grand Inquisitor took part in his own auto-da-fé. The Restoration was in full swing.

Bettino Craxi still languished in sun-drenched exile in Tunisia, ignoring his eight-and-a-half-year prison sentence and claiming that he was too ill to appear at the other trials awaiting him. Francesco De Lorenzo, the former health minister who had been charged with fraud, bribery, and extortion involving millions of dollars, was released from preventive custody. He was photographed with a friend of his emerging from lunch in a restaurant called I Due Ladroni, The Two Thieves. Gianni De Michelis was busy giving interviews in court about China, his new passion. The dodgy "Doge" had become a "cultural consultant" for Italian businessmen seeking stronger ties with China. It seemed as if the bloodcurdling morality play that was "Tangentopoli" had been rewritten after Act Two to become another lighthearted operetta. A country that had bayed for the blood of its rulers was already bored.

The anesthetic of corruption fatigue had begun to work. In October 1994 magistrates discovered that the Guardia di Finanza and SECIT, the Italian state tax auditors, had turned a blind eye to financial irregularities in return for handsome bribes. More than seventy officers of the Guardia di Finanza were arrested. Three committed suicide in the space of two months. The businesses involved ranged from a number of branches of Fininvest, the prime minister's company, to Milan's fashion houses. One damp Saturday in September 1994, the designers Giorgio Armani, Gianfranco Ferré, and Krizia all filed into Milan's austere Palazzo di Giustizia to be questioned by Antonio Di Pietro. Krizia admitted to paying $100,000 in bribes to the Guardia di Finanza in 1990. Giorgio Armani's lawyer told reporters that the eternally tanned high priest of haute couture had paid $60,000 to the tax authorities, and the corpulent Gianfranco Ferré, the chief designer for Christian Dior in Paris, said he "simply loved the judge's cashmere jacket." All the designers said they had become the victims of extortion, that their businesses would have been closed down if they hadn't paid the money to the Financial Police. What none of them mentioned was how many millions of dollars the so-called extortion had spared them in taxes.

A few months later the same argument would be used by none other than Prime Minister Berlusconi, who told the nation during a special TV address—how else—that he too had been forced to pay money to the Financial Police "like hundreds of thousands of other businessmen." This was an absurd statement, especially from a head of government who had vowed to clean up politics. But instead of unleashing a torrent of outrage, his admission was greeted with a quiet nod of understanding. Despite his undoubted mistakes, Berlusconi and Forza Italia continued to lead the opinion polls in a triumph of hope over experience.

The media tycoon embodied a nation, in which, it seemed, individuals from prime ministers to fashion designers, from tax inspectors to taxi drivers, cast themselves as victims of a flawed human nature, rather than as one of its practitioners. As sociologist Franco Ferrarotti put it, "If human nature is hopelessly flawed and perfection can only be achieved in Paradise, there's no point in trying too hard while trapped in the mortal coil. This profound sense of human imperfection has not plunged the Italians into a deep depression or driven them to self-improvement, no, it has freed them to be selfish and pragmatic. It is obvious from the way we drive, the way we park, the way we dodge our taxes and distrust the state and every one of its representatives." The spirit of pragmatism has spawned its own, very Italian, term—*possibilismo,* literally "possibilism." What it means is that everything can be achieved given the right degree of compromise. After 1945 even the Communist Party concentrated on establishing good local government rather than advancing the cause of the proletarian paradise.

Perhaps its leaders realized at an early stage that Italy, fragmented into an archipelago of interest groups from families, tribes, regions, cities, and village fraternities to trade unions and political parties, is, quite simply, unfit for revolution. This undergrowth of associations, loyalties, and affiliations has resisted the imposition of the state in the interests of society as a whole. It has undermined civic responsibility and obstructed reform, especially on a national level. But it has also prevented Italy from degenerating into anarchy.

Considering the wholesale collapse of the old regime, the arrest of thousands of politicians, bureaucrats, and business leaders, the eradication of entire political parties, the calamity of prime ministers accused of conniving with the Mafia, secret service agents plotting against the state, and the Everest of bribes that financed this system of corruption, Italy has remained suspiciously unruffled. My Italian friends used to boast about their *dolce* revolution. But this placidity had less to do with the self-restraint of an outraged people and more with the cynicism of a country that had always expected its politicians to sin. It tolerated their peccadilloes as long as they provided patronage, jobs, welfare, and a blind eye over tax fiddles in return. When they continued to take the bribes but stopped delivering the goods, this working relationship broke down. However, the most damning indictment for those who claim that the last few years have produced "revolution" or even reform is that the political debate has been dominated by personalities rather than issues and principles.

Italy has been called the laboratory chamber of European politics. The British historian E. P. Thompson first coined the term in an article in which he described the rise of Mussolini in 1922 as a taste of things to come in Germany and Spain. Italy has certainly experimented in recent years. Its laboratory has frothed and fizzed with everything from media-tycoon prime ministers to Fascists resurrected from the dustbin of history to wacky self-declared regional republics. As five decades of rigid *partitocrazia* collapsed, Italy filled the void with experiments and became a magnifying glass for nascent developments in other Western countries. The last three years have witnessed the decline of the political parties and philosophies that have ruled much of the Western world since 1945, the fragmentation of the nation-state into regions, the rise of citizen politicians, the invention of a new political language based on TV, soccer, and consumer culture, and the branding of the *partito d'azienda,* the business conglomerate turned political party. I wonder how many international tycoons have been inspired by Silvio Berlusconi to turn their companies into electoral movements. Shortly after Berlusconi's election victory in 1994, a delegation of Japanese businessmen came to Rome to study the genesis of Forza Italia. They were exploring the possibility of setting up a Forza Japan party. Regionalists, devolutionists, and secessionists around the world may have been inspired by Umberto Bossi's Northern League with its make-believe passports, its currency, and its historical pageantry. Italy, once the nexus of civilization, has become the hot tub of decadence.

Italian politics can inspire, frustrate, amaze, or entertain. But Italy is too idiosyncratic to be a model for any other country. Its experiments are best ignored. Because this country has achieved the near-perfect separation of state and people, because what happens on the political level barely impinges on the lives of voters, Italy can afford to dabble in experiments that would be dangerous elsewhere. Imagine the consequences of "Tangentopoli" in Britain, where something as trifling as the poll tax unleashed violent riots in Trafalgar Square. In Italy the poll tax would have been either ignored or briefly paid by those who were sufficiently intimidated. In Britain "Tangentopoli" would probably have led to the collapse of the monarchy.

The fact is that with its innate conservatism, its fragmentation into thousands of resilient family units, its petty provincialism, its inherited distrust of the state, its mystical dislike for logic, its unwillingness to respect the laws of cause and effect, Italy is not fertile ground for collective change. The country is unfit for revolution. This is an insurance policy against extremism and should reassure anyone who is worried about the rise of neo-Fascism. However, it is also a pity because Italy is still a long way from facing up to a real if mundane challenge: reinventing the relationship between the citizen and the state. The consequences of *this* "revolution" would be felt in a thousand tiny ways. It would shorten lines in banks, deliver letters on time, open museums, and improve traffic and the health system. If it can do that, Italy, with its culture, weather, beauty, humanity, humor, industriousness, inventiveness, unself-conscious eccentricity, and delicious food would surely be the closest thing to paradise on earth.

MATT FREI was born in Germany and educated at Oxford University, where he read History and Modern Languages. He started working for the BBC German-language service in 1986. Since then he has been reporting for BBC Radio and BBC Television from Jerusalem, Berlin, Bonn, Sarajevo, and Rome. He has been posted in Italy since 1991 as the BBC's Southern Europe correspondent. The author has also written for *The Spectator, The Wall Street Journal,* and the *Times of London.* This is his first book.